D1213692

THE CLASSROOM DISASTER

PUBLISHED IN COOPERATION WITH THE
HORACE MANN–LINCOLN INSTITUTE
TEACHERS COLLEGE, COLUMBIA UNIVERSITY
FRANCIS A. J. IANNI, DIRECTOR

THE
CLASSROOM DISASTER

How the outworn classroom system
cripples our schools and cheats
our children, and how to replace it

Leslie A. Hart

TEACHERS COLLEGE PRESS

Teachers College, Columbia University
New York

WILLIAM MADISON RANDALL LIBRARY UNC AT WILMINGTON

COPYRIGHT 1969 BY LESLIE A. HART
LIBRARY OF CONGRESS CATALOG CARD NUMBER 69–18133

SECOND PRINTING, 1969

MANUFACTURED IN THE UNITED STATES OF AMERICA

LB1025
.2
.H3

To
President Lyndon B. Johnson,
who has done more to advance public
education than any other president,
and perhaps more than all
previous presidents together.

89198

FOREWORD

There seems today to be a growing consensus that the traditional educational system is no longer responsive to the needs of a rapidly changing society. Critics of education are found in almost equal numbers inside and outside the establishment and on the many sides of each educational issue. Indeed, in some instances the criticism has already reached the point of protest, and we are almost certainly destined to witness increasing disenchantment with what we are doing as educators. That the protest comes from within our ranks as well as outside is encouraging, but as in so many areas of dissent we often find ourselves responding to demands instead of to evaluations, to denunciations rather than to alternative programs. In many cases the charges leveled at our schools seem made rather in the posture of the little boy at summer camp who wrote his mother complaining that the food was atrocious and besides there was not enough of it.

Leslie Hart has drawn together in this volume not just an indictment of "the system" but some carefully thought out appraisals of existing programs. He has done an excellent job in arguing that they can be a first step in the long journey to where we should be going. He has the advantage of looking at education from outside and being able to see it as a system. Refreshingly, his suggestions for new directions stress system-wide changes rather than unrelated and piecemeal reforms in curriculum, teacher education, or the administration of schools. His insights have the added advantage of his deep concern for what might be. This book should generate a breadth and depth of discussion that can refocus our currently diffuse approaches and innovative efforts.

Francis A. J. Ianni

Teachers College, Columbia University
April 1969

INTRODUCTION

This book is intended for parents; school board members; citizens interested and active in school and community organizations; teachers, and those contemplating a career in education; school administrators and specialists; public officials; and anyone else with more than a casual interest in what is happening and likely to happen in our public schools.

It is a protest, primarily, against what we suffer to happen to our children—almost *all* our children.

Its thesis is simple: that much of the disaster we have come to stems from continued reliance on a long-outmoded system of organization characterized by instruction in fixed groupings called "classes," the use of the ancient "classroom" as the principal facility, and progression of the student by annual "grade" steps.

This system is an anachronism retained from an earlier century, when it had considerable usefulness. In our present age, it has become a brutal, inhuman means of inflicting on our children planned restriction, suppression, discouragement, frustration, upside-down values, and humiliation. It is admirably designed to discourage the learning that children would achieve if merely given the means and left alone.

And it is a system which we no longer can pretend works. Criticism of public education is no new sport; but within the last ten years the volume and tone have sharply changed. Criticism is now urgent and alarmed. Among laymen, it comes from the President on down; among educators, from many of the most highly placed and respected. Both inside the Establishment and without, many people are, for the first time, taking a hard look at our schools. What they find tends to be hair-raising. The Education Act of 1965, calling for continuing funds in the billions and for a greatly expanded Federal role, won passage not because all is well, but because the inadequacies of our public education effort are painfully apparent. Urban riots have underlined the crisis.

That we are in process of changing from old system to new can scarcely be doubted by those who follow events. The process is popularly called "the revolution." Unfortunately, even those educators leading the way in this ferment of innovation and fresh thinking have little experience in how to behave during a revolution. Their training hardly leads many to mount the barricades and shout as a slogan, "Free the children — the classroom system must go!" On the contrary, perhaps for fear of arousing the natives too violently, they tend to present even major steps forward as isolated "experiments." Others in public education treat the revolution as "quite interesting" — a novelty to be looked into when time permits, as one gets around to reading a talked-about new book. There are also those who learn the bright new words as protective coloring and the mossbacks who smell danger to themselves and so heap invective on any critic.

But like not a few other revolutions, this one is not optional. Our schools have reached and passed the point of disaster. The revolution cannot be stopped; but it can be delayed and bungled by those who refuse to understand what is happening — to the further distress of our children and the nation.

It will cost billions to lubricate the change from outworn system to new arrangements. But to delay the change will cost far more. Even now we are putting up schools that are obsolete; the better they are built, the more it will cost to pull them apart and rebuild them to serve the future, not the past. Most of the teachers now in training are being prepared for what has failed, not what is to come. In only a relatively few advanced systems are personnel being selected with the revolution in mind.

Most of us, in our occupations, are used to rapid change. Educators are not. They do not know *how* to change, nor do they always have motivation. They are going to have to be helped, and shoved.

My hope is that this book will contribute to general understanding of what is wrong with the old ways and what is possible with the new. It is based on more than eight years of study, research, and thought. A variety of working educators have read it in script; they have found little to protest in the picture it gives of the present system — however much it may astound the trusting parent and taxpayer. A few of the ideas introduced as aspects of future systems are in some measure my own. By and large, however, what is predicted is based solidly on what is being done, somewhere in a few schools, or in some cases, many.

We are forced to abandon what we have — the sooner and more completely, the better. It will be helpful, I hope, to have some idea of where we are going. Part I deals primarily with our present system, Part II principally with what could be.

I owe thanks to the many persons who have assisted or encouraged me in various ways in bringing this book to publication, including those who have offered criticism. Without attempting a complete list, I should like to mention Judge Amos Basel, Harold and Janet Daley, Mrs. Robert L. Smith, Dr. David G. Salten, Stephen G. Birmingham, and Harry Wolff. Among those who kindly corresponded or sent material were Dr. John I. Goodlad, Dr. Jerome S. Bruner, Dr. Robert H. Anderson, Dr. J. Lloyd Trump (who was especially generous), Dr. B. Frank Brown, and the late Senator Robert F. Kennedy. The Office of Education and the National Education Association provided a variety of statistical data. Particular appreciation is due Melvin Bye, Dr. Maurie Hillson, and Dr. Francis A. J. Ianni for their interest and support. My wife, Jane S. Hart, contributed in many ways and gave many patient hours, and my daughter, Sara Hart Olson, and son, David M. Hart, helped bridge the generation gap.

CONTENTS

PART I

"Only a few children in school ever become good at learning in the way we try to make them learn. Most of them get humiliated, frightened, and discouraged. They use their minds, not to learn, but to get out of doing the things we tell them to do—to make them learn. . . . The children who use such strategies are prevented by them from growing into more than limited versions of the human beings they might have become. This is the real failure that takes place in school; hardly any children escape."

John Holt in *How Children Learn*

1

THE SCOPE OF THE DISASTER

Billy began school this week," announces a mother to a Saturday night gathering of neighbors.

The remark produces some smiles and nods in acknowledgment. Not much need be said. The other parents are well aware that for Billy this is a momentous occasion, one of the great transitions of life, and possibly the most far-reaching in its effects. They are equally aware that Billy's mother, love him as she may, fully appreciates the pleasure of having someone else take care of Billy several hours of the day.

The talk may turn soon to other matters. But suppose the announcement were to be put in other terms. "Today," says Billy's mother, "I committed my five year old son to a public institution. He will be compelled by law and by plan to spend a large share of his waking hours there for the next thirteen years. I realize what happens there can have enormous influence on how he develops and is (or isn't) prepared for adult living. Not only have I granted the school extremely broad rights to direct Billy, even to the extent of telling him when he may speak, what to think, and what to do in greatest detail, but I have also made clear to Billy that he is to accept this authority without creating difficulties for those who apply it, or he will have trouble with me and his father.

"I regret to say that while I have given this institution such power and influence over my son, I really know very little about it, nor do I have any practical way to find out. So far as I know, nobody outside the school checks on its performance in general; and the school does not even check and report on its own performance. Yet I have committed Billy anyway. It may sound awful, but isn't it what we all do?"

It is, indeed. Because the schools are *there* and seemingly always have been, in much their present form, we look at them but seldom *into* them. Intense local interest may be aroused for a time by recourse to double sessions; a narcotics scandal; an integration problem or Negro protest; a student incident that gets into the newspapers; a proposal to add sex education; or most commonly by a proposal to spend money and raise taxes. There may be flurries of interest in dropouts, or the way reading is taught, or pre-school programs. But seldom are the big and basic questions asked out loud or examined, even by those, such as school board members or PTA officers, who spend a good deal of time on school affairs. Interest most often focuses on fragmentary problems. Urgency seldom is felt about more than small adjustments or improvements within the existing structure. Nobody looks at the structure – which is the chief reason we have reached our present state of disaster. It is high time we did put the big questions, and insist on more than mumbled answers from those who run our public schools.

What I propose to examine is whether the way we *organize* our schools is not unendurably obsolete, and the source, perhaps the prime source, of most of the troubles that now so obviously plague the schools and our hapless children, like Billy, so blindly thrown to their tender mercies.

This subject of organization is so little considered, so rarely mentioned even in the now unceasing public discussion of our educational shortcomings and failures, that to most lay people and the majority of persons working in the schools the notion of studying alternatives for our individual schools and systems comes as a rather novel — and perhaps shocking — idea. Such arrangements as non-graded classes and team teaching have been fairly well publicized (although an amazing number of people involved in education seem to have only the vaguest understanding of what the terms mean in practice); but they are usually thought of as minor changes of the existing system, part of the "tinkering" approach so dear to educators and administrators, rather than as aspects or forerunners of a possible new system. In fact, the very concept that there can *be* alternative systems is not often put into words, even by those educators who are striving to build them. Perhaps they fear the thought is too alarming.

Yet, reasonably, we can hardly be startled to find that our class-and-grade system (it is so taken for granted that it does not even have a common name) is obsolete. It came into use in most larger communities well over a century ago, a time when the United States was a largely rural country with less than 25 million people and a railroad from coast to coast was a bold new proposal. It is slightly less modern than the covered wagon. We are still using, basically, the identical plan of organization. Classes, classrooms, classroom teachers, grades, annual promotions, subjects, marks, report cards, periods, recess, curriculum sequences — all these are still in daily use, along with a dozen more earmarks of the then radical system that Horace Mann did so much to popularize.

We shall examine, in chapters following, many phases of this now absurd system as it operates in actuality and as it exerts its dead weight to drag down student, teacher, specialist, and administrator — a process that may well lead us to wonder whether the education disaster is not worse than the harshest critics and most disenchanted observers have reported. Like a child's balloon that appears substantial until the first pinprick, the classroom system can be tolerated only so long as not the slightest probe into it is made. It is protected, however, by a layer of pomposity, encrusted age, disarming myths, and pious intent expressed in words of highest respectability.

For contrast and direction, we shall also consider at least the broad shapes alternative plans may take.

For the moment, let me emphasize that while the teachers and others who operate the schools are just as much victims of the class-and-grade system as the students, it is our children who take the brunt and who suffer the wounds, damage, and crippling, much of it permanent in effect, that it inflicts; and it is the disadvantaged children, who need the schools' help the most, who take the worst beating. In its earlier days, the class-and-grade system was in essence optional: those children who were least suited to it or who were most abused by it *by and large ceased attending.* Its aims at first were most modest — a few years of instruction (a "year" being less than a third of our present standard in terms of days attended) covering a very limited area of skills and fact. The system was generations old before the objective of free public high schools for most students became popular.

Today, teachers who have had a bellyful can quit, and each year a great many do; or they can try their luck in another school. But the students are virtual prisoners. They are treated much as are inmates in a prison — checked in, checked out, watched at all times, every movement controlled, every activity begun and stopped by signal. They are forced to march in files; to observe silence or speak only after obtaining permission; to suffer rude address and sarcasm; to obey orders, however arbitrary, without question or protest. Standard school punishment is simply to keep the pupil there longer than scheduled — an eloquent expression of how the school views itself! The prisons are softer-hearted, however, in that they give time off for good behavior.

After doing research in a number of high schools, Edgar Z. Friedenberg observed, in *The Dignity of Youth and Other Atavisms:*

> I had never previously realized that there was any building except a military installation subject to espionage in which people could not go about their legitimate business without let or hindrance. I knew about restricted areas, but not restricted people. High school students learn for four years that they cannot so much as walk down the hall to the library or toilet without written permission.

The six-foot tall, 180-pound senior who must prove his right to relieve himself or consult a reference work, even if he has no class at the moment, may a few months later be operating a

$100,000 machine in a factory, driving a huge truck, or wandering a college campus wholly on his own.

The penal aspects and regimentation of the classroom system are demeaning enough; but the mental and emotional bludgeoning is a good deal more cruel and hurtful. The preschool child from a reasonably good home environment manifests a forceful desire to learn. He sees with an eye sharper and clearer than an adult's because he has not yet learned what he is *supposed* to see, to be conventional. A myth holds that he has a short span of attention, a myth suspiciously convenient for the schools, but obviously contrary to fact, as any observant parent may know. He is impatient with interests adults force upon him, to be sure; but even a toddler will become utterly absorbed with what meets his needs of the moment. A sense of wonder, of joy, of spontaneity, of delight in "finding out" is natural in most children — until they reach school. There, in two weeks or two years, it is systematically crushed out. Not surprisingly, a recent research project on the "Head Start" preschool experience for deprived children showed that the substantial gains many made through this program vanished soon after they entered regular school. Throughout school, a child who shows enthusiasm for *any* academic interest becomes somewhat remarkable. Most enthusiasms lie *outside* the classroom.

The classroom school was never designed to arouse or permit individual interests. The basic idea was what we would now call thought-control. If children are to be handled constantly as *groups* (usually fixed groups), they must perforce be told what to think, when to begin thinking it, and when to stop. The poorer, lazier, meaner, or less confident the teacher, the greater will be the reliance on thought-control methods — and who will deny we have teachers in even the "best" and most expensive of public schools who fall all too clearly in these categories? The exceptional teachers, the ones who seek most to individualize instruction, must swim against the current. The school is not set up for them.

The classroom teacher's odd role in our society has been remarked on often in educational literature, even while it is suffered to continue. One of the bluntest statements, by Jacob W.

Getzels and Herbert A. Thelan, appears in *The Dynamics of Instructional Groups:*

> If one thinks of authority, control, and leadership in political terms, it is clear that the classroom group, at least in its formal aspects, is about as far from democracy as one can get. Not only do the students have no control over the selection of their leader, they normally also have no recourse from his leadership, no influence on his method of leadership beyond that granted by him, and no power over the tenure of his leadership. There are very few working groups in our society in which these essentially despotic conditions are legitimately so much the rule.

Since it would hardly be appropriate for our public school people to admit to methods which would do greater honor to a fascist or communist state, or a penitentiary, the realities must be glossed over with handsome words. To handle in fixed groups, following predetermined schedules, children who differ enormously, each child must be made to *comply*—at best, to act as though he were like every other child; and at least, not to challenge, upset, or impede the system as it grinds along its ordered course. It is not too much to say that the classroom school's very life depends on compliance, and the function of the first years is to beat the child (in some schools, literally) into compliance. The word is never mentioned. We are told, instead, that the child is being "civilized," "taught to get along with others," led into "democratic behavior," or shown how to act more "maturely." These words are hard to quarrel with, but we must remember that they are all glosses for "made to comply." What the teacher and the school want is plain enough. Being civilized, mature, and democratic all translates into saying "Yes, ma am!" and doing what the teacher directs. "Getting along with others," we strongly suspect, means ten percent getting along with the other inmates and ninety percent getting along with the teacher. Students might put the second percentage rather higher.

If we really intended to teach children practical democracy or the art of getting along with others, putting them into a highly regimented, autocratic situation would seem an odd way to go about it. In truth, the schools are still using a system that was originally set up without the slightest thought of being "democratic," or of recognizing individual differences, let alone honoring them. That administration commonly takes priority over education or respect for the child as a person is attested by the observations of many educators. A typical example is this, from a yearbook, *Elementary School Organization,* published in 1961 by the National Education Association:

> Efforts to meet the individual needs of children are frequently hampered by types of school organization that literally block the use of appropriate and efficient ways of dealing with the child as an individual. It is a discredit to us and a disservice to children to say that we believe in each child's working at the level of his own potential — and at the same time subject him to a common course of study, a comparative marking system, a predetermined structure within which to work, and general goals that may or may not be applicable to him.

The authors, referring to a "goodly proportion" of children, continue:

> We see children who are insecure, disinterested, irritable, lacking in self-discipline . . . aggressively negative in their behavior, and we see the "good little children" who just sit quietly and seemingly listen. True, the schools do not create all these problems. . . . But too often, instead of coping with the individual problems of children, we provide a framework that perpetuates them.

These blunt remarks occur frequently in more recent educational literature (usually safe from lay perusal), but only the top-drawer educators seem to appreciate the source of the troubles. In *Elementary School Organization and Administration,* by Henry J. Otto and David G. Sanders, a widely-used text, the respected authors lament "administrative convenience" and baldly observe: "Administrators and teachers often fail to see the inescapable relationship between school objectives and the details of organization." Pursuing the point further, the authors also note:

> For more than half a century there has been a quest by educators for a plan of grouping which would reduce pupil variability sufficiently so that all members of a class could profit equally from group instruction, thereby minimizing or eliminating the teacher's task of adapting instruction to individual differences. Such a panacea has not yet been found.

Nevertheless, despite obvious faults endlessly detailed in the literature, the classroom system remains in use. The school people still persist in using fixed grouping, as though there were no alternative. And they continue to prattle unabashedly about "recognition of differences" and "individual attention" even as these are daily brushed aside for administrative convenience. Even in superior classroom schools, the classroom system does not permit an individual approach to a meaningful extent.

We shall look into the effects of grouping from several viewpoints. Meanwhile let us note that the classroom situation allows extremely little "individual attention," as the innocent parent understands that term. In practice, it usually lasts, literally, only a few seconds, and even then the teacher must keep an eye on 25 or 30 other pupils. The idea that teachers "know" their charges, even though they may lack elementary facts about them and go months without a private, unhurried conversation with them, is one persistent myth we must discard to see matters as they are.

I need hardly point out that children desperately need personal attention, and especially private, sympathetic, and relaxed attention. In the classroom, they must compete for what few scraps are fleetingly available. The children most in need are usually those least able to compete.

The school virtually never considers a child as an individual, in the sense that a parent, a doctor, or a neighbor does. Rather, the school sees the child *comparatively,* as above average, as an underachiever, as high IQ, as below grade level, as oversize, as of average maturity, as exhibiting excellent "citizenship" (more compliant than most) or as a problem child (less compliant than most). Where the school does respond to the demands of individual differences, it normally does so by *a change in grouping!* So permeated is the whole school atmosphere with the grouping process, so frozen the thinking, that some teachers and principals cannot see why shifting a child to a different group is not evidence of individual treatment. It would be appropriate to have such persons go to a doctor who tells them, after examination, "I give out three standard prescriptions. In your case, I think Prescription B comes closest to meeting your needs." Or, perhaps, go to a service station to be informed, "We have five standard repair jobs. None will fix the trouble in your car—but choose one anyway."

We may wonder, at this point, why parents and children tolerate this outmoded system as well as they do. In *Toward a Theory of Instruction,* Jerome S. Bruner of Harvard University notes: "By school age, children have come to expect quite arbitrary and, from their points of view, meaningless demands to be made upon them by adults." Dr. Bruner's hint is a good one. At the outset, children are apt to regard the school's ways and authority over them as one more strange adult device that "is" and must be endured. As they grow older, they do, as any teacher can attest, resist more and more, to the limit they dare—by mockery, harassment of teachers (especially the hapless substitute), passive resistance, day-dreaming, evasion, lying, cheating, "apple polishing," underachievement, cutting, truancy, open resistance, and vandalism. What children like about school is being with other children and the extra-curricular activities. For the rest, the schools rely chiefly on fear. In the 1963 edition of *Principles of Guidance* by Arthur J. Jones, a passage expresses the traditional view:

> [Teachers] must provide the motivation necessary for the attainment of the objectives and administer such punishments as may be necessary for failure to study or achieve

academically. In addition each teacher is responsible for the behavior of children in his class.

John Holt in *How Children Fail* gives a highly perceptive explanation of how a school appears to the children in it: "Even in the kindest and gentlest of schools, children are afraid, many of them a great deal of the time, some of them almost all of the time."

The classroom school operates by fear, the means to effect compliance. Ironically, perhaps, the parents assist in creating and maintaining the pervading fear, by telling the child that he must comply or deal with their added displeasure as well. But the parents are trapped along with the child by the schools' irresistible weapon of control, the marking system. Most parents care about their offspring's success in the world. They know the child must get the school's blessing in the form of good grades, or be damned when it comes time to get into a chosen college, or handicapped in landing a desirable job. Evidence is sadly lacking that this marking system has any educational value whatever —there is much reason to suspect it is overwhelmingly harmful. But to the school it is an invaluable means of punishment and control, not only over the student but equally against the parents who might, without it, come to ask too many embarrassing questions. *If the school fails to teach the child, it need only give the child a low mark to, miraculously, make the child the failure, not the school.* The report card intimidates the parent: the neighbor's child got good marks—why not theirs? The child who brings home complaints is often discredited or pooh-poohed; or even if believed, told to suffer quietly. Though much evidence suggests that children are shrewd and reliable judges of their teachers and school, they have little in the way of standards, or knowledge of alternatives, to go by. Most soon learn that bringing complaints home is likely to be useless. They fear, as many parents do, that a protest to the school will likely fail and perhaps invite retaliation.

Most complaints to the school do fail. As we shall see, under the classroom system teachers, good or bad, "own" their classrooms. Principals have minimal authority over them (the idea that principals run their schools the way managers and executives run stores or businesses or departments is one more myth that obscures the facts); principals lack means of removing even atrocious teachers and cannot transfer many students out of their classes without having the whole system collapse. The principal defends the teacher, even though he would fire him or her in an instant if he knew how. So each year parents play educational Russian roulette, with their children as stakes, hoping the teacher will be good.

Fortunately, children are usually tough. But not all are. And even the most resilient, subjected to this vicious system, can have precious interests and talents choked off, their self-image badly damaged, their personalities permanently distorted. Perhaps worst, because it is commonest, they learn that gaining an education, high skills, and intellectual power is a dull, distasteful, demeaning process, to be broken off at the earliest opportunity. The joys of learning, the thrill of sudden insight, the satisfactions of mastery—these are routinely smothered by the very system we tax ourselves to support.

There is nothing sacred about this class-and-grade system. It is not mentioned in the Constitution, nor tied to any moral or religious precepts, nor hallowed by tradition. If we have anything in this last category, it is the one-room school, an arrangement antithetical to the one we use now. There is no good reason why we should not scrap it and replace it as rapidly as public pressure can bring about.

It seems reasonably safe to predict that this class-and-grade system has reached the terminal point. We can compare it to a worn-out vessel that, by patching and improvisation, has been kept at sea far too long. Under adverse pressures, it comes apart at the seams and goes down, its seaworthiness suddenly revealed to be pure illusion. The pressures on the classroom system are multifold; we may note them briefly.

1. *Population growth.* This is nothing new—our schools have always had to take on an ever-increasing load. The classroom system itself arose in response to the needs of growing communities. Yet it is startling to consider that since 1910 we have doubled in population, and added roughly a hundred million persons.

Such growth creates a basic pressure; but rapid changes in the rate of growth, as it affects the schools, add much sharper stresses. During the thirties, the birthrate sagged. After World War II, it climbed rapidly to a peak, and it has since subsided to a rate below that of the thirties. Whether the post-war bulge will bring us a similar increase in 1970 remains to be seen. With "the pill" and changing attitudes towards birth controls, prediction is difficult. The costly inflexibility of the classroom system becomes ever more burdensome. It is hard to explain to parents that their child must go through high school on double sessions because the school's load may fall in later years. Equally, taxpayers rebel at the waste and high expense of under-utilized units.

2. *Mobility.* When our present system came into wide use, most people grew up and died within a few miles of where they were born. An agricultural nation tends to stay put. Today a family that remains in the same neighborhood a dozen years is noteworthy, and one that has moved once every four years is not. The rising young executive or specialist is often transferred from city to city. The factory worker and technician, and not a few professionals, move where the work is. The small merchant yields as neighborhoods change and housing or other large projects sweep him out, and he may move his home, too. And among the poorest, mobility is often highest, especially within large cities—where in June a teacher may have few or none of the students she began with in September.

Our ancient classroom system, with its local-control aspects, assumes that students will move from the first through the twelfth grade continuously. *In reality, such a student has become a rarity.* Great numbers attend school in not one but three, four, even six or more school systems; but with typical indomitable will the administrators normally refuse to be confused by such facts. The transferee often pays a stiff penalty, particularly if he shifts schools during a school year. Here we see underlined the inability of the classroom school to deal with students as individuals—the child is pushed into whatever fixed group a principal decides on, often for the convenience of the school. As newcomers, the parents may well feel unable to protest or insist, even if they had enough knowledge of the new school to know what to demand. The child takes the brunt; and the school is likely to regard him as a nuisance if he does not "fit in." Since schools vary greatly in what they teach and how they teach it, his chances of a fit are rather small — but still far greater than his chances of being treated on an individual basis.

If the schools are badly organized to deal with pupil mobility, they are even less able to cope with rapid changes in population. Such situations rise continually in all parts of the country. In Nassau and Suffolk counties on Long Island, New York, for example, population increases of 89% and 97% respectively occurred between 1950 and 1958. California has had similar instances where aircraft or aerospace centers have developed. Near Cape Kennedy hamlets turned into bustling cities. Less noted is the reverse change, where communities lose their child-bearing families, and the schools stand empty or half used. Though state and sometimes federal aid may soften the blow, in some cases, sudden shifts may still create impossible strains on a system of organization that is above all rigid and slow-moving.

3. *The knowledge explosion.* This is a subject in itself: we need hardly attempt to deal with it here. We may note that the vast majority of scientists and experts who ever lived live *now*, and have facilities for creating and disseminating knowledge vastly greater than ever before. The effect on the schools is shattering. Textbooks may go out of date by the time they are put into use. Teachers, protected and lulled by a classroom system that encourages them to get in a rut and stay there, fall far behind current knowledge. New important areas in mathematics, social studies, languages, English, science, and vocational education open up, and teachers and materials cannot be found. The system simply is not organized to respond to such needs, routine as they have now become.

4. *The skill shift.* For long years, those who dropped out of school simply went to work. Suitable jobs existed. Today they don't: thousands of young persons with only a faint chance to get and keep employment constitute "social dynamite" in our cities, and make us wonder what kind of civilization we have spawned, that has no place for so many at the peak of their

vigor. The lack of jobs merely emphasizes an old failure of the schools—their flagrant inability to serve large sections of our population. In a talk to school administrators in February 1964, then Commissioner of Education Francis Keppel bluntly remarked:

> I have been amazed and dismayed to see how often the public's desire to do something to improve education in our slums has been interpreted by our profession as an attack upon the schools. . . . Let me say here as forcefully as I can that the essential step to progress is to face up squarely to our shortcomings. The plain fact of the matter is that we are simply not reaching hundreds of thousands of children who are now in our schools. You know it and I know it and the public knows it.

Unfortunately, the schools think in terms of classrooms, and the classroom system can't meet the need. Something has to give.

It is not only the "disadvantaged," however, who are involved. The schools have never paid more than nominal attention to creative thinking, which clashes head-on with the notion of teaching everyone the same thing. Educators are just beginning to hear about intuitive thinking, which gives most teachers the jim-jams and inclines them to hand out punishment. There is a good deal of evidence that many teachers, by intent or not, discourage intellectuality of the very kind that is priceless in many fields of endeavor, and in turn that administrators may fail to support those teachers who display this quality themselves. Vocational education is widely admitted to be in serious straits, because it cannot keep pace with the times. Again, the inflexibility of the class-and-grade system cripples the schools and cheats the children.

5. *Cost.* The bill for our public schools has gone up astronomically. There are more children, they stay in school longer, they need more of everything. Even apart from inflation, these factors multiply costs. With all the increases in budgets, which often force increases in local debt limits, there

seems to be no improvement in education—on the contrary, the problems of inadequacy seem to intensify. In all likelihood, we are going to have to devote a larger share of our national income to education, and spread it better—a process the Education Act has well begun. But we can hardly expect to pour endless new billions into a broken-down, malfunctioning system without arousing protest. President Johnson, during the 1965 White House Conference on Education, called for not merely more classrooms and teachers, but a "fundamental improvement," an educational system that "does not simply equip the student to adjust to society, but which enables him to challenge and modify and at times reject the wisdom of his elders." *That* is not the classroom system!

Title IV of the Education Act provides for, at last, substantial funds for research and means of getting findings into use. There are already twelve "laboratories" at work, and an Educational Research Information Center (ERIC) and scores of Title III regional centers to help get information around. As alternatives become apparent, the public, already notably skittish about voting additional money for a broken-down system, may more and more force school boards and superintendents to move ahead, willy-nilly. Withholding funds is the classic democratic way to influence bureaucrats.

6. *Minority pressures.* The clamorous and often militant demands of Negro, Puerto Rican, Indian, and Mexican minorities clearly provide some of the most inescapable and irresistible pressures for change. We seem to have a national tendency to "go to the brink" before we act with sufficient resolve and vigor. In civil rights the question is whether we have not slipped over the brink. In our inner cities the situation is now more usually desperate than not. But these acute situations should not blind us to the problems, tensions, and latent explosions that exist wherever there are minorities suffering oppression and the incessant provocations of discrimination.

Our black citizens are the most numerous victims, as well as the longest maltreated, even including the Indians. They are also the best organized and most vocal, though far from united or agreed on policies. This can hardly surprise us: whites are not agreed either, including those whites who have pontificated most loudly, or rolled up their sleeves to work on the scene in the ruggedest of ghettos. What many whites, including self-styled liberals, do not appear to grasp is that Negro leaders in the ghettos want to take charge of their problems. As Dr. Francis A. J. Ianni has summed it up:

> Paternalism, no matter how positive and sincere, has no place in today's urban education programs. In a very real sense, the people of the ghetto are demanding the right to make their own mistakes and not to have them made for them by others.

The resulting struggle, floundering, and frustrations on all sides will produce sparks, and loosen up many barriers long fixed and overhonored as immutable.

The black tradition has been that education, by and large, was of no great value in practical terms. As usual, the Negro got the least and the poorest—partly, we may suspect, to save public money, and partly as a convenient, continuous way to keep Negroes from getting uppity and wanting to enjoy constitutional and human rights like whites. Worse, the Negro often saw that those with the wrong color skin who did get more education still ended up with broom in hand, or not much higher up the pecking order. The rare Negro who "made it" via a better education usually departed for middle-class environs where his example was little visible to those left behind. (As with other self-made types of all ethnic origins, he often showed not sympathy but contempt for his ex-fellows—a problem now with not a few Negro teachers and principals when assigned to predominantly black schools.) Among deprived and oppressed people, "avoiding trouble" is often the most evident of motivations. The matriarchal head of a family might well regard a child's effort to excel in school, especially a white-run school, as only an invitation to insult and retaliation, and so would discourage rather than reinforce it.

The tradition is far from extinct. But the last few years have seen an astoundingly rapid change in point of view.

American Education in the issue of November 1967 reports on a survey made in Detroit in the summer of 1965, in which 1,175 persons were interviewed. Central city Negroes were found to be far more supportive of public education than headlines would suggest: 70% were favorable, even to the extent of willingness to pay more taxes, and only 14% rejected school support. Black support was far stronger than white in the metropolitan area.

The survey findings harmonize with observation and the reports of persons working in ghettos with whom I have talked. After the historic anti-segregation Supreme Court decision of 1954, the Negro leaders tended to stress physical integration—opening white schools to attendance by black children. Mere entrance was a triumph, a symbol of a new day. When "all deliberate speed" turned out to be more deliberate than speed, concern shifted to the quality of education received—usually in simplest terms: complaint that Negro children somehow all too frequently did not learn to read well, or do arithmetic, or generally prosper in the academic environments available. Negroes saw plainly enough that their children commonly went to dreary, dirty, overcrowded old schools, excessively staffed with inexperienced, weak, or antagonistic teachers but understaffed on the whole, and short of educational resources such as books and devices that were relatively plentiful in newer schools. The cure seemed simple. They began to demand that their children go to white schools not simply for "integration" but as a practical guarantee that these would not be inferior schools. While subsequent studies hint that some improvement does indeed result, the difference is rather trivial in the light of the whole problem.

Currently it seems clear that the older certainties about Negro objectives in education have faltered. The more perceptive see that small changes will not cure great difficulties. As yet I have not heard any Negro spokesman demand a new *kind* of school, or specifically attack the classroom system; but the day may not be far off. The assumption that all the black child needs is a white-type school is far too faulty to survive under examination.

Meanwhile, inner-city riots have brought needs into sharp,

hot focus; but still, if one may judge from published and public remarks, all too few realize the close connection between riots and education. The "Riot Report" of the President's Commission, published early in 1968, noted:

> The hostility of Negro parents and students toward the school system is generating increasing conflict and causing disruption within many school districts. . . . the most dramatic evidence of the relationship between educational practices and civil disorder lies in the high incidence of riot participation by ghetto youth who had not completed high school. Our survey of riot cities found that the typical riot participant was a high school dropout.

The Commission might have put the matter even more strongly. While defining the "typical" rioter as between 15 and 24, it laid little stress on the participation of even younger children, quite obvious and universal in news accounts, eye-witness reports, photographs and news films, especially during the initial phase. In the riots that followed the assassination of Dr. Martin Luther King, Jr., the role of youths of school age seemed to be even greater. *The Wall Street Journal* of April 10, 1968, reported: "In many cities, the violence apparently originated with Negroes in their early teens, or even all the way down to kindergarten age."

Quite recently, and hardly by coincidence, a number of former teachers in slum schools have turned author: Bel Kaufman, Jonathan Kozol, Herbert Kohl, James Herndon. Their work, whether hilarious or chilling, dramatizes the hopeless inadequacies and irrelevance, and the rampant racist prejudices, of many ghetto classroom schools. A variety of studies have brought other difficulties to light: the ghetto's different vocabulary and speech patterns; the lack of fathers as models; the number of disturbed children; the assignment of new teachers to "bad" schools because they lack seniority to choose "nice" ones; the now well-proved fact that children's performance in school is apt to reflect the teacher's expectations — and many slum teachers expect their charges to do very badly. To these must be added the overriding effects of poverty.

All this tends to obscure the basic problem: that schools

that work very badly for advantaged children must be expected to prove even worse for disadvantaged. *The basic problem is the classroom system.* The other problems are hardly unimportant, but secondary. Despite the considerable special effort made against ghetto school conditions, even the programs initially most promising have petered out or been quietly shelved as achieving almost nothing measurable. Pouring money into the ghetto school systems sounds like a better solution than it is: funding can merely produce larger failures.

Running his own show, fending off helpful whites who often lack valid answers, and probing with active disrespect for the traditional approaches, a Negro leader may well come to see the need is not for new school buildings, "improved" schools, or "better teachers," but for *new kinds of schools* — kinds that do not give the least to the children who need the most.

There is some delicious irony in the thought that our most educationally-deprived groups may play the key role in pushing and leading all the nation to new and far better schools!

7. *The cold war.* It would be unfair and disrespectful to world communism not to include it in this list. What other force can command attention, bring rapid action, and loosen purses so well? When in October of 1957 Sputnik I sizzled into space, indignation at our global embarrassment was directed, not at our military leaders, our scientists, our universities, or the administration, but quite amazingly at our public schools! While we must assume that this illogical outcome expressed a long latent and intense dissatisfaction, it remains a fact that Sputnik triggered the debate, reforms, and progress of the last decade.

The Russians, fortunately, have a regimented system even less flexible than ours; and the Chinese at the moment seem content to cripple theirs with overriding concern for political considerations. But this may not last. Late in 1966, the Soviet officials were reported to be worrying about dropouts, and to be instituting for the first time electives for older students. Reputedly, communists are much interested in revolutions. Just possibly they may develop a passionate eagerness for one in education.

It seems undeniable, if recent research findings are to be believed, that the schools of America are in urgent need of a fundamental reappraisal, and that an equally basic change in our modes of thought regarding students, curriculum, and teachers is the first order of business. For these researches show, in a variety of ways, that the schools of the country have simply been inadequate for a number of their primary tasks.

Melvin Tumin in "Teaching in America," *Saturday Review,* October 21, 1967. Copyright Saturday Review, Inc., 1967

2

BEYOND THE
EDUCATIONAL CURTAIN

Since we are about to penetrate the Educational Curtain and look around a good bit in the strange region on the other side, it will be well to clear aside some more myths that tend to fog the view.

Here I should point out that it is not easy to discuss our educational disaster in realistic terms without seeming to bear an animus, and to indulge in exaggeration, false generalizations, and incredible statements. As we shall see, an enormous number of people are engaged in operating our public schools, under widely varying conditions. We must make use of generalizations; but let us remember we are speaking of patterns and *not* individuals. My attack is upon the system, not the people in its clutches. To mislead ourselves about the people, however, and the way they work, think, and feel, can scarcely help us come to the understanding that is our goal.

Some years ago our Vice-President invited a camel driver from the Near East to visit him. We may suspect that when the good man returned to report his adventures and what he had seen there were many who regarded him, like Marco Polo centuries before, as given more to prevarication than reporting. This is the fate of those who visit strange lands. Because there is a school around the corner, and because we have been to school, we tend to think of public education as part of our current civilization. Yet in an important sense it is not. It is an enclave in which past centuries remain in force, and into which many of the concepts and principles and operating methods we take for granted have not yet penetrated. As a result, many a statement of simple fact appears a wild-eyed utterance. We cannot believe that sacred cows roam the streets of busy cities until we are told the cities are in India—then it is entirely credible. The same principle applies to any realistic discussion of our public schools. To help persuade the reader of this, I have made frequent use of quotations from educators and high officials.

The Educational Curtain is real. Indeed, I suspect a very large proportion of parents have become entangled in it at some time and found it extremely effective in blocking a satisfactory view of what goes on. Few communities care to advertise their school troubles. Most board of education members feel a conviction, which may rest on nothing more than ego, that they are doing about as well as anyone could, and that therefore difficulties and weaknesses may be easier to deal with if there is a tacit agreement to admit them only behind the scenes. Understandably, they may feel that critical examinations of the health of their system or its schools may make it harder to win approval of budgets and borrowings—and they are never more than a few months from the need for such approvals. Some hold it "unpatriotic" for a citizen to question the excellence of the schools. Won't it demean the community, keep newcomers away, and drive down property values? The superintendent and principals commonly join the board in a virtual conspiracy to accent the positive and conceal the negative, all for the best of motives.

The superintendent who feels an even stronger desire to "look good" may or may not tell his board all they might like to know. Except in quite small systems, the board will have to be both informed and astute to find out for themselves. Like other people, superintendents want to keep their jobs, build a good reputation and perhaps get called to a bigger job somewhere else. They are usually not eager to rock the boat. A notably daring exception, Carl F. Hansen, long the head of the schools in Washington, D.C., says in his book *The Amidon Elementary School:*

> Only an informed and unhappy public can bring about improvement in the quality of school service. Thus the public must have the truth, all of it, whether it is good or bad or mixed, and the responsible superintendent must face forthrightly his duty to reveal the facts about his schools.

He notes, however, that some of his associates locally and around the country viewed his announcement of the Amidon concept as "treason," which suggests they think "that a superintendent has a specific responsibility to defend existing practices. When he fails to perform this duty he degrades himself and his profession." When more recently Dr. Bernard Donovan, the head of New York City schools, gave out certain reading achievement results to the press, school by school, the action was regarded as of almost unprecedented boldness, especially since many of the ghetto school scores were distressingly low. It would be hard to find many parallel instances; and even this followed long agitation and demonstrations. By and large, it is difficult for the public to know what is happening within their schools, or to get useful information for evaluating them or supporting desirable change.

We must understand, however, that there is one excellent if alarming reason why the schools do not tell us more about themselves and our children. *They don't know.* Whether we speak of an individual school, a system, a state effort or that of the country, we must expect to find ourselves in the role of a traveler in a swamp, probing for solid land to stand on. The most elementary facts, figures, and findings are as likely as not to be missing or unreliable. Dollars can be accounted for (there has been amazingly little scandal in this area, in spite of the huge sums involved). But on the educational side, both statistics and results are at primitive levels. Parents and taxpayers who are in any way associated with or interested in the management of enterprises tend to take for granted that any sizeable undertaking automatically provides for checking on results, for exact controls, for accurate comparisons which reveal gains or losses and trends. The organization of the classroom school system makes this difficult. In addition, experience makes amply clear that most administrators are much more concerned with their own convenience and with having things run smoothly than they are with gathering, at some cost and effort, some idea of how effective the school is in achieving goals.

What is the educational output of our schools, and of a particular school? What do our children get for their time within this compulsory institution? What do taxpayers get for their money? How much goes undone? What could be achieved but isn't? In general, we get very little in the way of answers. For reasons we shall examine, the school often does not "know the score."

Examinations, even if state-standardized, tell us little. Students and teachers cram for enough right answers to get over these hurdles. Important exams become the educational *objective:* they create pressure on student and teacher to put exam-passing above any other consideration. "Achievement tests," although of value, are again essentially examinations, often very limited in scope. In practice, both are used primarily to test the student, not the school; both are employed to suit the school's convenience; and both are used as a rule in isolation, rather than as part of any effort to rate the school. Are the students being better taught, or learning more, than last year? Than five years ago? We have no information, none whatever, in most situations, other than piecemeal impressions.

Admittedly, measuring educational achievement or output is not simple. What amazes is that there has been so little productive effort in this direction, and even less desire by the schools to have yardsticks.

Naive citizens often assume that someone must check on their schools—the state, perhaps? State offices of education do, indeed; but largely in bureaucratic fashion. Classrooms must be a certain size, emergency exits of certain types, teachers must have taken certain courses to be "certificated." (Each state, incidentally, has its own requirements for teacher preparation—an expert teacher with years of good experience who crosses a state line may find herself unable to qualify for a license.) Dr. Robert L. Hopper, Director of State Agency Cooperation in the U.S. Office of Education, stated in an article on state offices in *American Education* (June 1966):

> They all lack enough employees with sufficient experience to pull the systems up to the levels of leadership and service they need to attain. In 1962, for example, the number of professional staff members per State education agency ranged from 16 to 271, and 21 states had fewer than 50 professional staff members.

(Though Dr. Hopper's figures were four years old, they were undoubtedly the latest available, even within the Office of Education. In education, figures only four years old are considered right off the griddle.) In general, state offices concern themselves with very low effectiveness only in extreme instances, and then primarily because bureaucratic requirements are not being met. Some states are putting in computerized systems, which may at least help get some of the statistics a bit more up to date. Beyond this, there seems little prospect of state offices providing any kind of continuous evaluation service which might comfort or distress the hapless parent who sends the children to school.

On the national scene, however, we will have had in 1968 the first approach to any such objective, independent measurement, the first "assessment." Incredibly, not until this time will we have the bare beginnings of such a control! An "Exploratory Committee on Assessing the Progress of Education" was set up in 1964 by the Carnegie Corporation, working with the U.S. Office of Education. Dr. Ralph Tyler, director of the Center for Advanced Study in the Behavioral Sciences, heads the effort, which has received over a million dollars in Carnegie funds. Since the assessment will use a sampling technique, and no teacher will have more than one student involved, preparation for the testing is prevented. But the assessment will give us only some very general bench marks: it will not report on any school, or system, or even state; and it will tell us only what students at several levels appear to know, not what they necessarily learned in school. Nevertheless, any such independent test is welcome, and the groundwork has been well laid.

Although Dr. Tyler and his many distinguished colleagues have been at pains to win consensus and to use methods above reproach, the assessment has drawn angry reactions in many quarters. One important official of a teachers' organization, asked if he favored periodic assessment, replied that it was being done every day by those who should continue to do it, the classroom teachers! Only in public education, I suspect, would we find a leader of this status suggesting that those who do a job are the ideal ones to evaluate their success. Some administrators announced that they would not cooperate with the project, a position they are likely to abandon, however, as public pressures build. As Dr. Tyler observes: "The need for dependable information on the progress of education in this country is now widely recognized by those legally responsible . . . and by the general public."

Noting that more than a fourth of our population is engaged in education, and more money spent than in any industry apart from national defense, Dr. John M. Stalnaker, president of the National Merit Scholarship corporation noted in 1968: "No activity involving so many people and so much money has done so little to find out about itself, the nature of its raw material, the effectiveness of its processing and the quality of its finished product." (*The New York Times,* July 21, 1968)

The probings of Project Talent (a massive study of high school students, based at the University of Pittsburgh) and the results of the Armed Forces "AFQT" testing in the last few years suggest we had better brace ourselves to receive the assessment findings. Project Talent found, in some parts of the country, that the majority of high school graduates could not meet ordinary requirements for *unskilled* labor — which agrees with the Armed Forces acceptance of high school graduates scoring as low as 16 on a test on which a score of 100 is readily possible!

We should not suppose that problems are confined only to those who do not go to college. Project Talent showed that a quite substantial proportion of students attending college had scored in the *lowest* third on the general academic aptitude scale. In the catalogue of a large university of medium quality appears this caution: "If a student's placement test shows he needs further training in the basic skills of reading, he must take the following course. . . ." Such notices, applying to reading or writing English, or both, are hardly uncommon.

Even if our public school educators do not know the score, nor apparently want to, we may and do assume that they are reasonably expert in their fields. Local educators do, indeed, present a public face of relaxed, Buddha-like wisdom, rarely acknowledging much of the human imperfection, doubt, and ignorance more common clay is heir to. We hope they are wise and able: we entrust our children to their authority, give them enormous amounts of money to spend, and rely on them for a major source of national strength. It is shattering to find that it is all too easy to credit them with more expertise than they possess.

Consider this appraisal from what amounts to an official source, the 1960 Yearbook of the American Association of School Administrators:

> Up to and including the present time, school administration has been based upon empirical foundations; it has evolved as a quasi-professional apprenticeship or folklore, with the techniques and processes handed down from one generation to another, through the trial-and-error and the hard-knock pattern.

While this passage, not intended for lay eyes, is blunter and more sweeping than most, it by no means stands alone. The better informed educators are not ignorant of their ignorance, though they try to keep their concern behind the Curtain. It might indeed upset the public to find those in custody of their children are operating by folklore — grandpa's folklore, at that.

In *Elementary School Organization and Administration,* referred to in the previous chapter, the authors observe: "Although much is known about learning in children, so much is still unknown that many practices must be based on the best knowledge available and the soundest guesses about the unknown." It might be amusing to find out whether parents prefer their children's education to be based on "folklore" or "soundest guesses"; but there is precious little room for humor in the situation. Even the reference to "best knowledge available" must be looked at askance. *Characteristically, new and useful knowledge circulates within the public school Establishment in the most haphazard of fashions.* To educators accustomed to trial-and-error methods and tinkering, the thought may simply not occur to try to obtain information that does not readily come to hand.

For example, a 1965 report by a task force of the National Council of Teachers of English, published as "Language Programs for the Disadvantaged," noted in the general recommendations that too few administrators and teachers seemed aware of help available: professional publications were rarely in evidence; professional libraries were poor, if indeed there were any; local leaders were often ignorant even of the existence of pertinent professional organizations! This, let us note, was in a "crash effort" area, where we might expect to find motivation and pressures to seek assistance strongest.

This is, of course, one of the factors behind the amazingly slow rate of change that has long marked our schools. In a major study, *Innovation in Education,* published in 1964 and one of the few books on the subject, Professor Paul R. Mort notes that studies going back some decades indicated that:

> Between insight into a need . . . and the introduction of a way of meeting the need that is destined for general acceptance . . . there is typically a lapse of a half-century. Another half-century is required for the diffusion of the adaptation.

Editor Matthew B. Miles comforts us, to be sure, with the news that very recently the rate of change appears to have speeded up by a factor of six or so. Six times nearly zero, however, is something less than supersonic. Professor Miles also notes that innovations may be seen as "ways of patching, splicing, adding accessories to or otherwise tinkering with the old mechanism to make it more tolerable." A doctor who let children suffer needlessly, because he did not keep reasonably abreast of new developments in medicine, would be looked on harshly. But the school official, or board of education member, who cheats the children by failing to keep up with progress suffers little opprobrium and usually appears to feel no sense of shame. Not to progress, in public education, is normal. As Dr. Francis A. J. Ianni, then research director of the Office of Education, has remarked, "the resistance of educators to the product of research is unmatched in other fields."

Dr. Ianni has also noted that educational research is in its "infancy" — a very strange place for it to be considering its advanced age. This brings us to a core problem. One cannot be a professional in any true sense unless one is using expertise *firmly based on a reliable body of theory*. Useful theory in turn rests on research. It is the absence of this structure, or cycle, which we take for granted in so many other fields, that makes our public school area a "foreign country." Without intent to be unfair to well-meaning, hard-working and often put-upon persons, we must realize that school "professionals," as they dearly like to be called, are not often entitled to that term. Those who operate and direct our schools relate to physicians, engineers and scientists about as witch-doctors relate to doctors. They are seldom scholars; they have no adequate body of theory to apply, nor much understanding of how theory is effectively used; nor do they work as specialists at their highest level of skill.

We have developed techniques for making very rapid progress in most fields by utilizing (to simplify greatly) two levels of interest, one conerned with day-to-day operations, and the other with non-operating, or theoretical matters. For example, a chemical plant will be run by operating people, while those on the other level are busy solving problems, working out new and better means of production, and developing new products. Those on the operating level in general do not attempt to solve other than routine questions — problems are sent to the theoretical level, solved abstractly, and then sent back to the operating, "practical" level for test or application. Ideas and useful observations may come from anywhere: from operations, from applied or pure research, from the literature, from outside fields, or quite commonly from accidental occurrences. Whatever the source, they are routinely evaluated at the theoretical level, investigated, and developed if promising.

In contrast, we have in public school education virtually only one level — operations. *The whole research apparatus is missing!* A lot of so-called "research" is done around the edges, for example, by candidates for doctorate degrees in education. It is notoriously bad, as a rule. In other instances, the *opinions* of many teachers or administrators are gathered, then solemnly tabulated, summarized, and published as research! Or a study will be made of how most schools handle a particular problem — a method guaranteed to exclude• the newest and best approaches.

Research costs money. It also requires people who know how to organize and administer a successful program, and there must be ways of putting the research to use. Our public schools spend annually well over $25 billion, perhaps as much as $30 billion. By best estimates, *less than one-fifth of one percent goes for research.* Most of *this* "research" is apparently for statistical and control purposes rather than efforts to solve problems or develop improved approaches.

Our program to put men on the moon calls for some $40 billion over a period of years, or less than our public schools cost in two. Even thus far, this fantastic venture has occasioned a striking "fallout" of side benefits: some 10,000 new patents, important new technologies, whole families of new products and materials, some already in wide use, and even valuable medical findings, not to mention a huge amount of other scientific knowledge. Perhaps most significant is the speeded development of a technique called systems management, heavily dependent on computers, which can be applied to almost any kind of very complicated problem — hopefully, maybe even our schools.

But from some $150 billion our schools have spent, we have
—what? Almost all of it has simply been spent, leaving us just
about where we were. Only in a small number of advanced
schools, and then usually with money from foundations or companies, have we achieved anything significant. To spend so
much money, year after year, and achieve so little advance is
a negative achievement on a spectacular scale.

The people who run our public schools may be the salt of
the earth and worthy of respect on many grounds; but let us
admit that they operate in deep ignorance, blundering along
as best they can by hit-or-miss methods oddly and disastrously
out of place in the twentieth century.

In very recent years, a considerable amount of valuable
research and experiment (using that term correctly) has been
done—more than in a generation before. It has not been done,
of course, by the schools, and not always in them. What most
impresses, out of these new findings, is the strong suggestion
that *the great bulk of what the public school operators think they know
is utter nonsense.* Again and again it has been proved that children can learn enormously faster and better than the old rules
permit. To discover that "folklore" is largely nonsense can
hardly be too surprising; but when we realize that we expend
vast sums and effort to commit our children to the schools,
themselves a haven of misconceptions and ignorance, we can
hardly be less than shocked.

What can we expect of these deluded, misinformed people
(I am generalizing, of course—let us bless the exceptions)
when the public more and more demands better results? All
many *do* know is how to operate the system as it is, guided by
the dubious principles they have long accepted. We may expect them, as any human beings would in such circumstances,
to cling to and defend and try to preserve the system we have.
Teachers, who suffer the most, and who often are youngsters,
offer a good minority willing to change at least to some extent.
But superintendents and principals run older and have a
greater vested interest in old ways. Only a few will lead. The
rest will have to be firmly pushed by a public that has seen behind the Educational Curtain.

If it is disturbing to discover the conditions we have here

briefly discussed, it may be still more distressing to look for a moment at our public school "system" nationally. To use the term "system" or any other which implies some sort of order or deliberate arrangement is misleading. Our schools form a hodgepodge, a disjointed and disorganized mass of confusion, nightmarish in its mad and pointless diversity.

In our public schools there are over 42 million students. To this, add roughly two million teachers, administrators and others, for a total of about 44 million "full time" persons—not far from a quarter of our present 200 million population!

The number of schools is roughly 100,000. They vary greatly in almost every respect. In size, they run from those with only a handful of students (there are still thousands of one-teacher schools) to elementary schools with up to a thousand pupils and high schools perhaps five times that size. I know of no figures purporting to show the *age* of our school buildings, but we get a hint of how slow replacement is from the fact that in fall, 1965, the total number of "schoolrooms" was officially put at almost 1.6 million, while in the previous year about 16,000 had been abandoned—just one percent! Only 65,000 new were added. Wherever we look in old communities, we find schools 50 to 80 years old, still in daily use. They tend to stay in use until they are too hazardous to occupy, and sometimes longer. In general, we do *not* seem to be making perceptible progress by replacing schools faster than they age. We probably are falling behind—this, after two decades of the most vigorous, least-interrupted prosperity we have ever experienced!

Public schools are supported by school districts, and operated as "systems." There are about 26,000 systems. Of these around half serve no more than 300 students. Over 400 systems have upwards of 12,000 students. At the top end, we have Philadelphia with about a quarter-million, Los Angeles with more than half a million, New York with almost a full million (but working on decentralizing).

Another way to look at the differences among schools is to consider how much they spend per pupil, not that this is necessarily directly equivalent to results achieved. The Office of Education provides data by states for 1965–6. For the country, the median falls at $532 per pupil. Mississippi comes in lowest with $317, South Carolina next with $349. At the other end we have New York, $876; Alaska, $775; New Jersey, $662. These are *state* figures. Some suburban schools in high income areas run well over the $1,000 mark; we may well wonder what the lows are in parts of some of the states at the bottom! *The top schools spend over three times as much per pupil as the bottom schools.*

The ratio of educational staff to students is another index. In suburban schools, it may run 70 to a thousand students; in a large city, 40; in very poor schools, even less. *The top schools provide twice the staff (and much better staff, we can expect), that the lowest do.*

Surprisingly few citizens seem aware of one of the most soul-chilling facts about our schools nationally and even locally. *How well a child does in school tends to be closely related to the income and social class of his parents.* The relationship is too complicated to go into in this book. *Education and Income,* by Patricia C. Sexton, the most recent large study, throws much light on the reasons. In a foreword to it, Professor Kenneth B. Clark, then at the College of the City of New York, stated that Dr. Sexton

. . . has presented concrete evidence which demonstrates beyond any reasonable doubt that our public-school system has rejected its role of facilitating social mobility and has become in fact an instrument of social and economic class distinctions in American society.

Horace Mann saw free, effective public schooling as "the great equalizer of men . . . balance wheel of the social machinery." For a period it did have that effect. But we are fallen on days of disaster. The very class-and-grade system that Mann did so much to foster is today the one consistent pattern amid the variations of our public schools, and it operates in exactly the opposite direction: to make the rich richer and more favored, the poor poorer, relatively more and more ignorant, discriminated against, and shut out from hope.

The class-and-grade system afflicts us all. It eats at our concepts of democracy and at our national strength as well.

"CRITICAL SCARCITY

OF TEACHERS HITS

NATION'S SCHOOLS

Worst Shortage in Decade

Follows Recent Gains—

Officials Are Surprised"

Front-page headline in *The New York Times,*
September 4, 1966

3

TOO FEW TO TEACH

There's nothing wrong with our schools that getting some more good teachers in wouldn't about fix up."

"That's right—even if we have to pay a little more to attract better people."

"The teacher is the heart of the matter. Say what you like about new gadgets, no machine is going to replace the teacher."

It is not hard to hear remarks like these in almost any community when neighbors get together. Yet there are few subjects on which the average citizen is apt to have less information and understanding in support of confidently asserted remarks. Though the "teacher" is a familiar figure, and the great majority of parents of school-age children know one or more at least by name and sight, the term is a semantic trap.

First of all, let us remember the numbers we are dealing with. Obviously, generalizing about some two million persons has its dangers. A particular teacher may be a brilliantly intellectual person, with an excellent education and a warm, outgoing personality, devoted to his or her work, and incessantly striving to improve on the results of years of on-the-job experience and training. Or, "teacher" may be the rawest recruit, graduate of a poor high school in the lowest quarter of the class, graduate of a miserably poor college, lacking in experience and background of every desirable sort, including contact with school-age children, and with the meagerest intellectual equipment and personal qualities one can imagine in a supposedly literate person.

"Teacher" is a title shared by all. It tells us nothing about qualifications, not even formal qualifications, for tens of thousands who hold the job and the title do not meet their state and local legal requirements; or even if they are "certificated" may be assigned to work for which they would not be acceptable according to the published standards. In *The Education of American Teachers,* Dr. James B. Conant has described in detail both the shortcomings of the various state standards and the ways in which even these are commonly circumvented.

Nor does experience tell us much. A young teacher with good training and a little time on the job may be far better on every count than one who has been working for years. Like other people, teachers fall into ruts, grow rigid in their ideas as they get older, become embittered and frustrated as hopes fail, suffer from arthritis, marital troubles, menopause, boredom, and not least, some special mental health difficulties which the classroom and lack of contact with other adults may generate. Many teachers are delighted to be teaching and would choose no other occupation. Others teach because they never found anything else to do, or as a stopgap, or because the hours seem short and the vacations long, or because bossing children nurtures an ego that shrinks from the competition of grownups. It is no dishonor to the able, dedicated teacher not to be romantic about "teacher." As we shall see, it takes all kinds to fill the schools.

To make the problem still more difficult, the concept of "teacher" has been changing steadily throughout the century, at first slowly and then with increasing rapidity. To grasp what the phrase "teacher shortage" really means, we will have to examine, however briefly, the nature of these changes. But for the present and at least the next few years to come, we can have little doubt as to the effect: there is virtually no hope that we can staff our schools as they are with enough teachers.

The figures of the National Education Association for 1967 showed that a record 227,000 persons completed teacher preparation programs — a jump of ten percent over the previous year's total. But by no means do all of these take teaching jobs. Of those trained for elementary schools, a shade over 80 percent usually find positions, and less than 70 percent of secondary people do. The loss bulks large: only about 70,000 elementary and 87,000 high school teachers were expected to enter teaching, a total of 157,000. (This "drop out" phenomenon has long been characteristic of teaching training. Most of the missing, apparently, never do teach.)

The NEA statistics use a "Quality Criterion" estimate, based on *minimum* needs to replace departing teachers, fill new jobs, and reduce overlarge classes to *maximum* "reasonable" size. On this standard, the year's shortage of supply was put at 172,000 teachers: 26,500 secondary, and a whopping 146,000 needed and not available for elementary schools. Considering the healthy ten percent jump in graduates, with either bachelor's or master's degree, this red figure was scarcely cause for joy.

Ironically, one of the factors in the shortage is the impact of Federal programs intended to help meet acute educational needs, and another is the tendency of systems to add curricular offerings, and services, in response to demand.

The teacher shortage is real, probably much worse than represented, and has long inspired a chorus of authoritative voices to gloomy forecasts and accurate but unheeded warnings.

The situation we are in was clearly foreseen. After a trip around the country in 1956, Dr. Alexander J. Stoddard, a leading educator, predicted:

By 1965, there will be needed nearly 350,000 more teachers than there are now. There are no signs anywhere that such a needed increase in teacher supply will be met by the total of all present or planned training programs throughout the nation.

About the same time Paul Woodring, a leading writer on education, reached a similar conclusion in *New Directions in Teacher Education:*

> If we maintain the present teacher-pupil ratio we shall need nearly two million *new* teachers for additions and replacements in the next ten years. Because good teaching is an art of the highest order, we cannot hope to find so large a number with first-rate ability.

Matters have not turned out quite as badly as predicted, in part because the birth rate halted its runaway climb, and to some degree because private foundations and the Federal government have poured billions into meeting the problem. But as some more recent studies indicate, the gains have been small, if indeed we have gained at all. *The prospects for having an adequate supply of teachers adequately trained even by existing standards to staff our present classroom system seem close to nil for as far ahead as we can see.*

What happens when a shortage of teachers exists? Any employer knows the answer. When he cannot get people of the quality he needs, he takes what he can get. A superintendent or principal who has to fill a vacancy someway does just that—someway; and it is hard to blame him. In some cases the lowering of standards comes to public attention. Residents of New York City were shocked not long ago to learn that more than half the city's junior high school teachers were not qualified by usual standards. California, as 1965 began, was seeking up to 3,000 language teachers to meet a program legislated in 1961. Standards had to be relaxed to provide even a hope that so many could be found.

More often, the standards are allowed to slip as quietly as possible. Neither superintendent nor school board are eager to broadcast the news. Various methods are used: certain shortcomings in preparation are overlooked, or emergency standards are resorted to. More substitutes are employed, sometimes as "permanent substitutes." A favorite method of concealing the situation is to employ a teacher who is technically qualified, and then to assign him or her to a job for which the teacher's record shows little or no specific preparation. A classroom teacher may be required to teach remedial reading or to conduct the music program. A high school music major may be put to teaching mathematics, a social studies teacher may be given English classes. Recently an artist of my acquaintance told me, in a state of shock, that his daughter's junior high art teacher had complained to his class that he really knew nothing about art, his field being physical education. On the record, however, all these teachers would show as qualified and certificated.

In two other practical ways the teacher shortage takes its toll of school operations. For one, it makes recruitment a major task. A significant amount of effort must be diverted to a never-ending struggle to fill the vacancies. Interviews must be granted any remotely possible prospect, and every mail inquiry must get the most careful attention. The less the school system has to offer competitively, the more effort it may have to make. For another, as we shall see, the shortage still further weakens the principal's authority and ability to control. When an employer has to take what he can get he learns to mutter most of his criticisms to himself — is it better to have a class covered by a poor or uncooperative teacher, or to have no teacher whatever?

Not the least of the sad aspects of the shortage is the lasting effect, however it may be resolved in due course. A teacher who is accepted into a system because none better can be hired stands a good chance of acquiring a permanent status, and in many cases tenure. Quite possibly, class after class for some ten years or more will add to the price paid for hiring incompetency.

The teacher shortage has been with us for virtually a full generation, even though it has come to public notice only in the last few years. So long as schools are organized on the class-and-teacher arrangement, it must grow acute, if for no other reason, when school population jumps. Consider a factory required to increase output by a third within a brief period. Probably, it can do so readily by adding some facilities and machines, but far less than a third more employees. Only where a pinch would occur need more hands be put to work. The same would likely be true of a food store, which might increase capacity with a very small addition in staff. But when we come to a classroom school, no such flexibility exists. If a 400-pupil school must expand to 530, it must add a third more teachers, unless it makes classes larger.

If the factory and store find the employees they need are hard to get, they can raise pay to attract more applicants. But they need only raise pay in those categories which are in short supply: milling machine operator, optical inspector, or meatcutter, let us say. In contrast, the schools have one overwhelming category of employee: teacher. A pay raise for teachers, plus the effect on future automatic increases and pensions, becomes a matter of staggering size. Again, the rigidity of the classroom organization creates an acute problem some other employers have to far less degree.

It is not our purpose here to discuss the incredibly intricate question of teachers' pay. Those who do, with some claim to authority, come to astonishingly varying conclusions. There is reason to suppose the whole argument is on the way to becoming academic — for the future will force a quite different basis for compensating school staffs and "teacher" will be but one of a number of job titles. We may note simply the fact that the NEA put the *average* instructional staff teacher salary at $7,600 for 1967–68, an amount which of course covers a good deal less than a full year of work and so might be said to equal $9,500. Many will agree that a really able person should get more, and that poor teachers are overpaid at any price.

Much more pertinent is to understand what has been happening to the term "teacher." Like many titles, it carries with it a good deal from the past; and we must take a brief excursion into history if we are to see the present clearly and at least glimpse the future.

If we jump back a bit over three full centuries to the famous Massachusetts law of 1647 which required certain classes of towns to establish *public* schools, we find the teachers' pay theme already a dominant one. The move to tax for schools brought much grumbling. What carried the day was the current equivalent of our fear of Russia and communism —fear of the devil: ". . . it being one chief object of that old deluder; Satan, to keep men from knowledge of the Scriptures . . ." Undoubtedly there were far-sighted citizens who saw in the education of all, at least to minimal literacy, a safeguard to our liberties and institutions; but these were hardly enough to force legislation. Moral and religious considerations had more weight in a day when an industrious and clever man might do very well with no formal education whatever. Since these public schools were attended only by the offspring of those who could not afford others, there was little tendency to be lavish with funds. On the contrary: the tradition of begrudging funds for public education and of paying teachers as little as possible was established even earlier than the schools themselves.

The term "teacher" as applied to publicly supported schools got off to a bad start for this reason, as well as the fact that in a pioneering society a male who spent his time managing children scarcely had a head start on commanding prestige. The early schoolmaster was apt to be an oddball type: an eccentric, a man with a distaste for other work open to him, one whose fondness for the bottle or even less charming lapses made it advisable to move often, or a lover of learning without means. That many of these persons and their like were not particularly interested in teaching and dedicated to finer things need hardly be stressed. So long as a candidate could make some pretension to literacy, had a strong right arm to beat the devil out of his charges, and would work for the pittance offered, he was acceptable. It was long the custom, as Ichabod Crane reminds us, for teachers to be boarded around from household to household in lieu of cash. The unwilling hosts were not always eager to set a good table. If at school their guests were unenthusiastic or slow in applying the whip, not infrequently they were turned on by boys as large as and much better fed than they. Such a life was hardly for women. Apart from the round-the-kitchen-stove dame schools, "teacher" then normally meant a male.

Between 1810 and 1840, when the population more than

tripled, the need for teachers became overwhelming, especially in the rapidly growing urban communities. Probably to no one's regret, this type of male schoolmaster began to disappear from the public schools, decorously pushed aside by a new flood of fresh-faced and innocent maidens. For the most part they were innocent of education, too; but since they would work cheap and at least had more schooling than their charges, they were welcomed to meet the emergency.

To what we would now term the upper and upper-middle classes, these teaching jobs held little attraction. To the lower class, they were unattainable. But to the lower-middle class, they were literally the answer to a maiden's prayer. Teaching was obviously far better than staying at home or working in the newly burgeoning factories or behind a counter. Association with books and learning and with a public undertaking not only promised prestige but was eminently *respectable* work, a factor of great weight in the society of the time. It is easy to see why the tradition arose that teachers, above all others in the community, must "behave" and offend no one—in sharp contrast to their ragged, disreputable, often laughing-stock male predecessors. We see, too, where the image of the old-maid schoolteacher came from. In truth, many *were* spinsters whose narrow and uneventful thread of life slowly unwound in the classroom.

But slowly the works of Rousseau, Pestalozzi, Froebel, and Herbart took effect. It was no longer assumed that children were evil and had to have all good beaten into them. The strong right arm was no longer in hourly use, and the first rays of what we would consider a modern approach were lighting the educational scene. Still, only the barest elementary education was attempted. And, estimable, respectable, and earnest as many of the young women were, we would find it difficult to consider them "teachers," even while they drilled their gigantic classes. They were by our poorest standards totally unprepared.

The first normal school in our country dates from 1839— teacher education is only 130 years old! The idea took hold and these institutions multiplied rapidly. Even in the light of history, it shocks us to realize that they were the equivalent of high schools. At first, one year at normal school qualified a teacher. Later, as standards rose, two years might be required, especially to teach higher grades; and eventually three or four years became a common requirement.

In a sense, public education and teacher education have played a sort of tag game. As public sentiment and the increasing complexity of our daily living demanded more and more schooling, teacher training had to be extended. After all, it is always desirable that the teacher be older, and know more, than her pupils! When free public high schools became common, during the last quarter of the century, the tag game began to be played at an ever-increasing pace. By 1900 most normal schools were requiring a high school diploma for *admission.* And only twenty years later, many had metamorphosed into teachers colleges, offering to at least some students a four-year course and a college degree. Standards now rose even more swiftly, as is nicely illustrated by the chart, based on data gathered by the Lynds for *Middletown in Transition,* the second volume of the famous study of a typical American city:

Teachers' Post-High School Training

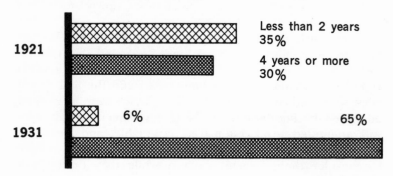

1921 — Less than 2 years 35%

4 years or more 30%

1931 — 6%

65%

The rapidity of the change is breathtaking. Clearly the meaning of "teacher" had altered more abruptly than ever.

Some modifying facts should be stated, however. The education degrees were scarcely the equivalent of a good uni-

versity B.A., and despite the increasing number of able individuals attracted to teaching in the spirit of social service,
the main source was still lower-middle-class women of limited
outlook and meager intellectual ability. Surveys found:

> . . . that students preparing to teach are, in general, of a
> lower economic status than students in other departments;
> that the teachers as a class are relatively inferior in schol-
> arship, and that their salaries are less; that teacher-training
> institutions are relatively deficient in physical equipment;
> that many of them are not adequately equipped with model
> or demonstration schools; and that public funds for
> teacher-training institutions are proportionately less than
> those appropriated to liberal-arts colleges and agricultural
> colleges. (Quoted from *Education in the United States*, by
> Edgar W. Knight, a widely used textbook published in 1951.)

Other authorities noted, as we might expect from the above
unblinking summary, that while the intelligence of teaching
candidates ranged from very low to very high, on the average
it was, as measured, the lowest of any group attending college.

The considerations which had sent so many into teaching
for a century were now enfeebled. Teaching had been one of the
very few respectable occupations for a young woman. Now there
were hundreds—most of them quite respectable, not that anyone any longer worried too much about that once dominant
consideration. More urgent factors now were "glamour,"
opportunity to meet eligible and prospering future husbands,
pay and benefits, working conditions, opportunity to travel,
general "fun," and perhaps we should add ease of parking.

What this highly compressed history of the meaning of the
term "teacher" shows is that a job that once was very easy to
get into, and that was particularly attractive to certain undis-
tinguished segments of our population, was by the 1930's no
longer to be so categorized. On the contrary, teaching now
commonly required a *greater* commitment in time, money,
and formal education than many alternative types of work,
many of which paid better.

True, if one wanted to go to college, preparing for teaching had its advantages. Admission requirements were less stringent, expenses usually lower, and competition and standards usually milder. But this cut both ways: abler persons had reason to feel that they might as well make a slightly greater investment and effort, and go to "a regular college." The proportion of men in public school teaching, which had been over 42 percent as late as 1880, had now hit bottom at below 15 percent. The teacher crisis had begun. A decade of economic gloom was to make it far worse.

The effect of the Depression was to bring almost to an end the "normal" supply of teachers which the schools had so long taken for granted. One out of four teachers in the land was receiving less than $750 a year. In cities of medium size, even in 1930, median pay for elementary teachers was about $1,600, for high school teachers $2,100, and for principals from $2,600 to $4,200, and depression economies quite generally cut these still lower. Married women teachers were regarded with disfavor, since they were keeping a male head of a family from a job, presumably. Where the law didn't protect sufficiently, ways were found to harass them or reduce their pay, and the tradition of the old-maid schoolteacher, which had begun to languish, was given fresh sustenance. Class size, which had been declining steadily for years, either stopped shrinking or began to grow: elementary classes were commonly over 35 and often up to 50 and more.

Even so, any job was greatly to be desired, and the teachers clung to theirs. Civil service waiting lists grew so long that those fairly well down from the top could figure from the rate of hiring that they would be lucky, indeed, to live long enough to be hired. To top matters off, population was barely growing, and enrollment in the elementary grades, where most teachers begin, was actually falling off—by a startling 2,500,000 from 1929 to 1939. (High school enrollment increased enough to balance a good part of this drop.) A high school graduate could find little reason to go to college to prepare specifically for an occupation in which employment seemed most improbable. The number enrolled in teachers colleges sagged, and at the end of the decade was no greater than at the beginning. Other colleges and universities felt no such pinch, for their enrollment climbed during the ten years from 1,100,000 to almost 1,500,000. While some of these students may later have entered teaching, there can be little doubt that the Depression choked off the already faltering supply, reducing what had been a flood to a trickle.

Scarcely had good times returned than World War II struck an even worse blow. Many male and not a few female teachers entered service. Those that did not had almost to fight off lucrative offers of high pay and overtime in all sorts of other occupations, including defense work blessed with the glow of patriotism, even if it was at a bench rather than a desk. *By the war's end, it was estimated that more than a third of the competent teachers at work in 1940 had left teaching.* Most never returned. Even in 1946 half of all teachers were being paid under $2,000 per year, pay that looked still smaller to those who had sampled wartime earnings.

For all the long-felt effects of these two historical accidents, however, we should not let them obscure the far more sweeping change that was taking place. As we have seen, around 1900 the normal schools were becoming more than high schools; by 1920 they were offering degrees; by 1930 many were changing their names to "teachers colleges," with outlooks changing to match. By 1950 many were taking the final step—dropping the name and concept "teachers," and becoming liberal arts colleges and even universities.

Dr. Woodring points out that the change was not nominal but actual:

> To continue to call such institutions "teachers colleges" because of their historical origin is as meaningless as it would be to refer to the University of Pennsylvania as an academy because it was so designated by its founder. . . . As a result of these changes the term "teachers college" is fast becoming obsolete. . . . It seems a safe guess that within twenty years, perhaps within ten years, the separate teachers colleges will have gone the way of the dodo.

The change Dr. Woodring refers to is far from widely understood. It is possible to listen to the great debate on education raging on for a month or two, and never hear even a reference to this earthshaking shift. Yet its implications seem both clear and relatively permanent: *teachers used to get a third- or fourth-class education; now they are well on the way to getting a first-class education.* And the number of persons who are attracted to and can accomplish a first-class education is smaller, and will remain smaller as far ahead as we can see.

Already there are many signs that qualification for teaching will soon require a regular B.A. degree *plus* at least a year of specialized training, instead of the present pattern of about a quarter of the usual four-year work being devoted to "vocational" subjects. "Teacher" will come to mean not a person with less than a "real" bachelor's degree, but one with at least a glimmer of true professional, post-graduate training.

It can hardly surprise us if those who accomplish such training prove more demanding when they seek work. For generations our public schools have kept pace with population growth and school expansion by hiring cheap help. There is still a disturbing amount of cheap help at work, with our children at their mercy. But clearly we have entered an era when cheap help teachers can no longer meet the requirements. The old source of teachers is useless now, and there is no adequate new source even in sight.

Paradoxically, even as the demands that teachers be better prepared and more able reduce the supply so desperately needed, these demands are progressively stepped up, in large part by blistering public attacks on the institutions that educate teachers or dictate what their training shall be.

In *The Miseducation of American Teachers*, Dr. James D. Koerner reported the findings of a two-year study of teacher education in blunt language. His conclusions in general are in firm agreement with other studies. There can be little doubt that education departments, even in highly regarded universities, usually attract an outsize share of students from the bottom of the academic barrel. Their faculties usually rate below the rest of the departments on almost any pertinent consideration. Indeed, one of the worst problems in raising standards has been a snobbishness, to avoid harsher words. Those not in education on college faculties have tended to sneer at and stay clear of their colleagues concerned with teacher training. The tendency has been lessened some recently by vigorous effort, as under sharp criticism administrations have moved to bring their education departments closer to their overall standards, and get the "educators" and "scholars" working together.

Much of the struggle revolves around control of certificates. Without a certificate, a teacher cannot get a job, at least not on a full-fledged and official basis. It is therefore a powerful club as well as a control. Even with one, a teacher may not be able to take a job in a neighboring state, for in most cases the requirements for certification are extremely detailed, spelling out exactly what kind of courses must have been taken, for exactly how long. Naturally, colleges within a state provide the courses the state authorities prescribe. An establishment results which can be exceedingly difficult to combat or modernize.

As Dr. Koerner pointed out, a typical high school teacher may have spent a full quarter of his time in college taking "education" courses rather than in subject or academic pursuits. An elementary school teacher may have taken up to half her work in such method and theory courses. Thus, for example, a teacher may have spent more time taking courses on how to teach English and how to manage a class than on English itself. To make matters worse, the education courses are often, if indeed not usually, of miserably poor quality. To quote from an article by Dr. Koerner:

> Not only are most prospective teachers inferior in quality to start with; the training they receive, with its heavy emphasis on education courses, only serves to stifle what talents they have. I recently managed to look into a good many of these pedagogical courses, to survey extensively the materials used, and to talk with many hundreds of students involved in them. The students' verdict is overwhelmingly negative—often bitterly so, particularly among the better students, the kind most needed in teaching.

The faculty members who teach these instructional courses are for the most part former school administrators and others whose background in liberal arts is often on the skimpy side. The pedagogical courses, however poor, out-of-date, and useless they may be, are nevertheless the base for what prestige they have, and their bread and butter as well. Only a bombshell can shatter their tight ranks and mutual support.

A pretty good bombshell exploded in September 1963, when Dr. James B. Conant published *The Education of American Teachers* with its 27 specific recommendations for reform or improvement. The very first of these struck what may prove to be a mortal blow. It proposed that, in effect, states certify any legitimate college graduate who in the opinion of his college was qualified to teach, thus wiping aside all the detailed requirements as to specific education courses. Although there is a long way to go, Dr. Conant's enormous prestige and the publicity his findings command has already had effect in more states than not. The combined forces against the state establishments promise to carry the day.

Tens of thousands more poor quality teachers from poor college education departments will enter the schools for years to come. But the requirements are steadily being raised. Colleges that have always accepted any student in the education department will more and more turn down the weakest applicants. Those that have almost never flunked out a student will begin doing so. Students taking genuine courses and studies rather than "serving time" in education courses will have to work harder. Higher standards attract better people; but there is every reason to believe that for a long time ahead the net effect will be better teachers, but relatively fewer. There will not be enough, nearly enough, to staff our present system.

It is hard to see any choice but to change the system. First, we have to get rid of the rigid organization that makes it mandatory to find another teacher for every 30 or so pupils. Second, since really good teachers are few, we must find a way of using what good ones we have as effectively as possible and not shut them into a room with the same number of students the poorest teacher in the school has.

While we delay, our children and our nation pay the price.

"By 1870, graded classes, graded content, graded textbooks, and even graded teachers meshed together in a school mechanism that has undergone little redesigning to the present."

John I. Goodlad in *School, Curriculum, and the Individual*

4

THE FUNDAMENTAL ERROR

School boards in some communities are composed of political hacks, serving to keep control in "the right hands." More often they are a small, valiant band of leading citizens, conscientiously trying to discharge a volunteer job that seems to enmesh them in ever more varied duties and ever more complicated detail.

On Monday evening a typical board of education member may pore over the pages of an inch-thick budget. On Tuesday he may meet with a neighborhood group to forestall complaints about changed districting. Wednesday may find him sitting in on a curriculum committee discussion with the superintendent, and Thursday may mean a board meeting which runs to 1 A.M. If he has nothing to do on Friday but worry about three new teacher resignations, Saturday morning may find him in the bowels of a school with an engineer, seeing at first hand the impending collapse of the heating system, which will mean that the funds for equipping the new laboratory will have to be found elsewhere. Even with a top-notch superintendent and a good staff to ease the burden, a board tends to be smothered under the constant demand of decision-making: on plant, on finances, on personnel, on curriculum changes, on planning, on taxes, on legal and legislative matters, on integration, on textbooks, on equipment for classrooms, gymnasiums, and lunchrooms, on pensions, on standards, on guidance, on disciplinary problems, on athletics, on health measures, on public and community relations, among others.

Where schools are in obvious trouble, the pressure to deal only with the emergency of the moment and plans for the immediate future is overwhelming. But even in those situations where the pace is gentler, boards commonly find, to quote one member: "We never have time to *think!*" The mechanics of school operation get attention, rather than education.

When those on the firing line, whether volunteers or paid personnel, do manage by some supreme effort to stand back for a larger view, their concern quite naturally is with their own *local* situation. Gigantic as is our national educational effort, it is guided and conducted by innumerable small units; and in relation to the whole, the central state and federal education offices are puny in staff and resources. Such a structure makes it easy to be over-concerned with matters of the moment and chronically behind in adapting to conditions changing more rapidly and sweepingly than ever before in man's history. Not surprisingly, major new concepts in education come almost entirely from the two extremes—those in "ivory towers" far from the battle, and those so desperately engaged and threatened with disaster that they damn the torpedoes, throw out the rules and improvise on the spot.

This book is concerned with stepping back, with examining some of our basic assumptions and habits of thought, apart from the innumerable variations local conditions may demand. Once we do, some of the concepts we may take for granted come to look highly questionable. Of these, I submit, none is more far-reaching, more the classic type of crippling idea, than the notion that our schools must be organized on the teacher-and-class principle, the student body divided up into the largest affordable number of equal groups, a teacher assigned to each group, and each teacher-and-class unit put in a separate classroom. The teacher-and-class arrangement is in such general use and had been for so long that the mere suggestion that there is nothing inevitable about it, and that it is only one of dozens of possible ways of organizing, comes as a shock to many persons, including, I have found, many persons intimately connected with education.

Schools without classes? Eyebrows go up, and that special tolerant expression appears, reserved for persons to be humored rather than argued with. Just so greeted were those who suggested that carriages might go without horses to pull them. Among those who had the open-mindedness and foresight to see what the motor car might soon offer, the term "automobile" soon came into use. But it is significant that for the public the term "horseless carriage" lingered on for years, each utterance testifying to continuing amazement that what had seemed so indispensable was now found not to be necessary at all. If our schools change in the ways that seem to be indicated, we will probably go through a period during which citizens will marvel at "classless schools" in much the same manner. (We already have "non-graded.") But I venture the prediction that a generation from now the whole idea of a class-and-classroom system will seem as quaint and antique as the surrey with the fringe on top. Children will listen with half-doubting frowns as we tell them how we used to spend an entire year in a group of thirty, with one teacher who tried to teach us everything under the sun, all in that one room. As they now say, "You *didn't* have any television when you were a child?"—trying to readjust in imagination to a life without the magic screen to command at the twist of a knob—so they will try to picture our present type of school.

Words can be paralyzing: we can think more easily if we get rid of the word "class" and instead think in terms of *fixed groupings* and *flexible groupings*. Whether we consider our elementary schools, where the pupil is put in a fixed group for a term or a school year, or higher grades, where the group may be fixed only in relation to a certain course or subject, our present system is organized almost wholly on the fixed basis. But the flexible system is by no means entirely unfamiliar to us. Most of our leading universities, for example, do not operate on the class principle. A freshman or sophomore may in the course of a day attend a lecture in a large, packed hall, go to a room to work with a group of fifteen or twenty, then to the library to work alone, then to a laboratory where attendance fluctuates, and finally to a discussion meeting with a tutor, limited to ten or twelve. It would never occur to the institution to count the students, divide the total by a convenient number, and then inform them that they would always gather in groups of the resulting size. Instead, it somehow seems obvious in the college environment that a professor can lecture to two hundred as well as to twenty, and that a discussion should be limited to a dozen and not attempted in a grouping far too large for the purpose. The college works on the exceedingly simple principle that the grouping should be suited to the educational *function* to be accomplished at the moment.

We take this principle for granted in most everything we do. For sports, say, we group by twos or fours for tennis, by nines or a few more for baseball, and by any number we please for bowling. In music we do not establish a grouping of thirty and suggest that at one time the group play a quartet and at another it play a symphony. It seems clear that for quartets groups of four are indicated, and for the symphony perhaps a hundred would be better. Even the army, which once worked on a rigid grouping plan, has largely abandoned the concept in favor of forming men, specialists, and officers into "teams" according to the function they are currently assigned. But our schools seem to be immune to such common sense as grouping for the function to be performed. Instead, our children are counted off into *administrative* groups, exactly as sheep might be loaded into cattle cars according to how many each can conveniently accommodate. If the groupings turn out to be thirty, then *the functions must be made to fit the groupings,* however awkward, absurd or downright impossible this may be.

So far as I can learn, no educator has come forward to claim that twenty-five or thirty is a grouping desirable for basic *educational* purposes. It appears, in fact, to be about as ill-chosen a figure as one could imagine. It is far too big for individual attention to the pupil; more than twice the limit usually set for true discussion groups; too large for individual drilling or recitation and unnecessarily small for mass drill; wastefully small for movies and the like; smaller than a desirable audience for lectures. It has no particular virtue for music, art, lab work, shop work, or physical education that is readily discoverable.

Even administratively, the fixed group type of organization brings a rash of tormenting problems as soon as the school seeks to make the mildest move towards modern education: *recognizing individual differences and trying to realize each child's full potential in spite of them.* "In spite of them" it has to be, for if the fixed grouping is to work perfectly, the children in each class must be as alike as sheep, and have the considerate decency to grow, in every respect, at a uniform rate. To the degree that children aren't alike, or stubbornly refuse to oblige by growing at a uniform rate, the fixed grouping is strained. To propose to recognize and realize the differences among children, and at the same time put them in fixed groups, is to embark on the frustrating program of simultaneously heading in opposite directions.

It seems absurd that we should have to set down, as a golden principle, that if we want to go North we should head North. Yet it seems essential to begin any discussion of the organization of our schools to state: *we should group children, not according to any artificial, administrative, or traditional scheme, but to enable us best to carry on the educational functions that will achieve our broad aims.*

Although it would be most difficult to find any educator who will not agree that our aims have changed radically in the past seventy-five years, we are still using the same rigid teacher-and-class grouping concept that was well established then.

It is interesting to take a look at a largely forgotten system that was imported from England around 1800 and that flourished in our burgeoning cities for a third of a century. The need was for some means of accommodating a sudden rush of children at (familiar theme!) a cost that would not rise, overwhelmingly, equally as fast. The education to be given was very simple, and the methods of the day depended largely on drill and rote learning. For this the Lancastrian plan was admirably designed. One teacher could preside over a huge room in which perhaps two hundred pupils (many more, in some instances) were arranged at parallel long desks, each row in charge of a monitor, an older student. The monitors put their charges through carefully prescribed drills, each group using its own wall area. While the students studied their next lesson, the teacher taught the monitors around his desk. The plan was splendidly cheap and worked admirably in many cases. The perfection of order and discipline enabled the large student body to be controlled smoothly; and yet there was a flexibility that permitted each pupil to advance to the next form and to the next monitor just as quickly as he could master his assignments. The system fell into disfavor only as the idea began to grow that children should be taught a good deal more than could be taught mainly by rote, and that perhaps they should even have some interest in what they were studying—a fancy notion that stemmed, as did more revolutionary and democratic ideas, from Jean Jacques Rousseau and others who held the strange view that there might be virtue in children that could be brought out, instead of being beaten in. Physically, the Lancastrian plan began to break up into classrooms, as separate rooms with assistant instructors were set up to handle teaching of the monitors. For all the limitations of the Lancastrian schools from our present point of view, they stand as an excellent example of organization serving function. And it is probably not too much to claim for them that they kept the idea of free public education afloat at a time when the rapid growth of cities might have sunk it for years to come.

More familiar, and dearer to our hearts because it has been so romanticized, is the one-room school so rooted in our national tradition—another example to show that "school" does not necessarily mean "classes," and one with features that a good many educators tend to admire wistfully today.

The little red schoolhouse (it was more often totally innocent of paint of any color, and a miserably unsanitary, unventilated, ill-heated, uncomfortable hovel) was small because communities were small and transportation limited. The teacher (usually a woman in areas where male labor was scarce) had the problem of instructing an extremely varied group, ranging widely in age, ability, accomplishment, and attendance. Except for such activities as praying, singing, listening to a story read aloud, and the like, dealing with the entire group as a "class" was impossible. If there were three boys at about the same level of skill in arithmetic, the teacher gathered them together for that instruction, then set them tasks while she worked with another grouping. We might consider these groupings small classes. But when she came to spelling, the groupings might be quite different. And as the children advanced at different rates, according to their energy, abilities, and attendance, her groupings constantly changed, too. In short, *each grouping this teacher formed was solely in terms of the function she was trying to carry on at the moment;* grouping was always for educational, not administrative, purposes.

We may doubt that some of these teachers, little more than barely literate themselves in many cases, could have explained their method in these terms; what they did "came naturally," out of the pressures of the situation. The one-room-school teacher usually had no training in teaching. She simply had to keep the school going, and there was no other way. And because function thus dictated organization, she accomplished a lot with an absolute minimum of resources. If her school failed to carry many pupils very far, at least it could be claimed that it held none back—a claim our best rigid-class school cannot make today, with a hundred times the resources. In the one-room school, the exceptionally intelligent student, the one with a thirst for more learning, was less likely to be regarded as a regrettable freak, upsetting regimentation the school was trying hard to keep neat. As our literature and history richly record, he left with enthusiasm undiminished by boredom, lack of personal attention, or systematic belittling.

Observe one of these schools now as it grows. The days come when the teacher cannot handle so many children unassisted. Again she does what comes naturally, and makes use of one of the older girls to instruct the youngest. Later, when this girl is ready to leave school, the town fathers agree to pay her to continue to assist the teacher. They also build a second room. And once more it is natural for the second teacher to take to the new room the children she was teaching, the younger and less advanced.

It is startling to realize that this typical progression has actually accomplished, de facto, three decisions that are still deeply rooted in our public school system. One is that the less skilled, newer teacher should teach the younger pupils. In a day when the older teacher differed from the new by being surer of how the harder words were spelled and how to divide a six-digit number by a three-digit number, this made some sense. Whether it does today, when the new teacher is likely to get not only the younger class but also the duller one, or the one with the acutest disciplinary problems, is an open question. When the town fathers obligingly built a second room, another decision was made: that a school should grow by multiplying similar classrooms. The third decision was that classes should be divided primarily by age and scholastic attainment. We have seen how this could have come about "naturally." It could also have resulted because the tradition of classes or forms in private Eastern schools, or in European schools, had influence.

But it was a decision, one of many possible. The division could have been made on the basis of separating the sexes—a plan that became popular, and that has some validity apart from "moral" reasons since male and female growth and learning patterns do differ. Or what we now call intelligence could have been the key factor, thus putting the fast learners all in the same room. Or size, age, and maturity might have been considered. Or no such division might have been made at all, with the school simply being set up as two one-room affairs, side by side. Or any basis of division might have been used with, in addition, the *teachers* dividing—alternating, or taking certain subjects, or certain groups. We have by no means exhausted the list, but there is little point in carrying the exercise further. Obviously, there were many choices. And when the school doubled, and had four teachers and four rooms, there were still more combinations possible both for students and for teachers.

The first division into two rooms foreshadowed another

principle of organization that now plagues our schools, the concept of "grade." There had to be some basis for moving children from the "lower" room to the "upper," some point at which he entered a new grade. "Grade," of course, was still vague. The teachers had the great boon of being able to promote a single child any time they felt he was ready, rather than having to move a group at a set time once a year, with the various members of the group at various states of readiness to advance. In fact, some moderately daring educators today eye this advantage with envy, and cautiously put forward the idea of "time blocks" instead of yearly grades. For if we truly are interested in each child as an individual, and recognize that each in reality goes at his own pace, then we have to agree it is absurd to promote children by classes and only in June.

As schools expanded, "grade" became more and more a dominant organizing idea. These early schools, we need to remember, had no such regular attendance as we take for granted now. As late as 1880, the average student attended only 81 days, although the nominal year was much longer. The rural student (and most of the country was rural) went to school a good deal less, when farm work, family health, and road conditions permitted. Nor did children necessarily start school at any fixed age, or quit school after a precise number of years. But as schools changed from almost purely local affairs to parts of larger systems, with state help and regulation an ever-increasing influence, the rigid class-and-grade system we now have took command. It was helped along by a sudden admiration for the way things were done in, of all countries to serve as a model for a democracy, Prussia! Flexibility was regarded almost with horror, as evidence of both laxness and backwardness. Good "management" became a fetish and a fashion in the later part of the century. School administrators boasted of the precision of their regimentation. The work each grade had to accomplish was minutely detailed and each child had to accomplish it within the same allotted period. Here, of course, arose another vexing problem still far from solved. What of the child who didn't accomplish it? For years, he was simply left back to suffer the exquisite humiliation and slow torture of repeating the grade's work. Later it became fashionable to humiliate and torture him the reverse way, by thrusting him ahead anyway. Either way, the absurdity of the rigid class-and-grade system stood forth nakedly, but as with the unclothed emperor in the old story, it was not polite to notice.

One further indictment must be levied, one all too familiar to parents. I have asked dozens of them, "Did your child ever have a teacher who was incompatible, who disturbed him, made him dislike school, slowed his learning, or killed his interest in a subject?" The answer has seldom been negative. More often it brings forth still bitter recriminations.

My next question then is, "Do you think it desirable that a child should be tied to a single classroom teacher, or even subject teacher, for an entire term or school year?"

To raise the question is to answer it. In the one-room school there was reason to tie the child to one teacher, whatever the limitations of that teacher in meeting the needs of the child. In a school that has many teachers, this relationship appears to be a senseless abomination, especially in these times when many a principal has to accept any teacher he can get, and deliver a hapless class into her clutches whether he believes her to be good, fair, or horrible. The system is justified by learned jargon about the young child's need for the "security" of having only one adult to relate to. If the schools are right, our habit of having two parents would seem to be wrong. And one wonders why in kindergartens, of all places, it is not remarkable to find two adults handling the group. The jargon seems to do little to disguise the apparent fact that the single teacher idea is part and parcel of the rigid class-and-grade system—the obvious thing to do for *administrative* convenience.

I am guilty, I must admit, of greatly oversimplifying the complicated history of our school system, which is crisscrossed by a thousand influences of one sort and other. But I think the vital point I am trying to make will scarcely be challenged: the class-and-grade system we have today and that we accept and tolerate without second thought is nothing ordained from on high, nothing resulting from the best judgment of trained people calmly studying the problem, and nothing inevitable. It is

simply a monstrous mistake, costly in every sense, wholly un-
suited to our present-day conditions, needs and views, which
grew up like a weed in the past, and which educators as yet have
not had the stomach and sense to cut down.

The one virtue this system had, up to about a generation
ago, was the old familiar cry. It was cheap. In its heyday, it permitted huge, regimented classes to be run by low-paid teachers.
But today, it isn't even cheap. Its rigidity year by year adds fixed
increments in cost, even while the inadequacy and irrelevance of
instruction may become more apparent. School boards, apt to
be clumsy and ineffectual even when things are going well, stag-
ger under the impact of one financial squeeze after another and
spend most of their time chasing funds or conspiring to win
budget approvals at the polls. Teachers, scarcely aware of why
they are so frustrated, toss their last pretensions to professionalism on the scrapheap and tote picket signs saying "Help the
children" until they win raises by the crudest trade-union power
plays, usually illegal. There is seldom prospect of relief, only of
worse next year. A school system that is not deep in money
trouble today is a rarity.

What price this "cheap" system now? Alternative measures
may not cut taxes, for the trend is clearly to more and more
years of education. But they do hold the promise of flexibility,
of ending the killing automatic jump in costs each year that out-
rages taxpayers, and of giving us all an enormous amount more
in *results* for our money.

The sooner this dawns on citizens in their role of taxpayers,
the sooner will we rid ourselves of the classroom.

The ideal teacher for a self-contained classroom of, for example, sixth-grade children, would be possessed of an impossible combination of virtues. She would . . . have a masterly understanding of the learning process . . . be capable of effective communication with children with I.Q.'s ranging from 50 to 150 or higher. . . . She should command a scholarly knowledge of mathematics, literature, history, science, geography, government, music, and art. . . . Ideally she will have insights, professional knowledge, and skills of a clinical psychologist . . . cooperate effectively with a wide variety of parents . . . be something of a public-relations expert . . . and be a leader in community affairs.

Paul Woodring in *New Directions in Teacher Education.* Reprinted by permission of the Fund for the Advancement of Education and the author.

5

ABSURD ASSIGNMENT

We have discussed some of the reasons why we should, with something faster than "all deliberate speed," abolish the class. We should also, I submit, and with perhaps greater haste, abolish the classroom teacher.

I am not suggesting, of course, that the good ladies and gentlemen be liquidated in the best fascist or communist manner, nor even that they be dismissed. I am merely tendering the idea that in all our broad land it is hard to find any common job more ridiculous in its conception than the impossible assignment we matter-of-factly give our elementary public school teachers. That of the high school teacher differs in some respects and is perhaps a few degrees less absurd from a rational point of view, but it shares many of the same basic contradictions and staggering demands.

The average parent and citizen, it seems safe to observe, has only a vague notion of what is, in theory at least, asked of today's teacher. For half a century the classroom teacher's job has been incessantly added to and complicated, with many of the new demands calling for an ever-increasing amount of training and ever-rising levels of skills. Were an unsuspecting management expert asked to write a job description, his findings might well leave him shaken. And were the description to be taken literally, it is a fair guess that not one teacher in 100,000 could be declared qualified.

Much of the criticism of our schools, when it involves the work of teachers, is unfair — precisely because one cannot give a person an impossible job and then demand performance. Even if all teaching salaries were to be doubled tomorrow, it would remain absurd to demand of each of thousands of rank-and-file persons the vast combinations of high and low skills that the textbooks solemnly inform the teacher-in-training will be required on the job. Yet criticism is an essential tool for management and for democracy. One of the worst features of the present classroom system is that it makes fair, useful, and valid criticism exceedingly difficult. The first need, then, is to examine the *job* critically. We should make each teaching job one that can reasonably be done by the people available to do it, before we evaluate how well it is done.

Consider the case of Miss L., on a bright September morning, as for the first time she faces a roomful of thirty boys and girls, newly washed and starched for the occasion. They will be her charges until June, for the entire school year of about 180 days. Her assignment is roughly to interest, inspire, teach, guide, develop, discipline, and protect them, covering single-handedly a wide range of subjects, mostly in this one room. Miss L. happens to be twenty-four years old. She is a graduate of a reputable college with a degree in education, she has a "half year" of practice-teaching experience (actually, a few weeks) and a year on this job, and her other work experience consists of summer jobs in a department store and in a college office. With similar training and experience in retailing, or in office work, or in a hospital, she would be looked on tolerantly as a perhaps promising beginner, ready soon for her first promotion from the bottom of the ladder to the lowest rung. But our schools, as we have begun to see, operate on weird and unique principles which ignore almost all we know and apply as sound sense and good personnel practice everywhere else. In our schools there is no ladder. Miss L. is a *teacher*. Miss R., who has ten years experience in three schools, is a *teacher*. Mrs. Q., who has had fifteen years experience and is regarded as an authority on several aspects of her work, is a *teacher*. Like the best and most accomplished teacher in her school, Miss L. has the highest non-administrative title and position she can get, and she had it from the first day she faced her first class in this institution! So far as *teaching* goes, she began at the top—a circumstance that may prove a little trying for her hapless class, even though Miss L. is (as not all youthful teachers are) eager, conscientious, and a cut or two above average in intelligence and ability.

If Miss L. should have a ruminative moment or two on this busy day, she may reflect on her chances for advancement. In store or office, and in many other occupations, she could feel some confidence that outstanding effort, skill, aptitude, and abilities will, with reasonable luck, carry her upward over the years. But so far as teaching is concerned, none of these will avail her much here. She can look forward to more pay and status:

- By growing older, since pay scales go up for years of service, almost regardless of performance.
- By going back to college and taking higher degrees or equivalent work, whether or not such courses actually improve her teaching.
- By becoming a head of department, assistant principal, or principal, *giving up teaching* to the required extent.
- By shifting from elementary to high school teaching, if this happens to be one of the few systems in which there remains a salary differential, thereby waiving much of her experience.
- By moving to another school system with a higher pay scale.

In general, these are the *only* ways Miss L. can progress, in all but a handful of school systems! If we were to try to devise a system better designed to attract and harbor mediocrity, to repel and discourage the more able and devoted, we would be hard put to surpass this.

But even more astonishing is the devastating fact that not only will Miss L. not be rewarded for exceptional teaching, but by and large no one will ever *objectively* know or much care how effective a teacher Miss L. becomes! I realize this statement may sound wildly exaggerated, but in the face of the evidence it is hard not to regard it as quite accurate. (The skeptical reader is urged to have a quiet, off-the-record talk with administrators in his own system.)

During the initial years, of course, before Miss L. has tenure or a continuing contract, there will be some degree of official concern about her competence. But today, it is highly likely to be an "in or out" concern—can she handle her classes or can't she?—rather than much of an attempt to measure her proficiency. If she is unable to control her classes, seeks help incessantly, can't conform to the school's operations, gives rise to too many parent or student complaints, makes a total mess of her records, shows marked emotional instability, is too frequently absent, or hopelessly antagonizes the rest of the staff, she may be dropped or transferred. Otherwise, she will be "in"— and the longer she remains in, the more impractical it becomes, as a rule, to attempt to remove her. As Albert L. Ayers points out succinctly in *Administering the People's Schools:* "It is difficult to clear a district of weak teachers; this, in itself, makes it important to hire good ones in the first place."

In large city systems, tenure is the rule. In smaller systems, the contract in some form is usually found. The smaller the community, the more will failure to rehire a teacher stir up a hornets' nest for the administration should the teacher have local friends and family. If the teacher can be tolerated, the powers that be are not likely to go looking for trouble. And with the teacher shortage what it has been, and promising to become far worse, most school systems are becoming progressively less fussy.

. . . Superintendents have found themselves in the embarrassing position of having to accept every qualified applicant for a position. Consequently, teacher selection practices have tended to become almost wholly controlled by the central administrative offices. In many systems the

principal does not meet the new teachers . . . until a day
or two prior to the opening of school. While this condition
is lamentable, it is in many instances understandable.

The quotation is from *Educational Leadership and the Elementary
School Principal*, by Spain, Drummond, and Goodlad, published
in 1956. In common with a number of other more recent books
on school administration, it is admirably if frighteningly realistic. Agreement among the authorities is high. With classes
to cover and schools to keep running regardless of high ideals
and fine theories, working administrators seem to have few il-
lusions. Even the reference to qualified applicants needs further
comment:

Let's be candid about the way teachers are selected. In
some small school systems, when a position is open, teachers apply and are selected according to the whims of members of the board of education or of the superintendent of
schools. In many large systems, the candidate must pass a
paper-and-pencil test at a certain percentile level and must
meet the personality requirements of a personnel interviewer. Of course, candidates in both systems must meet
the basic requirements of certification for the state, unless
an emergency exists. Sometimes, even the roughest match-
ing of qualifications and job requirements is overlooked.

The author quoted is Kimball Wiles, in the 1967 edition of *Supervision for Better Schools*. In many systems today, of course,
"an emergency exists" frequently or routinely.

Even in those favored communities where conditions are
relatively milder, and the principal can still maintain at least the
ceremony of interviewing new teachers before they begin work
in his school, his freedom of action probably is severely circum-
scribed. In practice he can object to a teacher only on blatant
grounds, or request an alternative on the plea that his locale
requires a person different in some way, such as one who can
teach woodwinds on the side, coach basketball, speak Spanish,
or demonstrate that the school is perfectly willing to hire Negroes.

As any personnel officer will testify, hiring people is a chancy business at best. But most employees work where they can be readily observed. *Teachers work in classrooms, behind closed doors.* And authorities agree overwhelmingly that there is only the scantiest knowledge of what attributes bring success in teaching. Intelligence and college records are not reliable indicators. Oftentimes, then, if a genuine choice is made between two candidates, it may be on the basis of which promises to get along better with the principal and his staff. The consideration is important, but not necessarily related to teaching ability.

The plain fact is that the principal, after he has a new teacher on the job, has almost no objective way of measuring her performance against that of any other teacher, unless one or both are obviously incompetent or impossible. How is he to tell? He can, of course, go into her classroom and observe her at work. He can see how she gives instruction, how she handles questions from the pupils. He can ask about various students and see how much she knows about them as individuals. From all this he can gain an impression, possibly even a fairly expert impression, if he himself is skilled and experienced and if he visits the classroom often enough. But the principal is not always skilled in the highly fallible art of judging other persons, nor does he usually have time for many visits. Even more important is that the moment he enters a classroom, the normal situation in the classroom ceases to exist. Both children and teacher are on special behavior until he leaves. If the teacher has serious faults or inadequacies, they may well be, in today's complicated, subtle classroom situation, exceedingly difficult to detect in a brief visit. Much of a teacher's best work cannot be judged save by careful and perceptive observation over a long period. Of this the principal or supervisor is well aware if he is truly competent to judge.

Walk down the corridor of a school while it is in session, and the most baffling aspect of this entire system is strikingly evident. What is going on behind those closed doors? There is almost no way of knowing, and, not surprisingly under today's conditions, almost no attempt is being made to find out.

Naively, parents often assume that teachers are closely

supervised and that how they teach is directed by the principal. Rarely is this the case. Today, a school is usually a collection of rooms in which individual teachers conduct their classes just about as they please. The beginning teacher who might like more supervision and help often finds it unavailable, while the more experienced teacher is likely to bridle at any more than a nominal effort of the principal or other official to supervise her, particularly if they try to "tell her what to do." In *The Teacher and School Organization,* published in 1962, authors Leo Chamberlain and Leslie Kindred summarize:

> In the majority of schools the quality of supervision given by principals and superintendents is exceedingly poor. . . . It is difficult or next to impossible for the taxpayer and school patron to detect the failure in supervisory work.

In *The Necessary Revolution in American Education* by Francis Keppel, recently U.S. Commissioner of Education, appears this conclusion:

> . . . To put it bluntly, teachers in American classrooms have received appallingly little direction or supervision. The ancient and honorable tradition of each teacher as king in his classroom may have to give way in the days of the necessary revolution.

A great many teachers are not visited for supervisory purposes for years at a stretch. The new teacher in the school and the beginning teacher in better schools may be visited a few times to see that they are "getting on all right," and others may be visited for special reasons not concerned with evaluation. Beyond that there is very little.

The literature on administration, and I have already pointed out that it tends to be frank, is quite unanimous on the topic. It agrees that evaluation of the teacher's work is a thorny and still largely unsolved problem, and that if any sort of plan is to be tried, it should be one that first is accepted by the teachers involved. It is not too astonishing that teachers in classroom schools show little enthusiasm for the whole idea of merit ratings, and schools that pay more for superior work in teaching are few and far between.

The standard attitude is neatly put in *Educational Leadership and the Elementary School Principal,* quoted above:

> The good elementary school principal will function in this area of responsibility [evaluation], as in all others, in conformity with principles of democratic leadership. If he does, the focus of his attention and energies will be directed not to past behavior, as rating scales are, but rather to creating situations which will produce more desirable behavior on the part of all teachers *in the present and the future.* Involving teachers, pupils, and parents in total-school evaluation seems to be a more fruitful way of stimulating individual teacher effectiveness than passing judgment occasionally on the teacher's work. *Acceptance of people as they are* and working with them cooperatively to bring about growth are sound educational practice. (Italics are my emphasis.)

The reader familiar with the realities of our public schools will likely find this statement honest, sound, and unexciting. Others more likely will find their hair beginning to curl. For here is a wide window looking in upon a vital area of the never-never land of public education. In every other activity, from baseball through business to the making of toy balloons or atomic submarines, we take it for granted that we obtain high effectiveness only if we constantly check on results, only if we move the able people ahead and reward them, and shift or cull out those who can't handle their assignments on the desired levels. One tries to picture a plant foreman saying of an employee who repeatedly ruins work, "One must accept people as they are!" Or a stockbroker, musing on the costly carelessness of a junior and observing, "We must try to bring about growth." The authors quoted above make sense, however, because there are two great differences in the situations. The foreman and the stockbroker have ample opportunity to observe, and to some degree measure, the effectiveness of their people; and they can fire, demote, reassign, or otherwise deal with their less satisfactory employees and show appreciation in practical ways of those who are superior. The school official can't. He is bound by a rigid salary scale that ignores merit. He is not free to hire and fire; he is stuck with his teachers. Under those circumstances, "acceptance of people as they are" is far from stupid, since there is little other choice. Those of us who do not have to work under such basically impossible circumstances should not pounce too impolitely on the term "democratic leadership," all too obviously a euphemism for plain helplessness. If there is one honored principle underlying democratic leadership, it is that authority must be matched to responsibility. It is one more of our basic rules of organization that is observed everywhere but within our school systems.

It begins to become clear, I trust, why we can venture to predict that no one will concern themselves very much with how effective our Miss L. becomes as a teacher. Since there is no way to punish or reward her, except by withdrawing her from teaching, why bother? When a typical principal assures a parent that "Mrs. G. is one of our best teachers," he does not mean that he knows she is a highly effective teacher, for he has almost no way of measuring her achievement with the pupils she is given. He means that Mrs. G. gets along all right with *him,* that her pupils don't misbehave or fall behind exceptionally, and that parents of her students complain rather less than average. He may also mean that Mrs. G. conforms to the proper pattern of in-service growth by taking courses or otherwise engaging in activities which look good, however difficult it may be to prove that they result in better performance within the secret confines of her class.

Principals can and do rate teachers for the guidance of the administration in appointing department chairman and other officials from the ranks of teachers. This power of recommendation is virtually the *only* control most principals have over their teachers, for power to control subordinates must ultimately rest on some authority or ability to penalize or reward them. But these recommendations often will not be based even on what the principal *believes* to be teaching effectiveness. Such jobs call for tact, popularity, ability to handle people, and both liking and talent for administrative work. "Politics" enter the picture heavily: certain teachers may be ruled out of consideration at the start, regardless of their estimated teaching effectiveness. Thus the teacher who is not interested in taking this route, or who sees no great possibility of achieving such a promotion, or who plans to stop teaching, can cooperate with or ignore the principal as she chooses, up to (and at times beyond) open contempt and insubordination. It is remarkable, indeed, that some principals manage to hold the influence they do; but even so, the typical principal in a good-size school may have to coax, wheedle, maneuver, flatter, and exercise the patience of a god over weeks to years to install the procedures and arrangements he wants. He can give orders, but he has little to enforce them with.

Oddly, principals in the largest cities are often better off. They sometimes can arrange to have recalcitrants transferred to far-removed or less desirable schools—a club that may command considerable respect, if the teacher's seniority or union is not too formidable. But since the principal has little knowledge of what goes on inside the classroom, it is seldom *teaching* that is at issue, but rather interpersonal relations or procedure.

The attitude of some teachers was voiced succinctly by one vice-president of a teachers' union: "An administrator, like the custodian or the heating engineer, is in the school only to make the job of the teacher easier." The viewpoint, or at least the phrasing, is extreme. A more moderate statement is found in *Improving Instruction Through Supervision* by Thomas H. Briggs and Joseph Justman, published in 1952:

> There is no criticism more frequently expressed of administrative officers than that they do not know or understand intimately the work of their subordinates. In consequence of this attitude teachers are often skeptical of the value of suggestions made to them by a principal who is attempting supervision.

Note the word "attempting"! But ironically, the mint-new and often very insecure teacher who would eagerly welcome advice, orientation, information, and supervision commonly finds such help hard to get. The novice classroom teacher, who in her probably skimpy practice sessions had help present or close by, now finds that the same four walls that imprison her

and her charges also shut out assistance. On most jobs, a beginner can learn rapidly by watching others and by the friendly
help of experienced workers with whom there is frequent contact. Team teaching provides this normal situation, but the classroom tosses the tyro into deep water alone, to sink or swim.
Even in well-staffed schools, pressures may not permit more
than fleeting supervisory attention, especially early in the term.
Suddenly and acutely aware of the inadequacy of her preparation, the teacher survives if she can—often embittered toward
supervision.

By and large, it seems safe to say that "democratic leadership" discussed above reflects the most common teacher attitude, and the usual practice. Let the principal lead, gently;
the teachers will follow, if they feel like it.

With, then, some idea of the autocratic, unsupervised
power over a large class of young children that our youthful
Miss L. is about to fall heir to, let us see what she is assigned
to do. If we seem to be already deep in absurdity, we are about
to plunge much deeper.

We can say that Miss L. teaches a class of thirty-odd children of a certain grade in a certain school: this will identify
her for public and payroll purposes. If we want to know what
she actually *does,* we have to consider and list in conventional
terms each function she normally carries out in the course
of the ordinary day and week. These include:

(a) *Teaching,* the prime function. It is helpful to divide
    it into "primary" teaching—presenting ideas and
    information, demonstrating, explaining, clarifying,
    awakening and maintaining interest; and "follow-up"
    teaching, which carries through the same process
    to each individual student—hopefully, to obtain the
    desired learning.

(b) *Drilling and practice*—developing skills and firm knowl-
    edge through repetition and exercises.

(c) *Guidance*—helping each child to develop as a person,
    and encouraging and directing each according to his
    own interests and abilities.

(d) *Evaluating*—checking on the child's progress in learning and personal growth, through examinations, observation, recitations, homework; and reporting it to the school and to the parents.

(e) *Discipline* — maintaining order, obtaining compliance and performance of work required; handling behavior problems, rewarding, and punishing.

(f) *Clerical* — keeping attendance and other administrative or teaching records.

(g) *Housekeeping* — maintaining the classroom in good order.

(h) *Custodian* — controlling, issuing, and recovering books, supplies, instruments, equipment, exhibits.

(i) *Shepherding* — taking the class from place to place; recess, bus, lunchroom, traffic, and study hall duties.

(j) *Money handling* — controlling "milk money," savings, and other funds for various purposes.

This is, of course, a simplified list, covering only those duties which relate directly to the class as a whole. The teacher is also supposed to assist in the extra-curricular activities of the students. She is expected to take an active part in faculty matters, which may involve assisting with administration, or helping to solve curriculum, teaching, disciplinary, and other problems. The textbooks invariably advise her to be active in the community to show her interest and demonstrate her good citizenship. Also, she must "grow" in service, by taking courses, attending workshops and conferences, or otherwise. Since some problems with students can be approached only on an individual basis, she should be prepared and equipped for such interviews. She should be equally equipped to deal with parents, whether interested, reasonable, and cooperative, or angry, anxious, and disinterested; and she is admonished never to forget the vital importance of building good public relations with the parents and the taxpayers who support the schools. She is expected to show imagination and ingenuity in devising her own teaching materials and methods, and in arranging special events such as trips, plays, or exhibitions, as well as parties and celebrations for gala occasions.

This is all we ask the teacher to do! But in addition to these

duties, we add a staggering load of responsibility. Both by
law and by custom, the teacher stands "in the role of the parents" while each child is in her care. She is responsible for
his physical and emotional well-being; she must protect him
from accidents; know where he is at all times; guard him
against older or bigger children, toughs, and intruders; observe his health and take steps if he appears ill; keep an eye
on his property; and if he is younger, "mother" him, help him
on with his overshoes, and instruct and assist him in the more
elementary forms of sanitation.

The teacher's job still *looks* much like the same job in, say,
1910, because there is still the same class and classroom organization. But the job itself has changed vastly. Almost year
by year it has become more demanding, more difficult to
discharge, as emphasis has shifted from running an "education
mill" to the present "child development" approach. In bygone
days the course of instruction was spelled out in detail, grade
by grade. Children were, in broad, put through the mill — they
passed or failed. Those children who had little taste or aptitude for learning dropped out as early as possible, with few
going as far as high school and far fewer to college. Far less
was taught, and probably less effectively, than is attempted
today. School systems in general were highly organized and
rigidly controlled; this was the heyday of the superintendent
and the mighty-whiskered principal whose frown caused teachers to tremble. They were told what to teach and they taught
it, as the students were told what to learn and, largely by
rote and repetition, learned it.

We must suspect that children then differed as greatly
in aptitudes, abilities, and backgrounds as they do today. But
the schools found the idea awkward. Children were taught as
if they were alike, so far as the teacher could manage. If matters
did not work out quite as badly as seems inevitable from our
viewpoint today, it was because the schools were attempting
a great deal less. An "elementary" education was just that;
and the emphasis was on what was taught and what was remembered, rather than on what happened to the child. For
a far simpler and less frenetic age than ours, the basic public

education was much less inadequate than it would be today.

Even though the progressive education movement is now dead and scarcely an issue, the changes that have taken place in the accepted view of what constitutes adequate public education is ample testimony to the potency of the ideas that William Kilpatrick and John Dewey and others put forward — and that some distorted or carried to absurd lengths. If parents today often have trouble understanding the schools, and older citizens especially carp, it is probably because this vast shift in purpose and content is only vaguely understood. Educators are in very good agreement, overall, that the development of each child is fully as important as what he learns: they bemoan the stuffing of knowledge down his throat, as geese are fattened in France. The premise is that each child is different, that he must develop at his own speed in each skill, and that his background, interests, needs, and potential all are unique to him. It is a premise that in the light of present-day knowledge is hard to argue with. But obviously it makes the teacher's job enormously more complicated: it is much easier to teach one class by the book than to teach thirty-odd individual children by one's own resources. Thus the level of skill asked of the teacher today is astronomically higher.

In addition, the school knows today that each child that enters kindergarten must be carried through to high school, not to be set on his own until the legal release age of 16 or 17 has been obtained, no matter whether he be a potential Ph.D. or be barely well enough endowed mentally to go to school at all. The requirement makes it all the more impossible to demand of a group of children that they all learn the same material at the same speed. Though vastly more is taught today, the assumption is that learning and development of the child as a person and personality must go hand in hand. For a while, as progressivism ran wild, there seemed to be a number of authorities who apparently believed that so long as the child was happy in school it did not matter whether he learned anything at all, or how much effort went into how little learning; but the pendulum has swung back to more reasonable proportions of effort. Aside from the most hard-bitten reactionaries, who survive in small numbers in almost any community, it is rare to find serious critics of the broad base on which our schools operate in this regard.

But though our schools today have radically different purpose and objective and a sharply different function from that of half a century ago, they still try to make use of the identical organization—classes, classrooms, grades, classroom teachers! Because the change in the teacher's job has been steady and gradual, the forms and structures of the past have continued in use. This is even physically true—the "egg-crate" design of schools has played no small part in preserving the class by providing classrooms suitable only for a class system.

It is apparent, I believe, that we ask a teacher to teach a class the way we once asked a shoemaker to make a pair of boots—doing every phase of the work himself, and by hand. If we still made shoes that way, a pair would cost from $60 up; and since it would be impossible to find enough persons with this combination of skills, most of us would go barefoot even if we could provide public funds to assist purchase. The situation in our schools is closely parallel, except that the skills needed are in many instances much higher than the shoemaker's. The organizational plan is pre-Industrial Revolution. We make shoes cheaply, plentifully and of excellent quality (and in vast variety!) by applying the twin principles of division of labor and use of technology, two of the cornerstones of our civilization and certainly of our abundance. In our schools we can find heating "engineers" who would not dream of mowing the grass, and grounds keepers who would become indignant at being asked to tend the furnace; but in our classrooms our teachers still essay the role of forty-armed goddesses.

Nor have the teachers, apparently, fully realized how ridiculous it is for them to insist, on any possible occasion, that they are "professional" persons, entitled to the status and pay of professionals. A skeptical but not unfriendly public observes that teachers don't *behave* like professionals. If a dentist used his time and skills as do teachers, he would spend part of his time working with patients, another part making

out his bills and licking the envelopes, and still other hours
cleaning up his office and equipment, and possibly washing
the windows. He might be a very good dentist, but his community could hardly help wonder why he did not hire people
to do the work that scarcely required his specialized talents
and years of training. An architect would not only make his
designs, but execute all the detail drawings and prepare the
blueprints, and then carry them personally to each contractor.
In modern life, a professional person is one with a high skill
based on theoretical understanding which he utilizes to the
full. He does not willingly or cheerfully do work that can be
done by persons of lower skill, nor does he expect to be paid
for his high skill when he is doing work that could be done as
well or better by an assistant, clerk, aide, handyman, or mes-
senger boy.

What is the proper pay for a teacher who is supervising
a lunchroom to maintain order? What is a good salary for
a teacher while she is correcting spelling or arithmetic papers,
which the brightest children in her class could do as well,
and give her the results to review? How professional is counting out pieces of red, yellow, and blue chalk, and then counting them back into the box so it won't be necessary to requisi-
tion more?

It is both amusing and in a way horrifying to consider applying to a hospital the kind of organization we have tolerated
for so many years in our schools. We would have to divide the
patients into "classes," and then put a doctor in charge of
each class. The doctor would now have to do everything for
his patients, from surgery through prescribing and administering medication, down to giving alcohol rubs and taking temperatures. How good would the care be and how much could
we expect such doctors to be paid? Where would we find
enough who combined in one person all the skills required?
In the context of medicine, it seems blindingly clear that
we can't expect to have more than a few extremely skilled and
able persons in each professional field, and that we must let
these persons specialize and be able to distribute their talents
widely. We must also arrange to pay them highly. And we must

provide other persons, at several levels of descending skill, to divide the work and perform it so that skills and the money to pay for skills are used most efficiently. The need for the same approach in education becomes equally obvious, as soon as we rid ourselves of the overage and overripe idea that children *must* be held in rigid class groups, in separate rooms.

If we consider the list of teacher functions given above and put them in new order according to the skills involved we come out with a list something like this:

Higher Skills

(a) "Primary" teaching.
(b) Guidance.

Medium Skills

(c) "Follow-up" teaching.
(d) Evaluating, where judgment and trained observation is required.
(e) Drilling, practice, and the like, where planning and skilled techniques are required.
(f) Discipline.

Lower Skills

(g) Evaluating, that part which is mechanical or clerical.
(h) Drilling and practice, where routinized or mechanized.
(i) Clerical.
(j) Housekeeping.
(k) Custodian.
(l) Shepherding.
(m) Money handling.

Even as I set down this division, I can hear the familiar anguished cry of teachers, raised whenever their accustomed ways are threatened with disturbance, "But you don't *understand!*" Most all of these activities, they will assure me, are part of the process of education. Counting back the crayons is more than a nuisance routine — it teaches the necessity of order, of cleaning up after a job, of regard for property. Collecting milk-money provides opportunity for teaching the value and use of money, and some arithmetic to boot. Such arguments, I submit, are besides the point. Since experience and learning are impossible to separate, it can easily be claimed that anything the child or teacher does has educational value in some way. The question, however, is *how skilled a person is required* to carry on this function, if it indeed has sufficient value to be worthwhile. We can hardly deny that the regular taking of temperatures in a hospital is an important function, but we don't have to take a doctor from other duties to do it. No business can survive if the mail isn't handled promptly and correctly, but we would be astonished to find an executive sorting or weighing in the mail room.

It seems evident that teachers must come to think in these terms. It is utterly unrealistic, I believe, for them to yearn for more professional status, more respect from the public, and more adequate pay, as long as they spend substantial parts of their working hours doing menial, trivial, and unskilled work. While teachers, like most other people, hate to change their habits of work and thought, it is hard to see how they can lose in any way by change that forces them to work at their highest levels of skill, and therefore become able to claim and obtain corresponding status and compensation.

Equally necessary, it seems obvious, is some form of "promotion ladder" up which teachers can move to highest skill assignments and greater responsibilities within teaching. So long as we give the title "teacher" to a raw recruit with a few weeks of experience at most, and give her the same responsibilities—charge of a class—as the best skilled and experienced, we make any claim to professionalism rather absurd. We need to provide a progression, such as apprentice, assistant, teacher, senior teacher, master teacher, with salaries to match, that can reflect ability, achievement, and experience beyond simple time-serving. The classroom makes such a ladder all but impossible. Team teaching and "open school" approaches make it entirely feasible. In addition, they attract the able, ambitious, and career-minded person (especially the male) who so often is repelled by poor promotion prospects and the dismal isolation of the classroom.

Following a White House Conference on Education, some years ago, the statement issued contained these conclusions:

The American public must be reawakened to the fact that teachers work with our most precious resource—our children. A good educational system requires good teachers and enough of them in each locality to meet its needs. We believe that, to increase the supply of good teachers from any source, three basic considerations must be kept in mind: (1) The prestige and status of teaching must be comparable to other professions within the community; (2) The salary structure must be high enough and flexible enough to compete effectively with other fields bidding for quality manpower; (3) The teacher's job must be so defined as to challenge and attract the interest of talented people.

The sentiments are splendid; but it is rather a pity that the language does not make more explicit that *changes* are required to bring about each of the three objectives. Wishing won't do it. Pointing dramatically to the importance of education won't do it. Making comparisons with other occupations won't do it. *Only reorganizing the schools and redefining the teacher's job will do it.* Since there is not enough money nor enough teachers now, and the shortages are getting worse rather than lessening, it seems inevitable that these changes *will* come about. The sooner, the better—not only for our children but for their teachers.

To see what is wrong with American (and foreign) high schools ... all we need do is take a close look at what goes on in the classrooms day after day during a school year. The ineffaceable memory carried away by a serious observer who stays for more than the usual fleeting visit is the crashing boredom that afflicts both the teachers and the taught.

Harold J. Noah in *Teachers College Record*, May 1967.

6

THE MASTER TEACHER

I have broken down the list in the previous chapter into three sections, but this is purely arbitrary. The more we study the actual, specific teaching job, as it is being performed, the more evident it becomes that many jobs are being rolled into one. Our management expert, analyzing what a teacher *does,* would simply conclude that, in a modern management sense, she does not have a job at all, but merely a collection of assorted duties. If we wish to sort out these duties, as a preliminary to re-combining them into a number of coherent separate jobs, we have to examine them in considerable detail. In the following attempt to do so, brief as it must be, we will get some idea of the tremendous complexity, the difficulties, the subtleties, and the frustrations involved in the classroom teacher's present assignment, as well as the lack of research, facilities, help, and administrative support, which adds greatly to the already crushing burden.

The imparting of knowledge and understanding, and the development of skills, is the key function of schools. That we now lay great stress on the development of each child as a person and citizen does not alter that fact. But there are two quite different aspects of teaching, which I have referred to briefly in the previous chapter using the terms "primary" and "follow-up." Because the classroom teacher is charged with doing both, the distinction at present tends to be overlooked. (It is further obscured by the gross assumption that teaching and learning are directly linked, and that the child learns what the teacher intends him to learn. The most casual check on this assumption reveals it to be contrary to reality — in Part II this question will be examined in some depth.) "Primary" teaching can best be thought of as the kind that stimulates the student and arouses interest and desire to learn, or that opens doors and invites him to enter new intellectual or skill areas. "Follow-up" teaching provides the student the content, explanation, guidance, coaching, and encouragement that helps him convert the aroused interest into organized learning.

The primary function of arousing interest and desire to learn clearly calls for both knowledge of subject and a certain type of personality — pretty much that which often characterizes the successful lecturer. We can hardly expect a teacher who has only a nominal knowledge and little enthusiasm for mathematics, and no flair for presentation, to inspire her group with a burning desire to learn algebra. Primary teaching calls for "spark." The person who has that precious quality usually does best with groups, especially large groups. The follow-up function necessarily calls for ability to be sensitive to and relate to the individual student, in a patient, sympathetic, and quiet way that lessens the student's anxiety and facilitates identification of learning blocks or failures.

Quite obviously very few teachers can be expected to combine these opposite attributes. They tend to conduct their classes in ways that reflect their personalities — whether this makes for desirable instruction or not. In *Teaching in High School,* by Hubert H. Mills and Harl R. Douglass, we find this observation on high school teachers, whom we might expect to have an edge over elementary school teachers in this "primary" ability:

It is unquestionably true that high school teachers, especially beginning teachers, are not good lecturers. Development of skill and effectiveness in explaining, telling, and lecturing requires time and much practice. . . . Probably the greatest limitations of high school teachers as lecturers are (1) failure to take time to prepare lectures carefully . . . (2) lack of skill . . . (3) the lack of background in the subjects, in life experience, and in ability to correlate and organize materials from sources other than a few textbooks or college courses. As a result of these weaknesses and underdeveloped abilities, teachers are prone to take refuge in lesson-hearing and oral testing in the class period.

It is only natural that the teacher who is unimpressed with his own talents as a lecturer and whose students seem to verify his opinion with yawns and restlessness feels impelled to turn to other methods. Since he is the sole arbiter of how he is to teach, there is little to pressure him into becoming expert through practice, even assuming he has the native ability to become expert. Just so, the teacher who is an excellent lecturer may rely too heavily on this method, and try to avoid the patient follow-up work which calls for more self-effacement.

Since it is hard enough to find persons with one highly-developed skill, it seems sensible to divide these two teaching functions if possible, rather than try to staff each classroom with teachers possessing these two conflicting abilities. And without worrying about such essentially meaningless questions as the "importance" of the two functions, since both are needed, we can see that the fine lecturer is much harder to find or train than the follow-up teacher. He is also likely to possess personality attributes that make him more valuable in the labor marketplace outside of public schools. Such persons can hardly be expected to take jobs in schools in large numbers, or to stay at such work, if their greatest talent is muffled by their being locked into a single classroom, and assigned routine work that forbids its use.

Thus the concept of the "master teacher" has come into

considerable popularity in the more adventurous educational circles, although it is still rather hard to come upon one in the flesh. Definitions will vary some; but basically the master teacher is a man or woman with a flair for arousing and holding the interest of students, *for inspiring them to seek learning* in a particular direction because of this interest, and for getting ideas across to them with the proverbial blinding flash of insight that betokens true understanding. In a word, this is what we perhaps mistakenly call "the born teacher."

Almost every reader will recall such a person from his own educational career. When I attended university, I jumped at the chance to take a course given by perhaps the world's greatest authority in the field. It proved to be a mistake. The learned gentleman was elderly, lacking in energy, and bored with his task. He read his lectures, and since he had a thick foreign accent and a partial speech obstruction, one did well to understand one sentence in three. In any case, it was faster and easier to read his book, which included precisely the same material. I am afraid many of us did just that during his lectures. Enthusiasm for the subject was rather dampened.

I also took a course with an unrenowned English instructor whose subject was Shakespeare. He appeared to be a frustrated actor: he used a towering frame, an expressive mien, and a rotund voice until his eyes bugged and the floor and walls shook. But his enthusiasm, energy, love of subject, and ability to communicate his feelings made him in the eyes of many students a master teacher. They took Shakespeare for credits and ended up enjoying every moment as a dead poet became very much alive.

These instances are extremes, to be sure. But the master teacher must love his subject, rather than teach it as a duty. He must know his subject in depth, however elementary the level at which he teaches it. He must have that mystic ability to hold an audience, to explain with exceptional and dramatic clarity, and to invest what seems to be the dullest assignment with vitality and interest. Such persons are not rare, but they are not common. It follows that when we find one, nothing could be more wasteful than to limit his teaching to a handful of students. Master teachers should teach as many children as possible. Fortunately, this type of person usually works much better with a large audience than with a small one. And fortunately too, modern technical resources make it simple and practical to provide the large one.

Once we make such a division of labor, and recognize the skill we are trying to hire, it follows that we want to see this person be truly a professional, by providing for undiluted use of his highest skill, and by providing all the conditions and aids for its use to the greatest advantage.

The classroom teacher, as we have seen, has a laundry-list of assorted duties. To expect her to devote hours to preparation of a single lecture-style period, to gather and check material for it, to assemble aids and props or have them made, to round up and prepare assistants or guests, is to ask the impossible. If a teacher makes even a portion of this effort once in a while, she is doing very well indeed. But for the master teacher, such preparation could be routine, a normal part of his or her job. Free of classes to cover, his time would be devoted partly to preparation, partly to delivery, and partly to working directly with various students and teachers to get feedback, learning how well his ideas had got across and what gaps need to be filled.

Consider the contrast. On one hand we may have, in a city, *two hundred* third-grade teachers duplicating effort, *each* explaining a fundamental operation in arithmetic. Even if we assume all are "qualified" by current standards, it would be remarkable if as many as one in six had any deep love and understanding of mathematics. It would be even more remarkable if one in twenty had a great flair for clarifying and creating interest in mathematics. So in most of the classes the lesson will be taught because it is called for by the book and the plan. In many classes it will be taught, if dully, at least diligently; but we can also be sure that in some, where the teacher dislikes or feels ill at ease in the subject, it will be taught badly, with aversion and lack of confidence that the pupils readily sense. For many students, a school year with such a teacher is often enough to kill their interest in the disliked subject for good.

On the other hand, picture the master teacher at work on the same assignment. He loves mathematics—he conveys his excitement with his first words. His knowledge is both broad and deep. He is experienced and he is a specialist; he has explained mathematics perhaps a hundred times more often than the average classroom teacher, constantly improving his methods and techniques. And he has the energy, the vigor, the personality, the combination of resources and skills that brings the subject alive, suffuses the simplest aspects of it with new meaning, relates it to the children's lives and interests—even while he is not afraid to treat it as an intellectual adventure, too. He is seeking not only to teach the process of the moment, but to inspire at least some students to want to know more, to *seek* it. And since he gives this same presentation many times, to many children, he can afford to have all the props and aids he needs. Does he wish to make reference to the pyramids of Egypt? A signal, and the picture is on the screen. Does he want to dramatize fractions by dividing a pie? Here's an actual pie. Does he want a few minutes of animated film to illustrate a point? Another signal, and the film rolls.

Can we compare the two levels of teaching? Will it surprise us if the master teacher in one hour gets across, unforgettably, basic ideas that the classroom teacher in many cases could not make as clear and vivid in ten, and in some cases not ever? In sports, in carpentry, in bookkeeping, in writing, in art, in executive work, in any field we wish to name, the difference between the "real pro" and the modestly trained and experienced person is enormous. It should not surprise us to find the rule any less binding in teaching.

The reader will not, I hope, jump to the conclusion that the school of the future is seen as one in which experts lecture one after another, to great applause, while the humble follow-up teachers hunt moments in which to do their work in dark corners. How the use of "presenter" specialists fits into possible new structures will become evident in due course. In drawing a picture of a certain type of master teacher, I am primarily seeking to illustrate the principle of *separating out* high skills needed in teaching. Persons who have them must be identified, and given the special preparation, training, and experience which will bring them to their peak usefulness. Then they must be allowed to specialize and bring their skills and talents to *many* pupils, not just one class. Just as "highly skilled doctor" may mean a brain surgeon, anesthetist, internist, otolaryngologist, general practitioner, or pathologist, so "highly skilled teacher" may come to have a variety of meanings in parallel fashion. In the pamphlet "Images of the Future," Dr. J. Lloyd Trump refers to "teacher specialists" and describes their work in these words:

> These specialists will teach subject matter for which they are particularly well qualified, usually to relatively large groups of students. At times they will serve as consultants to individuals and groups of students working in and outside the school and will assist with extraclass activities. Most of these teachers will be specialists in the use of such teaching aids as television, tape recordings, projectors, students' self-appraisal devices, and the like, although some may be particularly effective in working with smaller groups of students.

Other educators who see great advantages in the master teacher idea (the proposal in contemporary terms goes back at least as far as 1947) offer varying descriptions, but the basic approaches are in close agreement.

How much should the master teacher be paid? The usual view is, a lot more than the present classroom teacher: perhaps $10,000 to $12,000 to start in most systems, and up to $18,000 in the best-paying. For persons of high professional skill, based on talents and personalities that are none too common, such levels are hardly exorbitant. They appear necessary not only to attract the most able persons, but to give "pure" public school teaching what it has long lacked — both a financial and professional base for respect. By definition, we can never expect to have a great number of master teachers. But even a few in each school system will establish a top for a "ladder" up which persons interested in *teaching*, not administration, can climb. The ordinary person seeking a job asks, "How much does it pay?" The abler candidate asks instead, "How high can I go on ability?" If the answer is discouraging, he seeks other work. But while the proposed pay for master teachers may at first blush seem high, we should not think of it as necessarily being expensive. With modernized organization and improved use of personnel, any school may well be able to pay such top salaries without necessarily wrecking the normal budget. For, as we shall see, balancing savings occur.

Before we leave the subject for the time being, there is another point worth noting. It is no secret to our children that teachers are neither very highly regarded in society, nor well paid. As the brighter children grow older, they perceive quite clearly that not all teachers have first-class intellects, nor training, nor abilities. How much of our often-lamented national disrespect for intellectual pursuits, for scholarship, for bookish and abstract work, has its beginnings right here? For teachers personify such work and the people who engage in it, so far as most children have opportunity to see. It seems safe to assume that it will do no harm to have students discover, through master teachers, that at least *some* teachers are outstanding personalities, deeply rooted in their fields, highly talented, honored in their calling and in the community, and paid at least enough to give them some income tax worries. Without belittling the importance of keeping Johnny's feet dry, we can note that no parent will ever telephone a master teacher to say that Johnny's rubbers will be left in the office.

❝ Step by step, making their problems more complicated all the time, the children —not all of them, but a good many— worked out for themselves most of the rules for doing addition. In a week— working only a few minutes a day—they covered material that the school was prepared to spend years teaching them.❞

John Holt in *How Children Learn*

7

THE TEACHING FUNCTION

However skilled the master teacher may be, it is apparent that his job is primarily to start the ball rolling. It is an axiom of education in modern terms that no great amount of learning ever takes place until interest has been aroused; the amount of learning is likely to reflect directly the amount of interest. The master teacher's first duty, then, is to arouse interest in the particular unit of study he takes up. He must also use his special resources as a teacher to get across the key thought, the flash of insight that becomes the root from which all more detailed understanding grows.

For example, a master teacher may lecture on the rainfall cycle, showing how water is evaporated, forms into clouds, is precipitated as rain. To many of his young hearers the whole concept may be brand new: they have seen lakes and rivers (or perhaps they haven't!) and rain and clouds, but accepted them as simply "there," without any thought of process or cycle. The master teacher, if successful, makes them see the familiar with new insight, gives a section of their world new meaning. Such an experience is thrilling to most children. Having torn off part of the veil, they have no desire to stop. They want to know more, to consolidate and display and talk about their new understanding.

The stage is set for follow-up teaching. In the table on page 82 I have put this under "medium" skills. Let me point out again that we are not now concerned with "importance," since all essential parts of a function are important, and importance is at best a personal, often moral judgment about which we can argue forever. We are considering the matter of *skill,* and how to use personnel most wisely and efficiently in this light. If we ponder the question, we come to see, I think, that by "high skill" we invariably mean "rare skill." Most of us manage to develop remarkable skill in balancing a long, thin body on two small extremities, on which we contrive to stand, walk, run, dance, jump, and traverse irregular surfaces. Might not a seal view this as harder than balancing a ball on one's nose? Yet we do not, that I am aware, commonly think of our ability to stay erect as a high skill. Our civilization ordinarily pays persons possessing useful rare skills pretty much according to their rarity. Since we can find many more persons who can develop passable or better skill at follow-up teaching than we can find master teachers, it follows that we must define this work as requiring medium skill. There can be, of course, persons who come to have rare degrees of skill in methodology or follow-up teaching. Such persons might very well be made master teachers, specializing in using these skills.

On the whole, though, follow-up teaching does not require exceptional skills. Our Miss L., having patience and a friendly approach, plus training and experience that may improve year by year, can do rather well, especially if she is able to start with the learning readiness of her students at a high level, in terms of aroused interest at least. Miss L. knows how to ramify this interest into many areas, in which practice in a variety of basic skills will necessarily be involved. She may pose a science question: what experiments can the students devise to test whether water does indeed evaporate? Or a geographical question that calls into use library skills: what bodies of water are especially salty, what are they like, and what part does evaporation play?

She can form a team to visit the local newspaper offices, consult their files, and report on a flood of some years back—a project that increases understanding of community resources and employs skill in verbal and written communication. In arithmetic, there can be a dozen problems: calculating average temperature for a month; determining how much water would cover the playground to the depth of an inch; designing and building a gauge to measure rainfall. Still another team might do studies on the economic consequences of rain or drought, perhaps interviewing residents in a variety of occupations.

In all of this Miss L.'s skill in tying interest to projects and assignments and in guiding children into them on levels that allow each a good deal of successful achievement plays an essential role, as does her ability to find suitable projects, or invent her own, or let her students devise appropriate ones reflecting their aroused interest.

We can begin to glimpse, I believe, how a seemingly rather *rigid* program for the master teachers could be tied in with a much more *flexible* follow-up by teachers at the level of Miss L. The programming of the master teacher presentations, of course, will be influenced by experience and responsive to the reported needs of the follow-up teachers. In addition, the master teacher will of necessity want to maintain direct contact with at least a sample number of students, to get the invaluable feedback that tells him how well he is getting his ideas through to the pupils and how he can further improve his presentation. Splitting the teaching job this way does not rob the follow-up teacher of freedom to adapt teaching to the needs of her particular group of the moment, nor to use the methods she prefers because she has the best success with them. For the younger students especially, it can bring the enormous advantage of frequent exposure to a *number* of inspiring teachers and personalities, even while working routinely with only a few.

Making at least part of the master teachers' program rigid has one vastly important advantage. It is a convenient and relatively sure way of seeing to it that the few dozen "grand" ideas on which a basic education rests are positively and expertly covered, as early as practicable in a child's school career, covered enough times, in different ways, to raise the index of understanding to the highest possible point. It is a "grand idea," for example, that science does not accept anything on authority, but only on the ability of other scientists to reach the same conclusions from experiment or observation. The master teacher *says* water evaporates and condenses, but the students *check* his statement by devising and conducting experiments, because in introducing science the master teacher got across this fundamental idea and probably showed its startling effect on the course of civilization.

(In contrast, many so-called science courses in both elementary and high schools present as "experiments" what are simply demonstrations. The vital concept of an experiment as a "question to nature," a verification or disproving of an hypothesis, is often totally lost sight of. Students whose records show years of "taking science" often, at least in my experience, seem unable to state with any assured confidence the simplest tenets of the scientific method. In one instance, a group of students found in their biology lab microscopic work something quite unpredicted. The teacher, annoyed that this group was holding up the others, told them what they *should* have seen, and went on with the lesson! None of the students felt any scientific outrage, so far as I could determine.)

Similarly, in English, a master teacher secure in his scholarship and enthusiasm can get across the vitally important "grand idea" that words are not fixed in meaning, arbitrary, and inanimate, but on the contrary alive, changing, often rich in historical accretions, and varying in meaning according to when, where, and by whom they are used. Another grand idea is that we can represent a large object by a small, diagramatic drawing—a house by a plan, a state by a map. When for a time I taught map-reading in the Army, I was amazed at how many men, including some college trained, had never mastered this concept. In mathematics there are at least a half dozen such ideas. How many adults' ineptitude in arithmetic seems to stem from an imperfect understanding of zero! And I am among those who reached voting age and more before ever realizing that "two times two is four" is an *equation*.

Under the pressure of many duties, a classroom teacher may fail to cover some of these grand ideas adequately, or even at all; for usually it is quite possible to teach the subject matter so that it is "learned"—enough to give "right answers"—but not really understood. A child can become adept in doing arithmetic in the prescribed fashion without grasping the *why* of the process, for example. (Ask him to do mental arithmetic, and his dependence on the mechanical pencil-and-paper approach may become strikingly visible.) It is also customary for teachers to ask such a question as "what was the effect of the invention of the cotton gin upon the course of American slavery" in an examination, and deduct a few points if it is missed, even though missing it must raise the gravest doubts about the student's understanding of the period. On the other side, a child may often be able to parrot back remembered material that is correct, without ever grasping its full meaning.

If the teacher has had modern training, with its emphasis on mythical "readiness" and passively awaiting the "right moment," she may all the more easily skip a basic area, or perhaps hurry over it because she is behind schedule according to her unit plan. In practice, there is no adequate check on her, nothing to force attention to the omission at the time.

We can see the potential value of building the master teacher's program around these essential grand ideas, covering each not once but a number of times, so there is certainty of each child ultimately grasping them. It can then become the responsibility of the master teacher in each area to see that the students *do* understand. The interplay between master teacher and follow-up teacher introduces a check-and-balance relationship benefiting both.

There is much more to the process of teaching, however, than merely the area of "telling" and explanation that we have been looking at. I should like to offer here a simple and convenient division of the teaching-learning process into three stages. It is my own, I should perhaps explain, because the classroom teacher's job is, as we have seen, so complicated an assignment that "authoritative" break-downs of the work, where they are ventured at all in recent texts, tend to run several pages. Nor have I found any too useful for the purpose in hand: a division of the classroom teacher's work primarily by level of skill required. The three stages are these:

1. *Presentation.* This includes the arousing of interest, the conveying of information and the explanation of ideas. It is done *to* the student, who is passive.

2. *Repetition.* I have taken the liberty of coining the word, to include all the work which is primarily for the purpose of practice and developing facility, and which is more or less repetitive in nature. It is more than mere repetition, however, since it involves some insight, and usually means doing a *variety* of tasks with a common theme or object, rather than rote. Learning the alphabet, a multiplication table, or pronunciation of foreign words by drill come under this head; and so too do working an assortment of examples to master an algebraic process, learning the technique of playing the clarinet, or taking dictation to master shorthand. Repetition is done *by* the student, but usually at or under the direction of a teacher — usually a back-and-forth relationship.

3. *Personalization.* This is the step in which the student makes *use* of what he has learned, in or out of school, in a personal and original way, as by using mathematics to solve a problem in a model he is building; writing a report on a project he has carried out; or painting a mural based on study in history. Personalization takes place only if the student works to at least some extent on his own initiative, even if within the frame of a broad assignment.

In the examples of imaginative follow-up teaching given above we can glimpse how many ways there are that teaching can be carried through to the final personalization stage, in which the student makes what he has learned actually his own. "What you *know*, you don't have to remember." But the repetition and personalization steps should not be confused as to purpose. Personalization, of necessity, involves practice — one cannot write a report without further exercise in spelling and composition. But the exercise is not the purpose. Rather it is to find out, by the acid test of execution, how adequate the student's *understanding* is (from presentation), and how adequate his *skills* are (from repetition), for the project in hand. He has tried to devise a scientific experiment to test an hypothesis — does it do that, and can he set down, clearly organized and stated, what he proposes? He has designed a rain gauge — is it well conceived, is his arithmetic able to cope with the problems presented, can he make an understandable drawing? Was he able to carry out the interviews with tradespeople, ask sensible questions, and report in writing or orally in good style? Personalization tests, measures, proves what the student can do, at any point in his educational career. It does so not only for the school but for the student himself. He knows what he knows, and sees what he needs to know. *He,* not some other student; not "the class."

The object of repetition, on the other hand, is to compress a lot of practice into a short time. At this point, I believe, we can see why very "progressive" methods, now largely in poor repute, brought so much criticism on the schools that used them. Teachers had the children set up a store so that they might learn arithmetic by making change and keeping accounts. Possibly the children enjoyed it, and if so their interest helped them learn; but the amount of actual repetition accomplished in such periods tended to be reduced to perhaps a fifth of what might have been accomplished by a direct approach.

It is hard to believe that the avalanche of complaints about college freshmen who cannot read fast and well, or write simple declarative English, and business recruits who can't spell or do routine arithmetic, are without basis. Most of these complaints, so far as I can gather, seem to center on precisely the lack of crisp accuracy that is a sign of inadequate repetition. One office manager plagued with personnel problems of this kind told me of the perhaps illustrative comment of a girl in his bookkeeping department. He had called attention to the sad fact that her work was in error about five percent of the time. "Why," she responded, "that means that 95% of the time I'm right! That would be a very good mark in school."

I am constantly astonished at how frequently, in discussion of schooling, one hears plain old-fashioned *drill* spoken of disparagingly, with the implication that students hate it and would writhe if subjected to it, when there is such abundant evidence to the contrary. It is hard to find any school activity more popular and widespread than marching bands, which involve learning an instrument (largely repetition) and mastering intricate formations (wholly repetition). Further, bands set great stress on striving for perfection; and indeed, to "goof" while on parade is a painfully embarrassing experience.

In a great many, if not most, children's activities repetition plays a great part. Girls engage endlessly in hopscotch, jacks, ball-bouncing, and rope-skipping to doggerel or counting. What father has not found himself arm-weary and hot long before his boy was willing to give up throwing a football or baseball? A hoop and a basketball provide hours of entertainment. Almost as soon as a child is old enough to develop a recognizable skill, voluntary repetition to improve it becomes observable.

Even in a stricter context, it is by no means exceptional to find a class hugely enjoying crisply paced, rhythmic drill in learning phrases and sentences of a foreign tongue, when led by a teacher with energy and a personable approach. It is, of course, essential to enjoying drill that the learner has understanding of what he is doing and its purpose and that he can see that benefit can accrue. It would probably be difficult to get a band to drill its best if its members were convinced no audience would ever watch them perform. The same boys who eagerly practice baseball because they can see their skill improving, and know where it can be applied, will moan at calisthenics, which often seems to have no observable benefit or goal.

What levels of skill are required for repetition, well planned and carried out with verve and vigor? The answer, I am afraid, is not to be found in the textbooks, in part because repetition as such still does not seem to be a sharp concept, and also because the proper use of skills by division of labor is an approach as rare within our schools as it is common without. To some extent, we can make our own judgments. Clearly, it would seem, the *planning* of repetation must take place at a high level. It is hard to see why methods which prove best in practice should not be widely adopted, in each particular application—why should each repetition-leader act as though the problem were being met for the first time? By its very nature, repetition will often lend itself to considerable standardization, both as to goals and objectives, and methods to be used. That is not to suggest that the goals need be fixed, or that the door be closed to experiment in methods or use of alternative methods where there is good reason. *Once reasonably standardized, it would seem possible that at least a good deal of repetition does not require the full time and attention of a highly-trained teacher.* A student teacher, or an assistant teacher, ranking below the present classroom teacher level, might very well handle the job, under some supervision. In such case, a considerable saving in teaching cost may be attainable, for repetition makes very efficient use of teaching time to begin with. (Lest I be accused and forthwith burned at the stake for the heresy of saving money, I had better add at once that one main object of saving teacher time can be to use it for more small-group and individual teaching.)

We may also note here, for further discussion, that the nature of repetition suggests that some of it is capable of being done by teachers at one remove, that is, by some adaptation of technology. If "teaching machines" (in the broadest sense) have thus far aroused little interest and less enthusiasm among teachers, they have attracted a good deal more of both at higher and less hidebound levels, and a quite astonishing amount of technical and exploratory work is currently being done. Such machines, if economical enough, have one great advantage at the outset: they can be used by students *individually,* permitting them to advance at precisely their own speed. As we have pointed out, repetition demands constant evaluation of each child's progress, if he is not to be hurried or bored to tears.

In the process of *personalization* we can use few machines. What is required above all for success at this stage is a personal relationship between the pupil, or a very small group of pupils similarly engaged, and the teacher. Any teacher will agree, I believe, that nothing stimulates and inspires a child so much as the personal, genuine interest of a respected adult. "Gee," says the junior high lad, "Mr. Petersen is interested in *me!* He wants to see how I put my radio together!" A child makes a sharp and quite correct distinction between interest in him as a member of a class, and interest in *him*. But for the ordinary classroom teacher to give such interest to each child is impossible. There are too many children, too many duties, too little time. There is not even a *place* for a personal session during school hours, as a rule!

By and large, there is only one reliable way for a child in our class-ridden schools to get personal attention in private, and that is to get into more than average trouble.

Somehow we have to reorganize our use of teacher time to make the personal conference an unhurried, routinized part of teaching. We need to provide the small rooms in which teacher and students, not more than six at most, may meet. The actual number of minutes spent with each child need not, I suspect, be great — a few minutes to discuss an assignment, a few more some days later to discuss the results. But those minutes must give undivided, unpressured attention to each child. They can mean the difference between doing work because "we got to" and doing it with love and enthusiasm that builds a desire for learning and pride in accomplishment.

Whose attention should the child have? Here age is undoubtedly a key factor. For the younger child it should probably be dominantly one teacher, preferred by and selected by the child. But for older children, it need not be just one, nor necessarily his regular teacher. For the brilliant child, it may have to be the master teacher: it has long been observed that highly intelligent pupils begin at quite tender years to make less bountifully endowed adults uneasy and mistrustful. But regardless of how this matter is worked out, it is apparent, I think, that the teachers who meet with the child alone or in very small groups, and give him regular personal attention, will come to know and understand him far better than is possible in the typical classroom situation. And if two or three teachers so meet with him regularly, the chances of accurate evaluation of his potential and his progress are astronomically greater.

Personalization is the "pay-off" part of the educational process. Under the classroom system, it barely occurs at all as a warmly rewarding process between teacher and student, except in relatively rare special cases. (If you have a child in a classroom school, ask how many five-minute, one-to-one talks he has had with teachers—other than on "discipline"!) It needs to be made routine and effective for every child. Otherwise whatever teaching skill *is* available can never begin to bear full fruit.

Too often, schools reward only that which is most easily measured. And what is easily measured may be inconsequential in the conduct of human affairs. Children, like adults, see a certain expediency in doing that which is to be rewarded. Consequently, the world's children spend shocking proportions of valuable time on that which is of little importance.

John I. Goodlad in *School, Curriculum, and the Individual*

8

THE PROBLEM OF
UNDERSTANDING

The 1958–1959 Annual Report of the Carnegie Foundation for the Advancement of Teaching includes a summary of a discussion by the trustees, themselves a score of highly distinguished educators, on the education of the "academically talented." It begins:

> A basic aim of our society is to help each individual to fulfill the promise that is in him. Our educational system is the chief instrument for achieving that goal. To achieve it, the schools must recognize that children differ in their abilities and provide programs designed to develop the potentialities of children at each level.

The principle stated is today everywhere honored, though not always set forth so succinctly. As we have glimpsed, the organizational backbone of our schools, the classroom-and-grade system, has remained largely intact from days when the approach was quite the contrary—to treat each child alike and run him through an elementary learning mill.

Some of the schizoid strain caused by this anomaly is relieved in the minds of practicing educators by a resort to "guidance," a word as glowing as it is indeterminate. For the guidance counselor *is* free of the classroom. He *does* work with students one by one, with the fullest recognition on every hand that each is a separate personality and not either a "norm" or a "deviant." He is even likely to be given a small room or cubicle where he and a student may talk privately! Sometimes it was, or still is, the broom closet; but let us not quibble. The fact that guidance has entered the schools is a major beachhead, and that it has become established in many as a necessity (though still subject to occasional attack as a budgetary "frill") is cause for cheer.

The whole notion of guidance was forced upon our schools, however, *not* in response to the basic dilemma, but largely by historical accident—the rapid growth of high schools early in this century, and the universal enactment and later enforcement of state legislation making attendance mandatory for practically all children late into the teens. If we are going to keep a child in school because the law says we must, it is necessary to provide a program for him that has some hope of holding his interest, and being capable of his accomplishment. Previously, high school automatically selected those who were considered suited for further study or preparation for college. Others dropped out of public education somewhere along the way, in many cases because of lack of desire for more education, inability to do very well, or the availability of employment. But with compulsory attendance and child labor laws, this winnowing process all but ended. Public school education became for all a longer process, and one greater in scope, and appallingly more acute and more apparent became the differences in abilities, interests and achievement among students.

High schools, then, felt forced to offer different sequences of studies for those who would probably go to college, for those who might go to business, trade, or technical schools, or into some less academic occupation, or into homemaking. Further, many of these courses had to be offered on different intellectual levels. (We can see why Dr. James Conant, in his report

The American High School Today, offers as a prime recommendation the elimination of high schools with senior classes of under
one hundred students.)

As it happened, the popular discovery of "psychology," and
the development of psychological tests of some usefulness coin-
cided with the great expansion of our high schools. Testing and
guidance thus entered the schools more or less hand in hand.

To most students who come into contact with "guidance"
at all, the word calls up a picture of a counselor who can perhaps be seen after a good wait for an appointment, and who
advises on what studies to take, what colleges to apply to, or
what vocation to enter, and how. The counselor may also be
available on much shorter notice if the student is a problem—
the more acutely he is failing his courses or causing other difficulties, the higher the priority. The words "guidance" and
"counseling," which are more or less interchangeable, have to
be regarded with some caution: they are used to refer to highly
trained, full-time specialists in some cases, and just as glibly to
mean teachers assigned this work in addition to other duties,
with no special training for it at all, or those who are taking
spare-time courses to give them at least some background and
"professional" understanding. In school systems that lack
enough money to attract teachers to cover all classes, it is of
course difficult to clear funds to hire guidance specialists, the
more so because these persons are in a position to pick and
choose where they will work. In the middle and lower range of
high schools, then, highly trained "real" guidance people tend
to be sparse.

In junior high schools the trained guidance person is even
rarer, and in elementary schools, except for the top fraction,
guidance is little more than an intention. Going by Office of Education figures for 1964, about 30,000 guidance counselors
were working in secondary schools—or roughly one per school
on average (a good high school typically may have three to
five). *Of elementary schools over 100 students in size, three out of
four lacked a guidance counselor even one day a week.*

(It will help the reader to understand the woeful state of
educational statistics if it is pointed out that the long under-

nourished Office of Education was able to provide the above vague and naked figures only after four years of inquiry. Obviously it matters greatly whether a guidance person works one day or a full week, or is qualified or merely dubbed "guidance" so the school does not have to report "none." In general, even the simplest figures in the field of public education are lacking, disputed, biased, or dubious on mere inspection, to a degree one must experience to believe. In 1947, the U.S. Office of Education had responsibility for the relatively neglible sum of $29 million. By 1957 this had grown to $272 million, still absurdly small for such an office. For 1967 the figure was about $4 billion — an astonishing jump reflecting in good measure the educational interests and administrative skills of President Lyndon Johnson. We can understand if this bureau, at last playing the essential role it should, has not mopped up a staggering backlog of problems from an impoverished past. Aspects of the difficulties can be surmised from this paragraph in the NEA publication *Estimates of School Statistics, 1967–68:* "Some of the change observed from year to year partly reflects improvement in the states' ability to collect and process data. Some states are now able to collect and report actual data, rather than estimates, especially statistics of pupils and teachers." This mild and grateful note is too eloquent in itself to call for comment.)

At this writing, the latest available Office of Education figures, not yet published, are for 1965–66, and still very skimpy. They suggest that there may be some 25,000 full-time secondary guidance specialists, and 18,000 part-time. In the lower grades it would take some hunting to find 2,000 full-time, and a bit more than half that many part-time. The NEA points out that, on the "minimum" standard of one guidance counselor to 2,000 elementary pupils, a most modest target, 13,500 would be the need in the fall of 1967, against a mere trickle of supply, estimated at under 1,800. The secondary shortage appeared a good deal worse.

By and large, we can say that guidance, so far as it exists, is a high school function. The lower in grades we go, the less we find. In any specific situation we must ask what "guidance" attempts: perhaps as little as sorting incoming students onto "tracks" (all too often with skin color and ethnic background weighing heavily in the judgments), or inexpertly helping the departing to find appropriate colleges or employment. Only a few of what counselors there are systematically attempt much more than this sorting job, and make the effort to study each student, watch his progress, forestall failures and social adjustment problems, and even assist him in coping with home or outside problems when these interfere with his school success. Both programs call for skill, but it is apparent that the more thorough efforts call for highly skilled persons indeed.

We can summarize the present state of guidance best, perhaps, by an analogy. Consider a man who owns a $20,000 house, and has taken out $1,000 of fire insurance. We can congratulate him on having discovered the idea of insurance, and applaud him on having found some funds to buy some, but we must also recognize that the amount he has taken out is so inadequate as to suggest almost a lack of purpose.

To pursue the subject further it is necessary once again to come to grips with some fundamental lacks in our school system so basic and so familiar that they are not only often overlooked, but even concealed by contrary impressions resting on little more than empty assumptions and outdated rituals.

There is the highest agreement that we want our schools to be democratic in concept, which means we want them to be concerned with the welfare of each individual student. We won't for a moment accept the idea of trying to train an "elite," the sons and daughters of place and privilege who will automatically take over on coming of age. Even most of our private schools reject such notions, and deliberately give scholarships to children of the non-elite. Nor will we countenance thinking of our schools as a manipulated machine grinding out supplies for the State: so many scientists, so many engineers, so many poets. We instead insist that each child should have his chance to go as far and as high as he is able. And even while we are coming to see and accept the fact that as a nation we may perish if we fail to utilize the abilities of the highly able few, we have no aim to sacrifice the lesser intellects to the glory of the higher. We want to develop all to whatever levels each can attain.

One might assume, then, that our schools, starting from this truly magnificent premise, would set the greatest importance on checking continually to see how well the objective is being achieved. "Keeping score" is so indispensable a part of any purposeful activity, and even of sports and games, that the mind reels at the thought of trying to carry on a vast and essential undertaking without systematically measuring the results achieved. Yet, astonishing as it may be, *our public schools in general make almost no effort to keep score.* They have only the vaguest notion of how well each student is progressing, and almost no notion at all of how well he is doing in relation to his potentials — perhaps the most meaningful measure of the schools' success.

If the statement seems startling, let us merely ask a few questions. Joey Jones enters a school at the age of six, one of 400 students. He leaves it at the age of twelve to go to junior high, or at fourteen to go to high school. Who has checked in any detail on his *continuous* progress during those crucial years? Not the principal, unless the school is very small or very exceptional; for this officer has a thousand duties and pressures that make such a task for each student impossible. If Joey has been a *problem,* of course, the principal may have come to know him only too well. But aside from this, is there anybody in the school charged with following Joey Jones' career, and that of every other Joey Jones enrolled? *The job is not assigned, because the need for it is not even admitted to exist!*

In most cases, Joey will have a new classroom teacher each year. If she is diligent, she will examine whatever records there are to give her some idea of what kind of a pupil Joey is and how he had done thus far, as he enters her charge. Through gossip with other teachers, if Joey is "interesting" enough, she may gather something of his reputation. At the end of the year, having done her best for her class as she found them, she will turn Joey and the rest over to other teachers. Thus responsibility for Joey's *progress* will be divided among many teachers, each of whom feels her concern is strictly limited to the period Joey was in her charge. The *school* as such evinces almost no organized interest in Joey's progress and makes no check on it, unless and until Joey becomes a problem by his behavior or marked failure, or because of his parents' complaints.

The school's job is unquestionably to help develop each child as closely to his potential as possible. But the typical school has no apparatus, no routine procedures, no personnel to check on and measure how well it does its job. As we shall see, it almost deliberately makes it difficult for the parents to judge. Here, I submit, is one of the most intolerable weaknesses of our whole educational effort—a gaping hole in the foundations through which pours a substantial share of the vast amount of work, devotion, time and money that millions of persons put into it.

Administrators, I have reason to believe from conversations, will more readily agree with the acuteness of this problem than will many teachers. For not a few teachers acquire an enormous faith in their ability to "know" how well each of their charges is doing. Usually parents and principals go along with this faith to at least a considerable extent. But faith it is: for the weight of evidence makes it dubious that the teacher's evaluation is at all reliable enough to be of much value in itself within the present classroom system. It is essential to rid ourselves of the notion that "teacher knows" if we are to see where guidance can bring enormous improvement in our handling of pupils.

The classroom teacher, it is true, does have the greatest opportunity to observe the child at close range, over a considerable period. But we must remember that she is observing the child almost all the time in the same running situation: the class. Even when the child is serving as a class officer, or is on a special project committee, he is in relation to the class. How the child behaves in his neighborhood play group, or in his family circle, or in relation to his hobbies or interests, or when he is alone— these she has little opportunity to see. The great amount of observation possible can actually be misleading. Consider the situation of an employer who has ten employees who have worked for him for years, but who has had virtually no contact with them otherwise. For him to claim he "knows" these people is an exaggeration: there are vast areas of their lives and personalities that he is quite ignorant of, and that might sharply alter his judgments if he did know more about them. He is quite correct, however, if he says only, "I know how these people behave in my office." Teachers can be correct if they say, "I know how Peter and Alma behave in my class." If they claim to "know" Peter and Alma, they may fall wide of the mark.

The difficulty has long been recognized, as in these passages from *Classroom Group Behavior* by Mary A. Bany and Lois V. Johnson:

> . . . The behavior of a child alone in a situation is not the same as when he is embedded in a group . . . much of the behavior of children in classrooms is shaped by the class groups, or by the desire of children to be accepted and assimilated within these class groups. . . . Many of the acts of individual children that are labeled "problem behavior" by teachers are caused by pressures stemming from group membership.

To this obstacle must be added an even greater one: the child's behavior to an important degree *stems* from the teacher's, and is in response to her point of view, prejudices, manner, and method. Rarely, under the classroom system, does a teacher have opportunity to actually witness how a child acts in another classroom with another teacher or adult. Nor does the teacher really know what she is doing that affects the child:

> As with any individual a large part of the teacher's functioning is of unconscious origin. He is not aware himself of many of the feelings, attitude about things, and ways of relating to people that he is "teaching" to children. However skillfully he may think he is concealing his attitude towards individual children the teacher nevertheless conveys it to them.

The quotation is from *Elementary School Curriculum* by Aubrey Haan, published in 1961. The more recent research work headed by Robert Rosenthal has dramatically confirmed this finding.

The teacher is influencing the child on many levels, from those deeply subconscious to simply being a model:

It is difficult to develop students who are enthusiastic,
curious, and interested in growing intellectually, unless
they are taught by teachers who are enthusiastic, curious,
and interested in growing intellectually. The behavior
cues that students pick up from teachers are not limited
to the subject matter at hand.

The author here is Henry Clay Lindgren, in *Educational Psychology in the Classroom*. His observation suggests, perhaps,
why certain outstanding teachers seem to have unusual success no matter what methods they appear to use.

Clearly, the seldomly disputed tenet that the classroom
teacher "knows the child" does not stand up well under examination; yet it is one of the most holy of education's many
sacred cows. Nor can we afford to be trapped by *average* knowledge. If we agree that we are concerned with *every* individual
pupil, we cannot be tolerant because six or seven out of ten
are fairly well evaluated. Merely remembering that the three
or four misjudged and mishandled may include *your* children
is enough to make that point.

Even the most diligent, best trained and acutely sensitive
teacher runs head-on into two principles applying in the
classroom situation that make her judgments highly questionable at best. One is, *the judgments tend to be based very heavily
on what the child has done, rather than on what he can do.* This is
no great fault to be charged against the teacher: the record
speaks loudly, and potential in the faintest of whispers. Despite
the many hours she spends with the child under observation,
she may fail to get the merest glimpse of his potential. Since
she can't observe what isn't visible, we can hardly blame her
as matters stand. Years ago I had a clerk assisting me who
showed not a vestige of initiative. Some years later I met him
again as the head of a flourishing business built wholly out
of his own ingenuity and imagination. I still find it hard to
believe I was *that* wrong—I have to plead that he simply didn't
show those qualities while working with me! It is possible that
other circumstances brought them out, opening his own eyes
to what he could do. So it can be with children: those who

have small potentialities may behave in the classroom precisely like some others who have great resources to be exploited, visible only in a different milieu.

The second problem is that *usually the teacher has no way to check the correctness of her judgments.* "Robert could read much better with proper handling," thinks the teacher, and proceeds to give him special attention. He responds, and she has proved her good judgment. More often, she may attempt work with a child, and not get response. "I was wrong," thinks the teacher. Was she? Or did she use the wrong approach, or lack time, or were there factors holding back the child that she did not know about and therefore could not deal with? She may never find out. Lois, the teacher believes, is "doing quite nicely." Because she thinks so, she does not make the special effort she did with Robert—and she has no way of knowing whether Lois could do much better, or not. Because this "no comparable alternative" situation always obtains, the judgment of the experienced teacher may not be necessarily better than that of one relatively new. (The "old hand" teacher whose judgments have hardened into a tendency to quickly "type" pupils is all too common. "That Carl—I've seen a lot of *his* kind!") We see the problem clearly if we imagine a group of persons assigned to shoot rifles at distant targets, but never informed where their shots actually hit. They can practice for years, and quite possibly become poorer shots than when they began. Or, try the simple experiment of trying to place two blocks exactly forty inches apart. Do not in any way measure your results. In a few trials you will see the futility of attempting to improve your judgment when you cannot check your progress. The older teacher may indeed have developed greater ability to observe behavior, but any increase in her judgment and capacity for perceiving potentials may be more than offset by the encrusting effects of habit and prejudice.

According to legend, Ralph Waldo Emerson once visited a classroom and on leaving observed to the teacher, "Madam, you seem to be trying to make all of these children just like you. One of you is enough." Though today's teacher may be less guilty of such a purpose, it is quite impossible for any human being to be objective in the continuing classroom situation. Educational literature is heavily sprinkled with frank recognition that teachers *are* human. They tend to be greatly influenced in evaluating the child by the degree to which he does or does not appear to share the teacher's particular set of values. We may expect that the narrower the teacher's experience of the world, the more likely she may be to forget that her values are somewhat less than universally accepted. Horace Mann described the problem:

> To instruct the beautiful, the affectionate, the intelligent, the grateful, is unalloyed delight. A school, composed entirely of such, would not be earth, but elysium. But to take an awkward, gawky, unclean, ill-dressed, ill-mannered, ill-tempered child, and to work up an interest in it, to love it, to caress it, to perform a full measure of duty to it: — this draws upon all the resources of conscience, virtue, and religion.

Mann's use of "it" reminds us that, personally, he couldn't stand children; but his point is made well. The teacher's response to the child is complicated by other factors as well. Willard Abraham points out in *Common Sense about Gifted Children,* referring to studies made by Leta S. Hollingworth: "Gifted children may deliberately hide their lights in regular groups, but begin to shine and expand in special classes where their vocabularies, ideas, humor, and games can come out naturally and freely."

In another quote from *Teaching in High School,* the problem is seen to be even greater with older students:

> Students in the classroom are analogous to icebergs as far as the teacher's knowledge of them is concerned. Seven-eighths of the iceberg floats under water, leaving only one-eighth visible to the eye. Many of the student's attitudes, motivations, and perceptions are likewise hidden from the teacher's view. Unfortunately, because of numerous unpleasant experiences in revealing their personal problems and learning difficulties to their teachers and parents, many students have a strong tendency to

conceal rather than reveal their deeper feelings. In twelve years of public education, students become quite skillful in hiding their problems from their teachers.

In *Measurement for Guidance,* by John Rothney and others, the authors say: "High school grades are strongly influenced by teachers who tend to reward children of the higher social classes, give better marks to girls than boys, and become influenced by such factors as effort, neatness, or 'apple polishing.' "

To quote further is pointless, since it would be readily possible to fill page after page, not only with similar observations from competent sources, but also with the results of objective research. When we consider all the conditions, it is really cause for astonishment that we should accept even for a moment the fiction that teachers "know" their students. Curiously, almost every teacher I have talked with, including some quite new at the job, seems to feel that this mystic insight comes with daily classroom contact; yet, as we shall see, teachers universally detest and feel uneasy about marking and reporting on their children—a task we might assume would be fairly simple and comfortable if the insight were truly there. Principals and guidance counselors are well aware that teachers vary extremely in their marking of the same children.

We have not yet stated the whole case, however, for we have been speaking of the teacher as if she were more or less a passive observer. She is far from that. It is unrealistic to expect a teacher, with all the burdens and pressures upon her, to face a class day after day and not establish a whole system of personal interrelationships with the various pupils before her. Every teacher knows that trying to be "fair" demands a mighty effort and constant watchfulness to avoid the pitfall of the "halo effect." To quote Denis Baron and Harold W. Bernard in *Evaluation Techniques for Classroom Teachers:*

As a result of the "halo effect," or the tendency to believe that a child who is cheerful, clean and cooperative is also bright, teachers are often surprised when a quiet or a sullen lad achieves a high score on a test or when a blond, curly-headed little girl in a starched pinafore makes a low score. The element of subjectivity often leads to mistaken evaluations.

Because the teacher can never wholly disregard what *she* would find attractive in a child companion, she may also be quite in error in her impressions of what is going on between the various children in her room, as revealed by more objective tests called sociograms. The same authors note:

> Something of the value of sociometry is revealed by the very common remark of teachers, "I was surprised by the differences between what I thought were the interpersonal likes and dislikes and what was indicated by the sociogram."

The vast range of differences among children make it inevitable that certain children will rouse special emotions in certain teachers, often on the subconscious level. New teachers may feel panic as a result, experienced teachers may respond with antagonism. In *Guidance in the Elementary Classroom,* Gerald T. Kowitz and Norma G. Kowitz observe with regard to the gifted child:

> Many adults greatly fear him because he is in some respects more capable than they. From such a reaction, a field of conflict can develop between adult and child, and as a result, neither adequate guidance nor satisfactory teaching can be expected.

The difficulties of recognizing and "doing something about" gifted children are now widely realized, and happily increasing attention is being given to the problem. The quotation above will serve to remind us that teachers do not always jump for joy on discovering a gifted child in their class.

Emotional factors tend to be even stronger when mental health is the core of the difficulties. Teachers have been notoriously weak in recognizing even acute symptoms in their children for what they are. While there has been improvement in this respect in recent years, the problem certainly remains. Nothing is easier than interpreting the behavior of a disturbed child or even of one mildly neurotic as directed at oneself. In *Health Observation of School Children*, George M. Wheatley and Grace T. Hallock note:

> It is easy to feel personally affronted or disgusted by behavior we dislike—hard to realize that our feelings may lead us to make serious mistakes in interpreting and dealing with such behavior—still harder to admit that we may dislike a person because he possesses attributes we dislike in ourselves.

There is also the problem of social background. If I may use the terms "middle class" and "working class" loosely, almost all teachers identify themselves with the middle class, and most take middle-class manners, dress, speech, and attitudes as an unquestioned norm. Yet many of their students, and often a majority, are from working class homes and backgrounds. The teacher commonly struggles to force the child into a middle-class mold—all too frequently, perhaps, unaware that a struggle is going on: that the child is being pressured to despise and disavow the standards and customs of his home and environment. Thus a teacher may view middle-class morals, standards, and behavior as the only acceptable or "right" ways of life. A child may resist speaking in a manner his family and companions might regard as "fancy," while the teacher regards him as incorrigibly uncooperative, uninterested in "improving" himself, or just plain stupid. A project that seems cogent to a child from one home may seem silly or far fetched to a child from another. "At the art museum," says the teacher, "let's all pick out the painting we would like best to hang on the wall of our living room." On Joan's wall there is an original by a good painter; on Henry's are some prints and etchings; but in Judy's case the kitchen is the nearest approach to a living room, and there the liquor store pin-up calendar is tastefully hung to cover the largest hole in the sagging plaster. She may not readily enter into the spirit of the suggestion, but rather conclude that school is a place where people with backgrounds different from hers go—a place in which she is an interloper and had best get out as soon as possible.

On a broader level, middle-class people commonly assume that everyone shares their keen interest in education and success. The discovery that some lower-class parents hold no such notions and cherish few such ambitions for their children comes as a shock. Many teachers, I am not the first to suspect, never do come to realize that some of their students have other motivations than those their teachers assume "everyone" just naturally has. They can easily, again and again and year after year, misjudge the ability of such children, who don't exert themselves because they see no desirable goal to be reached. And they can readily misinterpret their pupils' reluctance to abandon their familiar standards as antagonism towards the teacher personally. The truculence of Negro children militant against white dominance often proves especially painful.

Considering once again our Miss L. and her training, experience, and knowledge of life (and recalling that we have drawn her as rather above average), it seems unreasonable and foolish indeed to expect her to make accurate evaluations of dozens of children, in a situation even a highly trained team of psychologists would approach with caution. Yet we continually ask classroom teachers to do exactly that, and to make decisions with regard to our children that can have lifelong effects on their interests, progress, and emotional and intellectual growth. Which is worse: the old-style teacher who made little effort to probe into her children and demanded rigid conformity to her standards, or the new-style teacher who is forced into judgments which she has not the time, resources, objectivity, information, or ability to make? Either way seems a poor solution. Is it not apparent that the kind of judgments we are speaking of involve skill at the highest level? That they require trained specialists who have the time and resources to apply to each decision? And that even then no single person should make such judgments without adequate check by others? None of these conditions obtain in our schools today except in rare instances. The classroom teacher simply plows ahead amid the hurly-burly and endless distractions of an impossibly demanding job. Every parent knows that teachers' mistakes can be damaging and often disastrous: it is only the fortunate resilience of many children that holds the damage down to being merely serious instead of frightful.

Here again we must hark back to the fact that the schools are problem-oriented. A common situation is that of the child who seems to get along nicely in school. Everyone is happy: the teacher, who has no trouble with the student and sees him moving ahead at the average pace or better; the parents, who are pleased with his report cards and the teacher's praise; and the child, who finds school pleasant and easy. It is only when testing or some other circumstance suggests that the child is underachieving that the bubble breaks. If such is the case, not only are the child and society losing the talents and abilities he is not developing, but the school is actively teaching the child how to get along without half trying. Unless and until something exposes the child's underachievement, it can continue, with teacher after teacher feeling content with his progress instead of worried by a failure. Even if the problem comes to light, it hardly is likely to find a place besides the more acute problems — the non-readers, the class-disrupters, the authority-baiters who cannot be ignored even if everyone so desires. Teacher after teacher can pass the underachieving child onto the next grade, concerned perhaps, but consoled by the comforting self-assurance that the failure didn't begin in *her* class.

It is fortunate for us all that teachers so commonly bring to their work an admirable devotion and perseverance in the face of impossible demands. But we need to remind ourselves that they are as human as other people, nonetheless. We know a good deal today about what is required to get people to do their best work, and what will cause them to do a good deal less. So we must face an even more crushing realization about our misbegotten school system in action: *it creates no adequate motives for closely checking on each student's progress, and does exert powerful pressures upon teachers not to do so.*

As we have seen, the teacher usually cannot get paid a nickel more for outstanding teaching, and there is no great official interest in finding out how well she performs. Even if she should do a fine job of keeping each child up to potential, there is no ready way to prove it, nor source of acclaim, nor tangible recognition. On the contrary, should she talk too much in the faculty meetings about her methods and their results, or should the principal single her out for too hearty praise, she may easily win the enmity or disapproval of her colleagues. When there is little reward in sight for being outstandingly good at a job, it is the part of wisdom not to strive too obviously.

But the teacher who is diligent in *trying* to find underachieving children in her classes even more directly piles up problems for herself. She discovers, let us say, three very able students and five more with significant abilities, all of whom are coasting. At the same time she has eight children who are lagging behind, two of them acute problems. How on earth is she to cope with sixteen pupils who need special attention? With all due regard to teacher devotion, let us recognize that emotionally healthy persons do not go looking for trouble for themselves. It is far easier for a teacher to persuade herself or permit herself to think she is doing a fine job than to dig for evidence that she isn't. It is vastly simpler for her to write on report cards, "Robert isn't working up to the level of his ability," or, "Susan is a slow learner and needs all the help and encouragement she can get," and then forget about it, than it is for her to add two more special situations to her already staggering load. In the less obvious cases, it is far easier for her not to see the problem than to recognize it. Teachers who find too many problems in their classes and too many inadequacies in their school do not always win the grateful appreciation of their fellow workers and the school officials. They are more likely to be given to understand that there must be something wrong with *them*. After all, Mr. R. and Mrs. M. down the hall are not plagued with so many underachieving children — why should Miss L. be? If there is a supreme definition today of the good teacher in our schools, it is the same as that of the good pupil: the one who keeps up with the average and causes no trouble.

Is it not apparent that our present class-and-grade system puts the teacher **in an intolerab**le and unworkable position?

The school, not the individual teacher, should take the responsibility for the child's continuous progress. Our Miss L. is forced to make innumerable evaluations and to attempt guidance, both functions likely to be beyond her solitary skill and resources, and she must try to be objective in situations in which she is deeply involved, far beyond any possible objectivity. She is constantly kept aware of the importance of her work, yet given an assignment in which frustration is unavoidable and made the principal judge of her own performance — hardly an arrangement designed to promote mental health or efficient work. Nor is it surprising that one comes across so many instances of teachers who seem to regard their classroom as their own private bailiwick, in which they are not to be challenged, questioned, instructed, or even observed. Protected by the privacy of four walls and a closed door, they arrive at some kind of guilty compromise with the impossible demands of their job, and often respond with supercharged emotion to any attempt to find out what they are actually doing. Inevitably under such conditions different teachers who are nominally doing the same job come to very different compromises. One superintendent who managed to survey, prior to instituting a new organization, how teachers used their time by subjects, told me that he found the weekly time allotted to a subject varied from 45 to 245 minutes! Teachers simply taught what they pleased, as they pleased, to classes of the same grade supposedly following the same course of study! Until the unusual study was made, what was taught, to whom, and how well, was a matter of total mystery within this school. The situation, I believe, is entirely typical. (Teachers do file "lesson plans," but they may follow them loosely or not at all.)

The way out, so far as evaluation and guidance of the progress of each child is concerned, seems clear enough. *It is to put this duty primarily into the hands of a few highly-skilled specialists trained and equipped for this work.* They can meet with and deal with children individually, free of classroom pressures. They can be objective about the child's progress, for they are not teaching the child. They can follow each pupil continuously, from first to last contacts with the school. They can have records and resources readily available, and time to use them, as the teacher cannot.

We should not jump to the conclusion that such skilled specialists are necessarily extra personnel, added to the existing structure. As with the master teacher, they make possible an efficient *division* of labor. As we shall see, there is reason to believe that this separating out of skills and functions, in the proper structure, can cost less rather than more, even as it helps make the teacher's job a realistic assignment rather than a perpetual frustration, and even while it gives each child a far better chance of reasonable fulfillment in his school career.

* . . . Many schools may not have any clear-cut policy concerning the use of standardized test scores. Furthermore, it is extremely difficult for a principal to know to what extent general policies with respect to tests, if they exist, are carried out by guidance counselors, teachers, and other school personnel.*

David A. Goslin in *Teachers and Testing*

9

THE PROBLEM OF TESTING

In the preceding chapter no reference has been made to standardized testing. The omission is deliberate: for if the teacher's ability to know the child and his capacities is highly dependent on testing, we do not want to confuse the issue by attributing it to classroom observation. That testing is useful as an aid to evaluation of student progress can hardly be doubted, but testing can just as easily "backfire" if misused or either over- or under-valued.

Standardized tests have proliferated until the number used annually in our public schools far exceeds 100 million. Hundreds of different tests are available, and new ones are created and marketed frequently. The impression given is that every child must be taking tests during a good share of his school time. But sober arithmetic and study of test use show that, while most students do take tests, the amount of testing given in even better schools to each child over the course of his school career is much on the skimpy side. Nevertheless standardized testing ranks as one of the schools' important activities.

The two most commonly used types are often spoken of as

aptitude and *achievement* tests. To the public the former is simply an "intelligence" test, and it would appear that many think of it as *the* intelligence test, not being aware that dozens of different aptitude tests compete for use. In the same way they think of the result as being *the* IQ or Mental Age. It is also common, even among educators, to think of the IQ type of test as looking to the future, indicating what the child can accomplish, while the achievement batteries show what the child *has* accomplished, and hence look backward. The experts take an increasingly dim view of this neat distinction. As Dr. Arthur E. Traxler, of the Educational Records Bureau, has noted:

> There is no clear-cut distinction between scholastic-aptitude tests and achievement tests. Scores on all these tests represent different combinations of aptitude and achievement, or of intelligence and environmental influences. Some measurement specialists insist that attempts to differentiate scholastic aptitude from achievement are futile.

One need only dip one's toe in the muddy waters of testing to find out that Dr. Traxler's views are representative. The popularity of tests dates from the great "discovery" of psychology in the 1920's, when no comedian could subsist without a notebook full of jokes about IQs. The intelligence test seemed to offer a golden opportunity to bring new order and simplicity into complex human affairs, and testing proliferated at a frantic pace. But in recent years the fine glow has faded, giving place to the sad realization that to undiminished human complexity has now been added the complexities of testing. It is standard practice today for psychologists to preface almost any remark about testing with cautions about their limitations and technical trickiness. Nevertheless, a good part of the public, and too many teachers, continue to regard testing as a counterpart to the public scale which for a penny instantly gives both weight and fortune.

We can glimpse the nature of some of the difficulties if we think first of a test to measure the relative "intelligence" of a mouse and a chicken. We construct a maze for each that we judge equally difficult to escape from, and provide food as incentive. The mouse, let us say, learns his way out after a few trials, but the chicken requires many more, and even then hardly convinces us that she knows which way to turn. The conclusion seems simple that the mouse is much more intelligent than the chicken.

But scientifically viewed, there are many questions to be asked. We remember that mice are used to small, tortuous passages much more difficult than our maze, while our chicken is used to an open barnyard. Mice are used to going to where food may be. Our chick is more used to pecking at the ground wherever she may be. Ordinarily this serves our chicken quite well; to expect her abruptly to change her most fixed habits for our momentary convenience in measuring her brainpower is to ask a good deal. Nor can we even be sure that the food motivates both subjects equally. It is even possible that one or the other has in mind not food but sex, a much more compelling urge. And there are a dozen other "bugs" one might find in the test. In the end, as good scientists, we had better simply report that, under the conditions of this specific test, the mouse got out faster. The less concluded about such broad and obscure abstractions as intelligence, the better.

Thus the testing experts are fond of pointing out that an intelligence test measures, to a certain degree of reliability, whatever it is that that particular test measures — and not necessarily intelligence in the abstract.

To test a roomful of boys and girls and then assume that their scores reflect their "true" ability is far from valid. As N. M. Downie points out in *Fundamentals of Measurement* (1967): "We have no intelligence test today that measures innate ability. The probability is high that we shall never have such a test." In the sense that these tests largely measure what a child has learned, there is an assumption, Professor Downie suggests, that each child tested has had an equal opportunity to learn. Such an assumption is obviously not tenable when we consider the variety of children's backgrounds.

This consideration must rank as major; and to it we should

add another: the attitude of the child toward tests in general. Middle-class children are more likely to come from homes where stress (perhaps too much stress) is placed on achievement. "Do well and get ahead" expresses normal aims. In less favored homes a quite different "push" may exist, particularly among minorities, who may with good reason resent both the school and this kind of slanted test. Experience in such homes may be that efforts to get ahead on white-majority terms bring frustration rather than reward. The parent may see education as a means to better living and higher status, yet still view the school as a racecourse on which his children are unfairly handicapped from the outset. To the child in school, any test appears just one more test—and why try hard on a test when the results are almost always unhappy?

Still another factor contributing to false scores on a test is that *anxiety* may be aroused in those who take it. Dr. Seymour B. Sarason, a Yale professor of psychology, observes:

> To the clinical psychologist, who usually operates in the face-to-face, diagnostic testing situation, it is obvious that individuals vary tremendously not only in their reactions to the process of testing but also in the ways in which their reactions affect performance.

A six-year study at Yale, he reports, suggests strongly that test anxiety is not infrequent, and the higher the anxiety the more adversely the score is likely to be affected. Every teacher is familiar with this anxiety factor in academic tests.

Those who administer many tests know that these are only two of the factors that may affect results. There are many more. What of the child who arrives at school the day of the test upset by a family quarrel, or in ill health, or simply tired? What of the slow reader, who on the many tests that involve reading is heavily handicapped and whose anxiety may be increased because he does not trust his reading ability? What of the child with a background different from "standard" children, or with a language difficulty? Or the child who is new in class, or one who fails to understand the instructions clearly? We must bear in mind that even in schools that use more than the average amount of standardized testing, a particular type of aptitude test may be given only once every three or more years. For example, tests intended to show IQ may be given in the second, fourth, and seventh grades, a fairly common pattern. Despite all the hazards we have so far listed, the score is set down in the record, there to stay unmodified for years. A misleading score in the second grade will stand unquestioned until the fourth grade score can be compared. An inaccurate fourth grade score may stand until the seventh grade score casts doubt on it, unless a special interim test is given for some pressing reason.

While normally the factors so far mentioned will result in a lower score, there are others that bring in an error on the high side. A moderately bright student who has opportunity to practice test-taking, or who is coached, may raise his score quite considerably. But more commonly failure to give the tests properly is the trouble. For example, Dr. Herman J. Peters, professor of education at Ohio State University, found that at least a third of almost two hundred teachers in a workshop he conducted indicated that in giving a standardized test they either guessed at the time allowed or changed the prescribed period! Allowing more than the standard amount of time, of course, would tend to elevate scores. Many experts agree that the failure of teachers to fully understand the directions, or to see the necessity of being meticulous in following them out, or to explain them adequately to the class, are prime sources of error. Here again we must note that often the test is given within the dread privacy of the classroom where no one can or does check on or supervise the teacher. The result goes into the child's record and has full effect regardless of whether the test was skillfully and correctly given or administered with the scantiest regard to standard requirements. Not all teachers are cooperative in giving tests. Particularly those who don't put much faith in testing, or resent the time taken for it, or who prefer some alternative test to the one being used, or who are exceptionally pressured at the time, are likely to brush aside "fine points" or what seem to them arbitrary instructions. But all that gets entered is a number. It tells no tales. And sad to say, even the number may be entered incorrectly, or the scores of two children may be switched. Since calculation and clerical work are involved in scoring most tests, the room for pure mechanical error or miscalculation is considerable. Rarely is real provision made for double-checking, although it is often recommended.

We begin to see, then, some of the severe limitations on interpreting tests as evidence of potential ability. They do *not* measure general "intelligence" as is popularly thought, but at best only certain sharply limited areas covered by the particular test given. Even these measurements are in all cases affected by variations in motivation and anxiety. Add all the other possible errors, and we are forced to conclude that a single test is far from being a reliable indication of what a child can do. (Let us remember that the *average* accuracy of these tests is for this purpose of little value, for the results are to be used in evaluating and guiding individual children, not classes.)

If we think of these tests less as measuring innate ability but more as predicting probable achievement in school, they become rather more accurate. For motivation and anxiety tend to continue unchanged unless there are forces that bring about change. Motivation that produces low aptitude scores will likely also bring low scores on quizzes and examinations. High anxiety will work the same way. A reading handicap will be an obstacle in taking *all* tests, in most schools. If the school or some outside circumstance lessens anxiety, increases motivation, or improves reading ability, we may expect aptitude test scores to rise. Roughly, the rise may reflect the amount of improvement. Unfortunately even educators who know better fall into the habit of acting as though they believed such tests as we have been discussing do measure intelligence, and that intelligence in an individual is a fixed quality. Little effort may be made then to raise aptitude scores by improving motivation or removing handicaps. On the contrary, a rising score is often taken as puzzling, or proof of error in testing! *The notion that it should be the function of the school to strive to raise the IQ of many children with motivational, emotional, or other handicaps is only now beginning to percolate in our school system.*

Even after the IQ or MA is entered in the records, it meets

a new hazard: the great range of teacher attitudes toward test scores. There are timid, conformist teachers not much given to questioning anything, and who therefore feel that Betty with a score of 114 is definitely brighter than Marie with a score of 109. There are those who are sour on a good many "modern" ideas, including standardized testing, and who refuse even to read the results, at least until some months have passed and they have formed their own opinions — quite a common attitude. There are multitudes who feel that their own mystic ability to "know" their children (which we have just examined in some detail) entitles them to accept test results when they fit in with their personal opinion of a child and ignore them when they don't! It is not at all unknown for a teacher, observing that Kevin with an IQ of 135 is doing just fair work in composition, to solve the discrepancy simply by raising the grade she writes in red at the top of his paper. Conversely, if George has an IQ of 90 in her records and shows exceptional progress in arithmetic, the teacher may conclude that he is somehow getting "improper" help, rather than that he may have special talent in this area and the aptitude is now coming to light. Such reactions must be looked for even in diligent teachers. By considerable evidence, many teachers tend to let their recorded testing and psychological information about their children lie undisturbed in file folders. A large-scale study supported by the Russell Sage and Carnegie Foundations, reported on in 1967 in *Teachers and Testing* by David A. Goslin, found a "surprisingly large percentage" of teachers had never used intelligence test data, to which they had access, in advising students about their school work. Of public secondary school teachers, only 11 percent reported frequent use. Dr. Goslin notes that it is "difficult to imagine" how a teacher could effectively counsel a student without these indications of abilities.

Since we can hardly expect teachers to seek out additional problems for themselves, or glory in proof that their vaunted ability to judge children is suspect, it cannot be too startling to find that when test results prove inconvenient they are often simply swept under the rug. This appears especially likely to happen with abler children. The authors of *Educating Gifted*

Children, Robert F. DeHaan and Robert J. Havighurst, quote a
fifth-grade teacher: "Mike here has an IQ of 132 on this test.
He is an average boy, all right, but he is not *that* bright. He
keeps pushing himself forward too much."

Much has been learned about the "gifted" child in the last
ten years. Almost all of it complicates rather than simplifies
the problems of fitting him into the conventional classroom.
Giftedness may not be an overall matter, but limited to one or
a few of many attributes; nor, in any case, may it show up in
that oppressive and essential hostile environment. The same
authors state: "Teachers have largely underestimated how much
gifted children can learn and how well they can perform." And
they explain: "Often a report of an IQ means little to teachers
because they do not see the kinds of behavior that have gone on
in the testing situation to produce that IQ."

The bright underachiever, belatedly the object of much
attention, further adds to the complexities. Recent studies tend
to agree that personality problems extending beyond the school
are likely to be involved. Underachievement can well be taken
as a warning symptom calling for investigation. But though
family or other non-school problems may be at the root, clearly
the school is deeply involved and implicated, the more so because it usually allows the condition to grow worse year by year,
punishing in various ways rather than responding to the child's
needs. The underachiever's woes are likely to peak in the secondary school years, when the usual adolescent self-doubts
are added to those he already has of his abilities and worth —
just at a period when pressures on him intensify to get into a desired college or a preferred occupation and to assume more
adult responsibilities. This is the time when the shook-up youth
(the underachiever problem is heavily male) may turn to a
variety of asocial and worse escapades: minor violations of the
law or actual crimes; use of drugs; wild driving; gambling;
violent behavior; sexual adventures; vandalism; arson, especially within the school. Shockingly often, the end is suicide —
there is almost a pattern of high school boys taking their lives,
with a display of failing grades set out to surround their body.
By no means every underachiever, of course, gets into serious
troubles; but from waste of talent to personal tragedy, the in-

cidence is high and the toll great. The classroom school's way and use of testing appear to aggravate the problems rather than help reduce them.

Most teachers and authorities agree that the "gifted" child often does not behave in the classroom in a way that matches his noble IQ on the record card (usually it will be high, but not always), nor evidence special talents that may ultimately come to light. Often bored, withdrawn, hostile or isolated, the child may dawdle, daydream, gold-brick, draw incessantly, make a general nuisance of himself, or give a very good imitation of a really stupid child — even a "non-reader." Because his differences tend to set him apart from children his own age, he may quite deliberately sabotage his achievement in order to fit better into his nominal peer-group. He may desperately want *not* to be different, especially if it means being isolated and made the butt of incessant verbal thrusts. Or, like Mike, he may be hungry for recognition of his abilities, and push himself forward to seek attention, by misbehavior if necessary. A teacher would have to be a saint or a machine not to find herself preferring and more highly regarding the bright, cooperative child who eagerly raises his hand while his neighboring genius glooms out the window. Certainly it can be said, rather hopefully, that the failure of our schools to recognize and fully nurture the rarer talents of the gifted child, particularly among black or other minority children, is widely looked on today as one of the most serious and acute problems in education.

Again in fairness to teachers, we must realize that when we are talking about children with intellectual ability in the top range *rarity* becomes a complicating factor. If a child's IQ makes him one in a hundred, a teacher in an average school may expect his equal to crop up only once in three or four years. A child at the one in a thousand level may never be encountered by the teacher, or only once or twice in a lifetime! It is hardly surprising that identification of such pupils is so often poor. It *is* surprising that teachers are so inclined to depend on experience in dealing with them when they are so unlikely to have had experience.

The achievement test, intended primarily to discover where each child stands at the moment, is subject to all the sources of error we have mentioned with reference to intelligence tests. Such tests also may be used as rough checks on the progress of the class as well. They often consist of "batteries," designed to measure skills or comprehension in several subjects or areas, the scores being shown separately for each, since children seldom achieve uniformly in all. If they are used for class evaluation, a strong temptation may also be put on the teacher to coach and prepare her charges for a good showing. Simply out of pride in her group, she may want them to do well. And she may well feel that a good class score cannot help but reflect on her own ability, while a poor showing might raise questions. To quote Professor Downie further: "In the long run, the type of evaluating device used determines, to a great extent, the type of learning activity in which students will engage in the classroom." If then achievement tests are thought of as another examination on which students should do well, some of the teaching is likely to be designed specifically for "exam-answering." If the teacher is familiar with the test or type of test to be given, such coaching is quite simple. More often than not she will know when the test is to be given and what test it will be, since many teachers either select the tests or participate in decisions. Such coaching, of course, can destroy the standardized aspect of the battery, which should measure what has been learned in the subjects tested, not ability to cram for a certain type of examination. But as Ruth A. Martinson and Harry Smallenburg observe in *Guidance in Elementary Schools:* "Rare is the teacher who can approach with complete objectivity the spring testing of a group that she has taught all year!"

If this mournful review of the state of testing appears to be an attack on it, such is certainly not my intent. To point out that a ferryboat is not an ocean liner is not to attack the ferryboat. Sending it out to sea is more likely to founder it. Most of the difficulties and shortcomings that put testing under a growing cloud today come not from overuse of it, but from doing far too little, and doing even that under less than adequate conditions and controls. I submit that these should be the ground rules:

1. *Testing should be done not by teachers but by specialists.* Good testing calls for expert knowledge and techniques, all the way

from selecting the test to be administered from the hundreds available, through giving it, scoring it, and interpreting the results. The specialists should actually do the testing, or at least closely supervise it if the situation demands that compromise. The giving of tests should not be forced into the classroom: there is much agreement that the typical class is often awkward for administering standardized tests. Particularly for younger children a smaller grouping is desirable; and in many situations individual testing is indicated. And there is always an overriding reason why the specialist should test: his ability to be far more objective than a teacher can be about her pupils.

It is hard to see why teachers should be encouraged to seek in-service training in testing if specialists can be obtained. The ordinary teacher administers few tests. There is little reason why the tricky business of choosing tests should fall upon teachers, or why they should even have opinions on so technical a matter. It is even harder to see why the teacher should get involved in scoring, which involves clerical accuracy and in some phases considerable expertness in statistical mathematics. On the whole, the technical side of testing relates less to everyday teaching than almost any other study teachers commonly pursue in service. The likelihood that the teacher will progress far enough in testing for her own knowledge to be reliable is small. Testing is a job for experienced experts, not willing amateurs, if it is to do good and not harm.

2. *The results of every test should be reviewed in detail with the teacher, for each child, and where lack of proper progress is seen, with the principal or other officer.* As we have seen, when the teacher gives the tests or is given the results without conference, there can be the widest range in the use made of the testing effort: from ignoring the results to taking them far too literally. Does it not seem clear that teacher and specialist should get together in a quiet room and review each score? For each child, each result should be considered in the light of all the school knows about the child, from the record, from the teacher's observation, and from all other sources. If more than one teacher taught the child, all who have had a share should be in the conference. The value of the exchange of views between specialist and teacher seems obvious: do the results of the test jibe with the

work the child is doing? Is there reason to question the test results? How strong is the child's motivation? Could it be improved? Have special aptitudes been revealed, or weak spots? Should further check of certain findings be made in the near future?

Such conferences should not be left to chance. They should be mandatory, and the specialist should be held accountable for a report on each child. Both he and the teacher should file a brief evaluation of their findings, independently, with the principal. Where there is disagreement, or where the child's progress raises questions, the principal or other officer can then carry the matter further. In some cases further testing will clearly be needed. Once the principle is established that an evaluation *must* be filed for each child, testing becomes a far more accurate and reliable tool. The teacher may still quarrel with the findings, but she cannot simply ignore them or brush them aside. When specialist and teacher must confer, each becomes a check on the other. No longer is the child's welfare left to individual caprice. influenced by uncorrected error, or forgotten under pressure of work.

3. *The school should have basic information about the child as early as possible in his school career.. Testing therefore should be thorough during the first two years, and especially at the time of entrance.* To have to set down such a suggestion in black and white may seem downright silly, for what could seem more inescapable? But as we have seen again and again, our school system is strong on historical accidents and woefully weak on rational procedures. In a vast number of schools that use testing, either none or almost none is done until the second grade! Even then the amount done is too skimpy to be at all reliable. While it is rather more difficult to give tests to children of kindergarten age, especially in large groups, meaningful measurements of even younger children can be made. In *The Psychology of Early Childhood,* Catherine Landreth notes:

> In addition to revealing the complex of factors involved in effective functioning, intelligence tests have practical usefulness in indicating how a child is functioning, relative to other children of his age, on a sample of performances. Be-

cause these performances are, from four years upward, related to success in school, they are some indication of the
kind of school experience from which a child can profit.

Testing younger children demands the services of a specialist
even more than later testing, and this becomes one reason why
aptitude measurement is so commonly deferred. On the other
hand, if competent staff is available and there is a desire to do
the job, there is no time when an effort to gather facts about
the child is more resultful than when he first enters school.
This is true not only of testing but of every source of information. The child's attitudes, interests, and abilities are highly
observable—he has not yet learned what is expected, approved,
or rewarded! The speed and extent of his adjustment to the
school situation can also be revealing in itself. He is less con-
scious of being observed or tested, and the relative freedom of
activity in kindergarten or first grade allows a greater range of
behavior to be noted. Peer pressures have not yet begun to
compel certain kinds of comformity. Further, information from
the parents is most easily obtainable at this time, and observation of the home most natural and readily achieved. That
most schools make scanty use of this golden opportunity is a
crime of omission hard to forgive. Months and years pass before the school learns essential facts about the child that it
could know at the outset. Attitudes toward the school form, and
problems begin, to grow steadily week by week, because of this
senseless, stupid, purposeless delay in getting the information
essential to launching the child on his proper educational path-
way.

It seems reasonable to assume that were our schools to
learn as much as possible about each child as soon as possible,
to continue testing expertly and reliably, and to systematically
weigh and use the findings of each test for each child, standardized testing would rapidly be transformed from a rickety structure that frequently brings harm rather than good, to one highly
helpful and distinctly more dependable. It is hard to escape
the conclusion that a good deal of the money spent on testing
now is largely wasted—much as it is wasteful and treacherous
to build a bridge part way across a stream.

“No scheme of school or curriculum organization washes away human variability or the manifold problems of dealing with it instructionally. This being so, much organizational effort clearly is misplaced. Organization cannot eliminate individuality—that is impossible and undesirable. But it can illuminate individuality so that human ingenuity will be more likely to come to terms with it.”

From *Schools for the Sixties,* a report of the Project on Instruction of the National Education Association.

10

THE TEACHER'S
MANY CHILDREN

Every parent of two or more children knows that children differ. But, in my experience, the average parent has little concept of the staggering problems individual differences present to every teacher. Almost always, the new teacher's great worry is about her ability to control a classroom. Once over that hurdle she begins an endless struggle with a new and unsolvable one — how to deal, single-handedly and in one room, with 30 or so wildly varying individuals whom she is supposed to teach, guide, and influence.

The situation is described vividly in *The Nongraded Elementary School,* a "landmark" book in education, by John I. Goodlad and Robert H. Anderson:

> The realities of child development defy the rigorous ordering of children's abilities and attainments into conventional graded structure. For example, in the average first grade there is a spread of four years in pupil readiness to learn as suggested by mental age data. As the pupils progress through the grades, the span in readiness widens. Furthermore, a single child does not progress all of a piece: he tends

to spurt ahead more rapidly in some areas than in others. Consequently, a difference of one grade between his reading attainment and his arithmetic attainment at the end of the second grade classification may be extended to a three- or four-grade difference by the end of his fifth year in school. The presence of a graded structure may disguise or distort such realities but it cannot remove them. In brief . . . a fifth-grade teacher . . . is not a teacher of fifth-grade children. At a given time, he teaches third, fourth, fifth, sixth, seventh, eighth and even ninth grades, as far as learner realities are concerned, even though all the pupils in his room may be labeled "fifth grade."

The layman may well ponder the picture presented—a teacher at the front of a classroom, 30 children before him varying from third to ninth grade in academic abilities. The teacher must conduct the class, day in and day out, so as to move them all along, maintaining interest and enthusiasm over a nine-month stretch!

But we are only beginning to see how ridiculous a problem the class-and-grade system poses for the teacher. In the grade classroom the elementary teacher normally handles all the "subjects"—reading, composition, arithmetic, science, social studies, and so forth. To quote from *Elementary School Organization,* published in 1961:

Few children are at grade level in all subjects. In fact, mid-year achievement test scores reveal that only three or four youngsters in an elementary school class of 30 are at grade level in all subjects, even when one defines grade level to allow a spread of one full year.

The problem of differences has long been obvious: efforts to solve it to some degree go back to the last century, long before the days of testing. Here again, the administrative convenience of the classroom system has survived over educational considerations, as one attempt after another was made to keep the class yet somehow reduce the spread teachers had to cope with.

One of the solutions familiar to parents is "homogeneous grouping," and many parents are apt to assume that the school somehow puts their children into a class with very similar peers. The impression is an illusion—sometimes rudely shattered when the child brings home a classmate who is not a neighbor. Homogeneous grouping is obviously difficult in smaller schools, and even in larger ones raises about as many problems as it alleviates. In any case it reduces variability by less than 20 percent.

To group children for likeness, it is essential to choose factors to group by. If "intelligence" is chosen, "achievement" scores are likely to scatter widely, for correlation between the two is often far from high. If "reading ability" is used, "mathematics ability" may scatter. If any of these are used, physical and emotional maturity will scatter. The hard fact is that children differ so diffusely that grouping for homogeneity cannot have more than a modest effect—and then mostly by luck, or exceptional guidance skill. Let us remember, however, that few elementary schools have any trained guidance officer. If the function is performed, it is very likely to be as one of many duties of the principal, and only as a special case will a child receive more than momentary attention. Just as children take "pot luck" with teachers who range from fabulous to terrible, they usually fall in a group determined to a great extent by a variety of variables, hunches, guesses, and luck.

We have been looking at the class mainly from the viewpoint of the hapless teacher who must somehow handle this ill-assorted lot. If we go deeper into the mysteries of personality, we quickly see that the problem is far worse. We must remember that the *scores* made by children on various kinds of psychological or achievement tests are not the same thing as the children themselves. The children are flesh and blood human beings. They have no necessity to be alike or even to be measurable. It is only the school that is trying so desperately to translate them from humans to numbers, so it can maintain a classroom system that is essentially non-human in concept.

Evidence is now overwhelming that each child is a law unto himself. His rate of physical growth, of social growth, of development of a variety of skills, will differ from the "norm" about as often as it comes near it. The slow child is by no means equally slow in all areas, nor the bright one equally advanced.

Further, as every observant parent knows, children do not grow, in any respect, on a smooth curve. On the contrary, they will shoot ahead; hold a "plateau"; perhaps retrogress briefly; show slow, steady advances for a period, then again a jump. The patterns are endlessly variable. Passionate interests arise and may suddenly cease. The growth of the child, infinitely complicated in itself, is made far more so by changes in his situation and chance interactions with his environment. The home, of course, plays the largest role: marital strain, the arrival of a younger child, serious illness, financial set-backs, moving — such factors in the family history can make the difference between high success or sorry failure for the child in school. But even "accidental" factors may have profound effects: the arrival or removal of a neighborhood playmate; a scare or beating by a bully; an athletic triumph; happening upon a certain book; an incident that brings praise or blame from the principal; an experience with death; even a conversation overheard and perhaps misinterpreted. All of these can affect how the child develops and his ability to learn. Nor can we fail to note that the school itself is another area of influence, second only to the home, which affects the child in innumerable ways, both by plan and by chance, both for good and for bad.

The child, in a word, does not come to school as a clay blank which the school can unobstructedly mold to its desires. To quote *The Role of the Teacher in Guidance,* by Edgar Johnston, Mildred Peters, and William Evraiff:

> Even the simplest learning of subject matter or skills is difficult for the unhappy child, the one whose past experience has given him no sense of achievement, the child disturbed by emotional conflict, the one who sees no purpose in the tasks he is asked to perform. The successful teacher can never forget that "the whole child" comes to school or that the group of pupils with which he deals includes an infinite variety of different patterns of home background, neighborhood environment, emotional and intellectual

and physical characteristics. His goal — effective learning —
is dependent on constant awareness of these differences,
and adaptation of the learning situation to them.

It is the fashion in some quarters to pooh-pooh this whole
approach, on the grounds that it is not the function of the
school to be a psychiatric center, nor a personality-development
"success" school, but to give the child an education. The confusion of many laymen (and some educators who should know better — especially those at college level) is no doubt honest. And
to be sure, much nonsense and verbiage has been attached to
the rather silly term "the whole child" by sentimental and fuzzy-
minded educators who confuse the use of jargon with thinking.
The essential point is simple, I believe: *the school is concerned
with the child's whole welfare and development precisely and unavoid-
ably to the extent that effective learning and teaching is involved.* The
school does not have the option of ignoring the fever that makes
Hugh's head swim, the myopia that prevents Claire from seeing
the work on the blackboard. It cannot say sternly, "Ignore your
fever, ignore your nearsightedness — do your work!" Nor can
it say to Albert, "Ignore the problem of your mother's attitude
that shows she expects you to fail," nor to Susan, "Ignore the
fact that every time you attempt to read aloud you are exposed
to public embarrassment that makes you want to sink through
the floor." If the school wants to do its prime job of teaching,
it *must* recognize and to some extent at least deal with obstruc-
tions to learning.

Today our knowledge in this area is so great, supported
by so many tens of thousands of case studies, that it would be
as sensible to debate the possibility of atomic energy or the validity of the germ causation of diseases as it is to argue this
question. We can say flatly that to attempt to teach without
taking into account and dealing with the kind of factors we have
been discussing is to throw time, money and effort down the
drain in the most wasteful fashion. The school cannot "just
teach," because the child cannot separate "just learning" from
everything else that is happening to him. Adults are no different. The executive who is worried about his wife's illness finds

it difficult to concentrate on his work. The machinist who bitterly resents his foreman may find his spoilage rate climbing or end in the accident ward. If you knew an airline pilot had just been rejected by a club he wanted to join, would you climb as happily into his plane? The adult's working efficiency on the job is much the same as the child's working efficiency in school. Neither can be isolated from the rest of his living.

A school cannot adopt a "just teach" attitude, nor can it try to be "neutral" towards these other factors. For if the school does not recognize and deal wisely and sympathetically with these factors, it may easily compound them — and let us remember that many such problems begin in or directly involve the school. Such extreme difficulties as stuttering or outright delinquency may be school-caused. And even if the school does not attempt to evade the burden of these factors, but the teachers are insensitive or unskillful in dealing with them, the damage to the child can be violent and lasting.

From an administrative point of view, it is certainly inconsiderate of children to be so different, to develop so many various ways, and to bring such an assortment of concomitant considerations with them when they come to learn. But the school is in the guidance business whether it wants to be or not. Guidance, we see, must be thought of basically *as the effort on the part of the school to deal with each child not as a fictional average or norm, but realistically as an individual,* whose growth patterns, attitudes, motivations, and relationships must be meshed with the school's program. Admittedly this is staggeringly complicated. But there is no choice. It would also be much simpler, say, for the Army to issue the same size uniform to all recruits; but it has to choose between this kind of fictional "efficiency" and the hard, irritating fact that the men *aren't* the same size. Once we recognize that the only meaningful measure of efficiency in this instance is the accuracy with which the uniforms fit each individual, we can begin to make the complexity manageable by finding better ways to get better fits, with less effort and error. To carry the analogy a bit further, we can see that it is futile to attempt a distinction between "issuing the uniforms" and "fitting the men." It is equally difficult, I believe, to make any clear separation between the guidance need and the educative function. As we have here defined guidance, measurement of its success can only be in terms of educative success. We can readily note *who* is charged with either function, but the functions themselves are not separable in the sense that either can exist alone. *Guidance is not optional, not a fancy "extra": it is an aspect of the fundamental assignment of today's school.*

The full complexity of dealing with children on this realistic, individual basis is set forth in a monumental work published in 1957, *The Child in the Educative Process,* by Daniel A. Prescott, long director of the University of Maryland Institute for Child Study. Dr. Prescott's findings are backed by more than 15,000 studies of individual children, over at least a sixteen year period. One might expect that so large a study might have led to a grouping or classification of children according to repeatedly recurring patterns, but such is not the case. Rather, he stresses that each child study: ". . . has turned out to be about a unique personality following his own idiomatic pattern of growth, learning, development and adjustment." The suggestion is strong that we should, once and for all, free ourselves of the urge to force children into "alike" groups, when there are now mountains of evidence that such groups are illusory, unless we want to ignore all factors but one at any given time, and even then we have trouble. It is not too much, I submit, to define the modern educator as one who has stopped trying to deal with children in defiance of their differences, and whose constant effort is to de-group them when custom persists in trying to find alikeness where it does not exist.

Referring to the work of H. H. Anderson and his associates, Dr. Prescott emphasizes the staggering task that the classroom teacher has in attempting to deal with students as present-day knowledge of them requires. Studies of the actual number of interactions between teacher and individual student show results that sound incredible, yet are thoroughly researched. In the course of an hour, these contacts ran as high as 300, and at times almost 400 per hour! A great many of these obviously involve decisions: to praise or criticize, to permit or forbid, to take up or pass over, and so on without limit in variety. And many of these decisions can have significance to the child involved. What parent has not seen a child come home aglow because of a favorable word, or in despair because a special effort went unnoticed or unappreciated? It is hardly surprising that: "Many teachers, after a year or two in our child-study program, have felt overwhelmed by the immensity and significance of the professional tasks and opportunities that they discover are theirs." Indeed, if there is one book that shows rather than tells more than any other how vastly the concept of "good teaching" has changed and grown since half a century ago, it may well be *The Child in the Educative Process.*

The facts I have set forth are in very little dispute among educators, and they have long been recognized. The lay reader may wonder: why has the class-and-grade system so long been tolerated, if grading is so unworkable? Why do teachers tolerate so impossible an assignment without rebelling?

The questions are good ones, and the fact they have recently been asked in louder and louder tones is helping to bring about the Revolution. But we must realize that children combine sensitivity with a sometimes amazing toughness. The school, while a major and long-continued influence, is only one of many. What happens to a child in his first three years of life usually affects his personality more than all his schooling put together. Even while in school, he relates to playmates after school and on weekends, and to his family. He has his private world of activity, sometimes kept a close secret. And in our heavily organized world, he likely has many regular or scheduled activities, that range from dancing school to gang membership, from candy store to summer camp.

Overall, most children like school. Even for those to whom many aspects of attendance are a form of slow torture, there are offsetting attractions. The school provides the peer social contacts and variety of activities many children want, and at least some attention by adults who are *not* their parents. Except in some large city situations, the junior high and even more, the high school are the focus of social relations. In thinking of children of all ages, we should remember that not all homes are good homes, and not all good homes happy homes. The whole process of growing up is one of finding more and more sustenance *outside* the home. School is a center, even for the ghetto child with good reason to hate it, for finding some of the things he seeks and hungers for.

The healthy child has a great ability to select. He suffers what he must, and gathers what he needs wherever he can find it. He learns to "get along" in school, and a useful and important lesson it is. One of his most valuable discoveries is the usefulness of dissembling: year by year he becomes more expert in concealing his thoughts and feelings. Girls especially learn to conform and be docile in school, and so get better grades — though they may weep at home. The slower students pretend their failures do not hurt. The ones who can easily outrun the class learn to loaf, follow their true interests on their own, or turn to more or less humorous harassment of teachers to gain more acceptance by their classmates.

We must bear in mind that the great majority of the people involved — students, parents, teachers, and administrators — suffer the system without ever giving the slightest thought to possible alternatives. The classroom system *is*. They have no knowledge of any choice. On finding out that there are alternatives, the first reaction is often astonishment and disbelief. Thus those in the grasp of the classroom, like millions of others around the globe who have never known anything but misery (by our fat standards), come to terms with the inevitable and somehow survive. Revolt comes only when the "inevitable" is suddenly seen not as ordained but as a bad choice.

Significantly, children who have experienced an alternative arrangement, even if only a partial departure from the classroom system, typically prefer the newer choice overwhelmingly. The same is not always true of teachers, who must change their habits and procedures, learn new ways, and enter new interpersonal relationships. Even so, after the initial shock has passed, a majority of teachers also prefer the new, and their preference is apt to grow rapidly with experience and as they become secure in the new situation.

Rare is the parent whose child does not experience major difficulties in the course of a school career, in the area we are discussing. The beginning of each term brings a period of anxiety: has the child got a good break in teachers? If the problem becomes acute, there may follow an effort to effect a change. But principals resist this solution for one all too obvious reason, among others—unless opposed, the good teachers would end up with staggering loads and the poor and disliked teachers with empty classrooms. Every classroom system school operates on an unstated but firm principle: *each student must suffer a fair share of the school's weak teachers,* much as he must eat spinach to get his dessert.

When we speak of "good" teachers, we are of course speaking relatively. As we have seen, the elementary classroom teacher's job is beyond doing. In the departmentalized high schools, where students have a different teacher for each subject, the job is somewhat simplified, but only to a degree. Variations among children grow wider and more distinct as their years increase. Later all the magnificent and zesty problems of adolescence are added. A high school teacher may have in one class, to illustrate:

—A student who knows more about his subject than he does and who has superior intelligence.
—A student who reads only at fifth grade level.
—A student in violent rebellion against authority in all forms.
—A girl student who has a violent "crush" on him.
—A student far bigger than he who wants to be working and resents being kept in school by the law.

The list is fragmentary, but enough, perhaps, to give the idea. No classroom job is easy.

The teacher survives the impossibly demanding assignment either by not caring, or fortunately more often by scaling down effort to a practicable level. "I can do only so much," the teacher says, in effect. "If you were there, in my place, you would see why." Not all teachers survive, of course. Some are shattered and leave for other occupations. Some find nowhere else to go, and stay on. It is an exceptional faculty that does not boast one or more "nervous" members. And among teachers with many years of service it is not at all uncommon to find those who will admit they are simply serving time until they can retire on pension.

That teachers do as well as they do is perhaps remarkable. To use what skills she has, a teacher plainly needs far more time to deal with students individually or in small groups, time to maintain and study records, and time to think. And most of the skills she needs she cannot obtain in advance, any more than a woman can become a skillful mother before she has children. But once trapped in the classroom, the opportunity to gain skills and adapt them to her needs becomes minimal. She can attend a college at night, if she has the stamina and opportunity. The high school teacher can deepen and widen his knowledge of his specialty, if he has energy left. But what the teacher in each case needs most is the chance to see what the expert does in the same situation she must face, and this is almost totally denied her.

At best, the prowess of the teacher is apt to be exaggerated. Successes tend to be marked, failure or inaction is attributed to impossible pressures. Basically, nobody keeps score. But the inability of the teacher to respond to the individual differences, interests, and problems of her students is frustrating even if she is outstandingly able. The less able teacher may be far less sensitive to the situation, and care less about the students besides.

The damage to the children can be enormous, even while they survive. Interests are killed, talents are squashed, originality made a misdemeanor. Reading problems grow worse under the stress of embarrassment. Abler students are literally taught to loaf, near-geniuses to hide their ability. The less able and disadvantaged children are discouraged, persuaded they are stupid, led to hate the whole idea of education. (Several studies have shown that when these latter are better handled in a suitable program, even their IQ's move up!) The younger the child, the greater the damage is apt to be. But it is precisely the young child who is kept in the self-contained, single-teacher classroom; and much of the time the less able and experienced teacher is assigned to the lowest, most impressionable grades.

It seems clear that the need for basic guidance, in terms of leading the child into the right path of development, and encouraging natural growth, is far greater in the elementary school. But this is precisely where trained guidance experts are rarest. The delicate, enormously intricate task is left in the hands of the far overburdened classroom teacher. The guidance people are found chiefly at the other end—in the high school, where the guidance function is relatively trivial in impact on the child. *The damage has long since been done.*

What is the solution? It seems hardly necessary to say that the classroom is the villain, and that the classroom must give way to a far more flexible organization if each child is ever to get genuinely personal attention, a true opportunity to develop as a unique individual, not a 30-at-a-time compromise. Each child's program must be adapted to his ability, his needs, his talents, and interests. *Each child must, some of the time, get the undivided, undistracted attention of one or more teachers. Each child's progress must be continuously followed and evaluated.* All this is impossible in the classroom situation, but attainable in an organization designed for these objectives.

What the teacher needs, plainly, is a job that *one* person can do. The job must be broken down, divided, simplified, clarified, and teachers must be released from the dismal, distorting loneliness of the classroom, to work with, see, and be seen by other adults. Again, new organization of the school can make this readily practicable. As a solo worker the teacher is swamped. As part of a team, she can function far better with less strain.

It is worth noting in passing that a shocking fraction of the energy of any conventional school goes into "discipline." It takes much of every teacher's time, at all levels, and even more of the time of the administrative staff—often more than half. This need for discipline springs very largely, we are being forced to see, from the students' natural rebellion against the inadequacies of the classroom. Where schools have moved away from classroom organization, discipline needs have dropped precipitously—indeed, have all but vanished.

For the moment, let us forget the grinding restrictions the classroom style of organization puts upon schools, and consider only what specialists are required to provide the services "guidance" in its broadest sense calls for.

(a) *The Evaluator*

If each individual student is to progress on his own terms, the school must "know the score" for each, continuously and expertly. As we have discussed, schools today do not as a rule have anybody charged specifically with this function. Teachers keep score to some degree, but only while they have the child; and principals may play some part, but usually only incidentally unless major problems arise. And we must also note that the score-keeping is almost always *in terms of the class:* the child is lagging behind the class, or running ahead, or disturbing it, or "does not fit in." It is precisely this attitude — that the child is a problem if he doesn't fit neatly into the administrative system — that we must blast to bits if we are to have adequate, modern schools.

The function is so important, and the need for continuity so great, that it seems rather obvious that proper organization demands this job be given to a full-time, highly competent, and properly supported specialist. "Evaluator" might be a suitable title. In a small system, he might operate only with clerical help; in a larger one his office might include a psychologist and perhaps an assistant evaluator. According to the situation, an evaluator might have this responsibility for from 400 to perhaps 1,200 students.

The evaluator would at once lift from teachers the often back-breaking job of gathering, recording, maintaining, and reviewing information about each child. In his office would be gathered all information, from a variety of sources — far more than a classroom teacher would likely have, and in much more accessible form. Centralizing information in this way makes practical the use of a computer to eliminate tedious and expensive clerical work. A computer can readily be programmed to "keep an eye" on each child's record of progress. Instructed to report any one of dozens of variations from normal expectancies, the computer will print out the pertinent data, which the evaluator can then review. Whatever is put into its elephantine memory is recallable in microseconds. The evaluator can have better control of information concerning each of 1,200 children than the classroom teacher has for 30.

The evaluator's record would be continuous, an enormous advantage in itself. Having no dependency on the instructional staff and reporting only to higher authority, the evaluator can also be objective. It is nothing to him that Miss L. is an experienced teacher, or a lovely person, or has been distracted by a sick parent; his concern is only with how each child is getting along.

Another onerous job would be lifted from teachers by this new officer: the issuing of reports to parents, and almost all routine contact with parents. It is a job most teachers will happily part with. And with an evaluator in the picture, teachers may also give up the whole nonsensical, time-consuming and trouble-causing task of "marking," of continually giving out grades on work done, routine exams, and conduct.

We shall come later to a clearer picture of how a typical evaluator may operate. For the moment, we can readily see the advantage to the child, who is observed continuously as he progresses through the school system, expertly and individually. For the parents, the evaluator is a source of more and dispassionate information on how the child is doing. For teachers, he can provide any specific information wanted, almost instantly, as well as regular reports. And for the administration, he can provide any sort of summary data, usually without troubling teachers for clerical work.

(b) *The Test Officer*

The case has been stated for taking testing out of the hands of the teacher and letting it be the expert function of experts. But we must realize, in any discussion of testing, that it has been one more of the many devices employed to hold on to the anachronistic classroom system. "Psychological" testing was seized on with great glee as an instrument that would *facilitate* sorting each student into the "right" grouping — not as a means of freeing him from the educative cattle-car system.

Thus the teacher or guidance officer or principal says to the underachieving student, "With an IQ like yours you should be doing much better than you are." The implication is that the school is wholly right and the student wholly wrong. That the child may be bored, that his true interests and talents are being brushed aside, that his intelligence gets no real challenge — these are beside the point. The test enables the school to "prove" the child is at fault. Few are the parents of bright children who have not encountered this smug attitude.

It works in reverse, of course, with the child considered less bright, who may be actively discouraged from tackling work he is quite capable of doing, or may simply be given subtly to understand what his "place" is (especially by the insensitive, bigoted, or racist teacher) and so never stimulated to major effort. Many teachers, perhaps even most, can be deaf and blind to talents which intelligence and achievement tests fail to give even a hint of: artistic, dramatic, inventive, athletic, technical-manipulative, intuitive, social, business, and so on. The tests that are used, let us always remember, are called "standardized" because they are just that. They narrowly test mainly what the child has done, or is likely to do, in the existing classroom school. They do not test anything absolute, or anything "real," although that assumption is naively made by many both in and outside of education.

Once a school breaks free of the classroom system and begins to fit education to each child, it will have to move to quite a different pattern of testing. One objective will be to discover early those talents and interests which now so often go unnoticed. Much more individual testing will be called for, to be conducted with imagination.

Whether the test expert should be in the evaluator's office, or indeed even the same person, will depend on the size of the unit and its resources. Ideally, perhaps, the functions should be separate, for even if highly cooperative they can then serve to some degree as mutual checks.

(c) *The Visiting Teacher*

This odd term has long been in use. Apparently its purpose is to conceal, rather than reveal, the nature of the work.

The visiting teacher is, or should be, a specialist who goes to the home, usually to help solve or get information about an acute problem of behavior. This specialist need not be a teacher at all, but ideally should have social work experience. Although visits by classroom teachers to pupils' homes are hardly unknown, there are obvious reasons why in some cases they are hardly desirable, especially if the teacher is young, female, and rather innocent of some aspects of the world. In addition, as a recent survey, *Guidance Services: Organization and Administration*, points out: "To be of value, home visits require persons skilled in interview techniques and observation of behavior. In fact, if conducted by unskilled persons, home contacts can cause great damage to the pupil and to home and school relationships."

As has been noted in several parts of this book, the school's greatest need for information about each child comes at the moment of entering the school. This is true even in the graded classroom school. Rigid though it is, it can still take some advantage of such information if it has at least a few persons eager to use it. In the non-classroom school on the other side of the Revolution the need is far greater, for this flexible school must and will use all it knows about each child. Much of this knowledge must be obtained *before* the child comes to the school.

We can see, then, that the concept of "visiting teacher" may change a good deal. Likely, the specialist will still need similar training; but the emphasis will be on visiting *all* homes, and on preventive procedures intended to introduce each child smoothly to the school, and vice versa, rather than on efforts to deal almost exclusively with desperately difficult situations.

(d) *The Health Officer*

President Kennedy sounded a warning on the state of the nation's health. Some of the details that were brought out regarding school children shocked many into realizing that our schools do far less in this area than they might.

Here again we come to the philosophical argument as to whether the child's physical development is a function of school or home. We can avoid the dispute by recognizing that there are certain health areas that the school must take action in, including any condition which affects the child's ability to learn and participate.

Meaningful guidance requires not perfunctory, widely-spaced examinations of the child (often done outside the school), but full, reliable, and continuous information, obtained not merely by rule, but with insight. Many conditions develop slowly and subtly, or lead to behavioral symptoms easily misinterpreted. Teachers often fail to see what is happening before their eyes, even as may parents.

On the other hand, a doctor brings far more knowledge to the examination, but far less contact. Usually he never sees the child in a normal situation. He may easily miss conditions that have not developed to an acute or evident state. In most schools today, doctor and teacher seldom confer regarding a child, and then only *after* serious questions have arisen.

Thus it comes about that some children suffer for years from conditions vitally important for the school to know about. Hearing difficulties, which affect about four percent of school children (almost one to a class, on the average), are notoriously often overlooked or interpreted as stupidity or bad behavior. The child himself may not be aware of his handicap, and his efforts to compensate may hide the problem.

Speech defects present a delicate problem, especially in the early grades. Many young children speak poorly, and even the expert therapist may have difficulty determining whether a genuine defect exists. Some authorities say that stuttering becomes serious *after* it has been diagnosed, and that the diagnosis, by formalizing the problem and multiplying anxieties, appears to be one of the most potent causes! A teacher takes a great risk of creating a problem by calling attention to any speech condition. Even a chance remark can have a shattering effect on the child's self-consciousness, setting off a chain of difficulties that may take years to break.

Defective eyesight is another condition that the child tends to mask and the teacher to misinterpret. The child who sees a blur instead of a sharp image has no way of knowing what normal vision is. Color blindness, too, sometimes goes undetected even into adult life.

Perhaps the most common condition among young children is simply a lack of energy. The causes can be many, ranging from a chronic condition to lack of adequate food or sleep, or even, according to one recent report, excessive watching of television. The child's poor performance day to day, and in responding to testing, may lead to a grossly wrong estimate of intelligence and ability. Behavior may be interpreted as un-cooperative, hostile, or withdrawn — instead of indicating fatigue.

With rare exceptions, schools check on the health of their students only intermittently, and often with very loose control. Yet continuity is not difficult to put into operation. A number of systems have been worked out to organize and simplify the observation of children's health and growth. Here, too, the computer offers new help. It can easily hold and in seconds review thousands of records, calling attention, as instructed, to any deviations from normal patterns. The whole idea of rating the energy of the child in comparison to others and to the previous record is one the schools have scarcely even examined. (The classroom school wants no more evidence of variations.) But in newer, flexible schools, we can anticipate that both teachers and evaluator will take a keen interest in "EQs" — Energy Quotients. The energy children can display is often frightening to adults. Channeled and used, it can have prodigious results. Undirected, it is a pressure that creates enormous discipline and other problems for the school, and in adolescence, for the community.

Emotional problems are all too familiar to classroom teachers. In the typical class of 30, there is likely to be at least one obviously disturbed child, often one who perpetually disrupts the class and drives the hapless teacher almost out of her own mind. But other children in need of help may be excessively quiet, highly compliant, or even the "perfect" child type, who seems ideally adjusted until he or she suddenly lands in an institution, or when of high school age, commits a shocking crime or sexual act. Only an observer with some training and with the opportunity to see a good deal of the child alone and with others is likely to read the indications correctly. Though many schools now have some psychiatric resources, they are often inadequate, under-used, or restricted to only the most serious cases.

In the last few years another major concern has been loaded onto the already bowed back of the teacher: drugs, especially "pot" or "grass" as youngsters casually call marijuana, and a variety of "pills." Typically, most school administrators respond to charges of wide use by students by first ignoring the assertions, then denying them as "ridiculously exaggerated," and finally in at least some instances admitting the problem and doing something about it. How many children use drugs cannot easily be determined, but the persistent estimates that in some high schools a third of the students have tried marijuana are not readily put aside. The need to recognize symptoms of use, and of the personality problems, alienation, and acute boredom that may precede it, is obvious. Exactly how harmful marijuana may be proved to be is besides the point—its use by children must shock us to our core.

We have examined some but not all of the health problem, but amply enough to make clear that there is room for vast improvement in the way the school handles it. Basically, the school needs a sharp, full picture of each child as he enters. This is the time to spot problems, as well as to note the individual characteristics of the child. But a few quick, "get it over with" tests will not produce the information needed. Part of the health picture is given by the home: what is the build and activity of parents and siblings, what are the family standards of diet, sanitation, health care? Part must come from careful observation, continued over many days: how does the child move, how much energy does he show, how readily does he tire, how emotionally secure does he seem? And part can be fairly objective: his weight, height, build, eyesight, hearing, and so on.

Assembling this information is hardly an overwhelming job for several specialists working together as new children enter —however far it may be beyond a single teacher. With adequate records to start, and a proper continuous system to follow up, the school need not do a great deal more than it may do now, nor need the cost be excessive. But in the flexible school, especially with an evaluator to coordinate the information, we can expect far better health development, much more use of health information in guidance, and prompt discovery of health problems.

(e) *The Counselor*

This officer, already functioning pretty much outside of the classroom system if trained and full-time, will have no great shift of duties in the flexible school, but will become, very likely, parallel to the evaluator, and so in evidence throughout the system rather than only in the higher grades.

The job of the counselor is to deal with children individually, to guide Johnny and Susie not only through the school career but also into college or other training, and perhaps to vocation and employment. Like the evaluator, the counselor must have an independent posture to do the job. Though it is common to say that classroom teachers do a guidance job in the lower grades, it is evident that a teacher can hardly be effective in solving a child's problem if she herself is part of the problem. The counselor must stand *apart* from the instructional and administrative functions.

Counselor and evaluator can form a close-knit team: the evaluator measuring and reporting the progress of each student, and the counselor adjusting and advising to help keep the progress at the most rewarding level. This is anything but a "frilly" activity—it parallels very closely the function of able personnel people in any large corporation. Unhappy and mishandled people cost money and raise problems in both cases.

Where counseling begins with the student's entry into school, we may expect many difficulties to be caught at early stages, and far fewer to become the serious, complicated, established kind counselors must wrestle with now—often too late. With the evaluator able to spot problems almost before they arise, the counselor does not have to wait for overt symptoms.

There is perhaps no aspect of the classroom school more repelling than its failure to recognize and deal with problems in their early stages. The work of Dr. Francis Ilg and her associates at the Gesell Institute suggests that even in kindergarten the warning flags are flying for those trained to see them. Almost any experienced elementary teacher can point out a dozen or so children in her school whose problems are becoming worse year by year, with little or nothing being done to halt the process. Not long ago I heard a superintendent proudly tell a meeting he was seeking three remedial reading teachers—not for early grades but for junior high school!

In President Johnson's historic message to Congress on education of January 1965, he observed:

> We now spend about $450 a year per child in our public schools. But we spend $1,800 a year to keep a delinquent youth in a detention home, $2,500 a year for a family on relief, $3,500 a year for a criminal in a state prison.

The President was referring specifically to the high drop-out rate, but the principle is the same: the failure of the school to adapt to the needs of many of its students presents the community and the nation with a mighty bill, in dollars, in waste of talent and ability, and in racial bitterness and disorders.

But even this must be judged minor compared to the universal suffering of child and parent that the school causes because of its absurd classroom organization, an ever-present obstacle to allowing the child to be an individual. The classroom overwhelms even the good teacher, forcing her to do not her best, but the best she can and survive. To preserve the classroom, the school bullies the child, pushes him around for administrative convenience, demeans and belittles his abilities, forces him into lockstep, ignores his differences, fights down his strengths, and cruelly perpetuates his weaknesses. By the time high school has been reached, the student is in many cases in open rebellion; in others an avowed opponent; and even for many who by the record do well, the school is seen as a stupid monster to be outwitted, ridiculed, and despised.

The student is no fool. He is right. The school *is* against him: it is designed to teach classes, not persons. Unfortunately, all the students are persons.

❝For many—perhaps most—teachers the unhappiest moments of their careers come when they must make out report cards.❞

R. Murray Thomas in *Judging Student Progress*

11

A MOST UNHAPPY DUTY

That the whole business of marking, grading, and reporting is a perpetually gnawing and upsetting problem for the schools can hardly be doubted. One plan after another for solving it has become popular, only to give way to yet another brave hope. Even the descriptions of various schemes in books on school administration have a distressing tendency to argue against their own merits as they run on page after page.

Mrs. Q., for instance, has two girls in her class who do very well. One child is from a wealthy family, blessed with every resource of background and a sharp incisive mind. Her grasp and command of the subject is hard to doubt and seems to come with scarcely an effort. The other child is from a home with few advantages. She is a rather anxious, plodding girl whose diligence passes all normal bounds. Mrs. Q. rather resents the first girl, but sees little alternative to giving her anything but an A. Nor does she see how she can give the other student anything less—even if she were not aware that to do so would break her heart and perhaps discourage her seriously. But Mrs. Q. is astute enough to see that the two A's represent sharply different achievements.

Mr. P., next door, is marking a B on Albert's card, and a D on Warren's. Albert, he reasons, doesn't deserve a B, but he seems to have given up his role of class clown recently, and Mr. P. feels that encouragement is called for. The D, he decides, is a lower mark than Warren's work really calls for, but he believes Warren could do much better than he does. The D is experimental: it may jolt Warren into doing much better. Mr. P. hopes so. If his gambit succeeds, it may make a minor topic of conversation during lunch with other teachers. If it simply angers and discourages Warren, Mr. P. probably won't get around to mentioning the matter. The use of marks for manipulative purposes doesn't strike Mr. P. as wrong. He considers his power to give or withhold good grades one of his more important disciplinary resources.

Dear Miss T., who is near retirement and much loved by all, has always thought it more genteel to give high marks than low. In years past she and the principals sometimes had chats on this weakness of hers, but her delight in pleasing her children was seldom tempered for long by these encounters. Her neighbor in the next classroom, Miss R., is equally noted for strict marking. Mrs. A., nearby, has a different approach. She marks duller classes generously, brighter classes much less so. Mr. L. is known around the high school as a brisk fellow who "marks on a curve," giving a set number of A's, B's, and so on regardless of the nature of the particular class. That using a probability curve for so small a group is an outrageous violation of the basic statistical concept of a curve doesn't bother Mr. L. one bit. He stopped thinking about the whole marking question years ago. That year after year his method embitters students against his subject and school in general doesn't bother him either.

Joe, Saul, and Luis are students of about equal ability, but they have landed in three different classes in the same year of a junior high that groups to some degree "homogeneously." Joe is at the bottom of a "bright" class and gets low grades. Saul is in an "average" class and makes better grades. Luis is in the "slow" class and gets very good grades. All are doing about the same level of work and working about as hard. The parents who see their report cards are totally unaware of the way the classes are set up. Martha, who lives on the favored North Side, brings home B's from her school, while South Side Sylvia gets B's from hers. Were the children switched, however, Martha would easily get A's while Sylvia would do well to get C's by North Side standards.

Mr. Y. is a counselor in a big city high school. His biggest task and worry is getting his students into colleges. He is wondering how he could point out to certain teachers that marking a little less harshly would help him a lot. After all, how can a college entrance committee tell whether those grades on the record came from easy-marking or hard-marking teachers? He is not unaware that some craftier students entering his school deliberately spoil their scores on aptitude tests — to get put into a "slower" class in which high marks will be easier to come by and where they might win comments on how they have done better than expected. A transcript is a transcript.

Miss Y., working at home at a pile of report cards, is near tears of frustration. She is an earnest and conscientious girl in her first year of teaching, totally unprepared by training or experience for the circumstance that more than half of her children are from distinctly lower class homes. Right now she is trying to separate her evaluation of Nina's work from her all too great awareness that Nina has twice had nits in her hair, and her judgment of George's dubious English achievement from his colorful way of blowing his nose and the playground language she has overheard. Miss Y. realizes she has led a sheltered life and that distinguishing classroom work from the personality that does it is harder than it seemed in the textbooks. She would be comforted some, perhaps, if she reviewed the ample evidence that teachers are influenced by social status, appearance, and certainly sex — even in the finest neighborhoods. It is common knowledge that boys during much of their public school careers lag behind girls of the same age in both maturity and academic ability, and they also tend to be less compliant and more restless. Boys also get marked more severely and failed much more often.

The multifarious problem of marking bothers not only teachers, but students and parents as well. Children commonly are aware of what marks their classmates get and have a shrewd idea of their abilities. The cry, "She isn't *fair!*" is loud in the land. Parents are given both to protesting and resenting grades awarded and to misunderstanding the often intricate symbol system itself, especially if it differs from that which they knew as students or that used in another school their children attended.

In bygone days, children almost always were ranked. Ranking had its brutal aspects: those less well endowed or handicapped for any reason repeatedly had their failure publicly displayed—if they came to regard school as a place to escape from at the earliest possible moment, one could hardly blame them. Nor was ranking always a blessing to those who scored at the top. If the competition was too easy, the temptation to coast was great. Since ranking was based almost wholly on mastery of subject matter, modified by pleasing the teacher, some of those at the top by no means enjoyed the respect of their classmates. Yet to parents ranking had a simplicity that often proved practical—if the child seemed to be falling lower than usual or than seemed reasonable, investigation was called for. Of course, not all parents chose to investigate. Some chose the whip or put other pressures on the child, with results often about as fruitful as might be expected from beating a five-foot man to encourage him to stand six feet tall.

When the progressive movement was in full swing, the pendulum veered to the other extreme: it was nothing less than wicked for children to compete (although wickedly they persisted in running to competitive games the moment school was out). The report to the parent soon took the form of an essay or a face-to-face conference. Unfortunately, fresh difficulties arose. While this non-symbolic form of report offers greater freedom and directness, it tends to increase sharply the burden on the teacher. Writing an essay to sum up a child's progress is far from simple, and teachers' ability in this respect varies enormously, not only in knowing what to say but in fluency in writing it. To have to compose 30 such essays is not only time-consuming but nerve-wracking. It is hardly surprising that a teacher, knowing that each word may be studied by the parents, becomes loath to set down negatives about the child. She may fear not only parental wrath or hurt, but rupture of her rapport with the child, who may feel she has betrayed him. In some cases, she may with reason anticipate that parental pressure on the child will only make matters worse, and so the teacher may turn from efforts to report to efforts to outwit or circumvent the parent instead.

Essay reports thus tend to be bland, for the more negatives there are to report, the less the teacher may care to set them down in permanent form, and the fewer the specifics, the less ground for argument. The parents also acquire an additional problem: guessing whether the teacher composed her report carefully, candidly, and after much thought, or whether she scribbled it off in a few minutes to get the odious job done with. Sadly, reports done both ways may look much the same to a parent.

The face-to-face method seems to offer advantages, but once again practical problems appear. To have value, a conference should be unhurried. For 30 children, at least 12 hours must be allotted, quite apart from preparing the content of the teacher's report. If conferences are held in the daytime, either class time must usually be taken or overtime put in; in most of these cases, the father would, unfortunately, be excluded. If held at night, a quite substantial burden is put on the teacher, who still must prepare the next day's lesson, attend committee meetings, perhaps take a course, read, assist in community affairs, counsel a club or coach a team, and conceivably rest or have some private life.

But the greatest trouble with conferences can be put in one word by teachers: *parents.* As children vary enormously, so do their parents. Sometimes teachers are hard put to tell which they find more trying—parents who want to help, or those who don't. In *Administration of Elementary Schools,* Harlan L. Hagman states the matter eloquently:

> In the teacher's deep concern for the good education of children it may seem sometimes that the parents of school children are themselves the greatest problems to

be overcome before the educational achievements of the children can become all they might be. The overly anxious, the overly protective, the careless, the accusing, the interfering, the demanding, the patronizing, or the busybody parent may annoy or anger the teacher. The harsh or neglectful parent may arouse indignation; the ignorant or simple arouse sympathy for the children or despair about them. The dirty and "shiftless" parents may repel the teacher and dampen enthusiasm about the potentials of the children. The parents whom the teacher might regard as "best" may disturb the teacher and seem to challenge the teacher's role as the expert in the education of children.

The hard fact is that interviewing is a high skill in itself, even in situations less charged with emotional considerations. No personnel head, I believe, would expect an interviewer to become very expert with less than a year of full time experience under supervision, more interviewing than a teacher is likely to do in a lifetime. Picture our Miss L., who has never had any training in interviewing beyond, perhaps, some classroom discussions during teacher training, and who has never met or had any but the most superficial dealings with persons such as many of her parents. She must now deal with them on the touchiest of topics — the abilities, progress, and shortcomings of their children. To make matters worse, most parents come to the interview also with little experience in the situation, and with attitudes ranging from awe to blazing indignation. To plunge all of a system's elementary classroom teachers into such a program is to add one more burden to their already overflowing load. And the burden is potentially a shattering one for some teachers.

It is a tribute to the stuff many teachers are made of that a minority of schools do actually use the conference system, especially in communities where the parents have a high level of education. We may well wonder, however, how widely suitable the conference method is, and whether part of its apparent success in some instances is not due to parental pleasure at hearing what a sweet child Susie is, or that Howard (whom his peers insist on calling either Stinky or Stupe) is showing signs of a better adjustment to reality and a healthier emotional set. If an essay report is too permanent, a private conference is conveniently evanescent. If the parent goes away happily or at least quietly, the teacher can hardly help but regard it as more successful than if the parent storms to the principal, or leaves in a huff sure to be relayed, duly elaborated, to the neighbors. No one is apt to check up on what the teacher told the parent unless a vigorous reaction occurs; the pressure on the teacher to mollify is great. Further, let us note that in any type of reporting, the teacher is commenting not solely on the work of the student, but on her own work, too. Because teachers are commonly diligent, sincere, and horribly overburdened, they may approach many a report with guilt that they have not done all for the child that might have been done or should have been done. Others less suited for teaching may blandly ignore their failure.

At the higher grade levels, where subject teaching becomes the rule, the conference system is complicated by the fact that a teacher may have 150 students, and a student many teachers. At this level, too, a permanent record becomes more necessary for referring the student to a college or other school or to an employer. The slowness of these higher institutions to demand and accept better reporting methods than the grades now used adds to the already ample confusion and frustration. In transfers and matriculations few profess to trust grades very far, yet virtually everybody insists they be supplied.

For the purposes of this book, there is little reason to follow the vexing question any further into its murky depths. Let us note one facet illumined by Professor Hagman, however:

> Perhaps the greatest cause for inadequate or unsuitable reporting practice by schools is failure to recognize that reporting is part of an educational task relating to the child but enlisting his parents in service to his education. The report to the parents is an invitation to them to participate in the school's effort, yet the invitation is often neither clearly extended nor plain as to what the parent might do.

Unprofessionally but almost universally, teachers tend to feel that what parents might best do is go jump in the lake. The reasons for their lack of warmth in any other invitation we have just glimpsed. Reporting is for teachers not only technically and emotionally difficult in itself, but if successful in educational terms it is likely to involve the teacher with the parent on a still more tricky level!

Once again we are brought back to the prime source of most school troubles, the classroom teacher-do-everything system. Is it not painfully evident that teachers should not directly do reporting at all — that no system that calls for them to do so can escape the inherent contradictions? Teachers cannot be expected to be skilled in reporting, nor in interviewing, just because they are teachers. Still less can we expect teachers who vary greatly as individuals to achieve any great uniformity in reporting, the more so when they are reporting on their own work, directly to parents whose attitudes vary even more widely than teachers'. Nor can we expect them to solve the dilemma of wanting parental help and support at home on one hand, and on the other being afraid of what action they may arouse. Finally there is the problem of time and energy — the teacher is already assigned far more than one person can be expected to do. The answer seems clear: *take the whole job of reporting off the teachers' bowed shoulders, and give it to a specialist, the evaluator we have already discussed.*

Many schools with guidance personnel have moved much of the way in this direction. They give the delicate duty of talking with the parent to the counselor, who is more expert at interviewing, has fewer or no teaching pressures, is not reporting on his own work, and can readily coordinate a report when a number of teachers are involved. To move to the evaluator is but a short step. It is in the elementary school, however, that the need for the evaluator appears greatest. As the class-and-classroom-teacher system begins to expire and young children are no longer left to the variable mercies of a single teacher, the need for the evaluator becomes imperative. Whatever system of reporting the school then chooses to use, it may be expected to function far better because an expert specialist will take over the job from overburdened amateurs. Instead of each teacher marking on a basis that seems proper to her, we shall have reporting coordinated and unified by one qualified and closely supervised person. The evaluator can be impersonal, free of guilt and fear to a far greater degree, and both important and skillful enough to give parents less sugared and more useful reports with minimum risk to life, limb, and job security. As a third party, he has at least the opportunity to enlist parental support and interest without giving the teacher an immediate additional complication.

We need not assume that under such a system the parent would be prevented from talking directly with a teacher when good reason or great desire dictates. Indeed, such contacts might be fairly frequent. But they would be channeled through the evaluator, who would still conduct the initial interview and control the situation. No longer would parents be apt to feel that the school is fending them off. No longer would a teacher be haunted by the spectre of an unexpected anxious, angry, or obtuse parent waiting to disrupt her schedule and upset her emotionally for the day and more.

One can almost hear the sigh of relief arising from schools across the land.

"Use of teacher aides ... stands out as one of the many ways to achieve individualized instruction. The aides attend to classroom administration and the general wants of each child and thus free the teacher to use her skills and training in leading the pupil to more successful learning."

Clayton Braddock in "Suburbia Takes a Cue from the Slums," *American Education*, February 1968

12

THE LOWER SKILLS

We have discussed ways of dividing a number of higher-skill functions so that the burden on teachers may be brought down to reasonable proportions. (The reader may wish to refer again to the outline in Chapter 5, page 82.) Separating out the lower-skill tasks is a good deal simpler, in theory and probably in practice.

It is amazing to contemplate the attitude of our schools toward using clerical help at clerical salaries. So inescapable is the need, so glaring the payroll waste of not using clerks, that one would think administrators, teachers, and school boards alike would join in a common outraged howl for instant correction. Howls enough can be heard, but they seem hardly the kind that bring action. The 1955 Yearbook of the American Association of School Administrators lamented:

> The teacher spends four years or more preparing to do a good job of teaching and then, on the first job, finds a comparatively large proportion of the teaching day and a lot of home time must be devoted to work which calls for no professional competence or training.

As usual, reliable research on what actually happens is hard to come by, but there are many estimates and some limited studies of how much teachers' time goes to essentially clerical activities. The findings vary greatly, most likely because definitions of "non-professional" also do, and of course considerable variation would be expected from one situation to another in any case. But there seems to be agreement that the percentage of total schooltime is large—at least 25% would be a good guess. For example, a study in San Diego in 1952 showed that correcting papers, filling out forms and reports, filing lesson plans, attending meetings, and other such non-teaching work took about 20% of the school day. A substantial analysis of the time used by 137 elementary teachers in Bay City, Michigan, in 1953 showed more than an hour a day was used in making out report cards, putting materials on the blackboard, correcting papers, making reports, housekeeping, and fund collection.

One need only talk with teachers at random to find out they are almost universally exasperated with "clerical" demands upon their time and upon their nerves—for many teachers, perhaps to their credit, detest such tasks. As the Kowitzes sagely observe in *Guidance in the Elementary Classroom:*

> Few teachers are trained clerical workers. There are many requirements of the teaching profession that are counter to the requirements for a good clerk. As a result, clerical accuracy frequently is not found in excellent teachers.

The point is worth noting: when a $7,000 teacher is put to tasks that should be assigned to a $2,000 part-time clerk or helper, not only does each hour's work cost over three times as much, but the teacher is made unhappy and the work is probably done less well and more slowly than the clerk could do it. We also see why teachers' enthusiasm for fuller records about their charges is often dimmed—it is much easier to find value in complete records when one does not have to sit up nights compiling and entering them. And undoubtedly some of the feeling about report cards stems from the same wearisome source.

When we use the word "clerk," we are speaking ordinarily of a person trained and competent to handle records, figures, filing, and routine but not necessarily unimportant detail, with speed and accuracy. Much of the teacher's non-professional burden falls in this clerical category. But there are at least two other segments. One is work that can be turned over to a "teacher's aide," a term that has come into standard use. Typically, a teacher's aide is a woman from the community, probably a mother, who likes children and has some skill in dealing with them, and has a suitable personality and enough education to be at ease in a school room. She is often employed only for school hours. Such persons are seldom hard to find in most communities. Often they are college graduates, and some become interested enough to take qualifying courses and become teachers themselves. More do not wish to work full time, but welcome activity to fill the middle of their day and the extra income it brings. To the teacher's aide can be given a long list of duties, which can include classroom housekeeping, giving out and taking back supplies and equipment, escorting children, lunchroom and bus duty, putting material on the blackboard, handling audio-visual equipment, helping small children with clothing, and such exotic chores as feeding the class animals and overseeing a variety of windowsill horticulture.

The second segment that can be split off is the often dull and routine business of "mechanical" evaluation and correcting of student work. It is important here to make the distinction between "right or wrong" correcting and the much more subtle and complex evaluation of how a child is doing as evidenced by *what* he gets right or wrong. In spelling, Albert may receive a mark of 80, or five words wrong out of twenty-five. The degree of accuracy Albert has achieved is of interest; but the teacher, looking over his corrected paper herself, may note that Albert's errors follow a common pattern, such as not knowing rules about plurals. A few words to Albert may set him on the right track. Just so, in arithmetic, the teacher may want to know what kinds of mistakes are being made: errors from carelessness, from sloppy writing, from not knowing basics, or from not understanding problems. In a social studies class, she may want to check essays to see whether her ideas got across, or got garbled. Just as it is important in learning to know as quickly as possible what one got right or wrong, so in teaching feedback is essential to know how well the teaching effort succeeded.

It is still possible, however, to split what we can term lower-skill and higher-skill evaluation. A great deal of routine correcting need not be done by the teacher: it can be done by any competent person, and then given to the teacher for review. So long as the teacher must correct all work she gives out, she is under practical pressure to hold down the amount. This is particularly true of individual work, such as essays, collections, or projects. As we have added burden after burden to teachers, the effect of this pressure has become all too evident. For a time one got the impression that school was to become a place where answers were invariably given by making a checkmark on a "mechanical" test, the "objective" type which requires a student to indicate True or False or choose the right answer from several offered. Such tests are delightful so far as correcting is concerned: they can be marked swiftly and accurately by use of a template, or when given on a larger scale, by machines that read the checks electrically. But the limitations of this useful type of examination have been realized, and an outcry against its overuse has had some effect. There is now at least a good deal of lament about the need for balancing mechanical tests with those calling for essay type answers. These discourage the guessing and superficial remembering that mechanical tests are apt to foster and reveal the student's depth of comprehension much better. They also give him invaluable practice in organizing his thoughts, communicating in writing, and developing a personal and perhaps original point of view.

Simple arithmetic will give us some notion of the size of the correcting problem. If an elementary teacher asks her class of 30 for an essay, and allots each response no more than five minutes, she has given herself two and a half hours of work merely to correct it. If she follows up on at least some of the results with brief discussions with a dozen of her pupils, another hour is accounted for. Further, good teaching demands that results be given as quickly as possible. The teacher then can ill afford to push off the correcting task to a convenient time. Much of it gets done in evening hours, which otherwise might go to better preparation of the next day's sessions. For a high school teacher with 150 students, one essay type assignment a week, corrected at the rate of one every ten minutes, means 25 hours of correcting—plus any conferences! In *The American High School Today,* Dr. James B. Conant recommended that:

> The time devoted to English composition during the four years should occupy about half the total time devoted to the study of English. Each student should be required to write an average of one theme a week. Themes should be corrected by the teacher. In order that teachers of English have adequate time for handling these themes, no English teacher should be responsible for more than one hundred pupils.

(Dr. Conant is speaking of the situation at the time of his survey; he stresses elsewhere in the report that it would be "most unfortunate" if his conservative recommendations in the report "should lead anyone to believe I was in favor of freezing the development of the curriculum or the organization of the high school.") Putting this recommendation into effect in most schools would mean cutting the pupil load of English teachers by at least a third. In some, it would be nearer half. We may well wonder how many high schools can find the funds and the teachers to put this ratio into effect, and we may further question how many teachers will, under conventional organization, find the sixteen or more hours of correcting time even the reduced load calls for.

To solve this problem of correcting in English and in other subjects in which essay answers are desirable, a small but increasing number of schools have begun to use "readers." Often these are well-educated adults in the community who welcome such part-time work, which can be done at home on a piece-work basis or at the school. Or the readers may be college students qualified in the field; or as we shall see, assistant teachers can carry the function. When readers are used, some simple provisions insure feedback to the teacher—a plan for rotating the pupils whose work the teacher still corrects herself so that the work of all is seen, and arrangements for the teacher to review and spot-check all reader-corrected papers. With a reader assigned, a teacher is under pressure to assign themes. Without a reader, the pressure is the other way —themes are not assigned, and the student gets little practice in writing.

So far as I have been able to observe, English teachers show little awareness of or enthusiasm for the reader idea. Perhaps this attitude should be considered in conjunction with the 1959 report of Professor Harold Martin, head of the College Entrance Examination Board's Commission on English. Describing the working conditions of English teachers as "unbelievably bad," Dr. Martin also pointed out that qualification standards for English accreditation are low, and yet nearly a third of high school English teachers do not meet these standards. Only half had even majored in English in college. Dr. Conant's solution hardly seems imminent.

The basic organizational concept in the use of clerks, aides, and readers is so simple that we need hardly examine it further. We organize almost everything else this way, dividing labor and counting costs on an hourly basis as a matter of course. For schools, the potential saving in dollars is something to conjure with. If only one-third the work now done by teachers can be done by other employees at half the cost per hour, *the saving would amount to one-sixth of the entire teaching payroll.* The cost-per-hour saving in practice may work out to well above half the teacher rate. All told, it is conceivable that *one-quarter or more of the payroll might so be freed for other uses.* Even in a small city, such a saving would run into millions each year.

Unfortunately, the class-and-classroom system again stands squarely in the way. True, it is possible to use clerks, aides, and readers to a considerable degree within the framework of the classroom system; and it is being done in various ways in hundreds of places. But let us sympathize with the principal, superintendent, board, or whoever else tries to bring about this kind of change.

First, there is the peculiar and little-discussed circumstance that the classroom system can make genuine economies appear to be added expenses. Suppose, for example, that a school with twenty-four overburdened teachers adds twelve aides. The educational output of the school could as a result rise a third or even a half; but educational output is far from easy to measure. What shows up in the financial report and the budget on which taxes are based is a visible cost increase of about one-sixth.

But there is more to the matter. A school is organized, as we have seen, by dividing the total number of children into classes and assigning a teacher to cover each class. From this point on, according to popular habits of thought, every additional person working in the classroom or with the children or teachers elsewhere is automatically a "frill" — an extravagance in the eyes of budget-choppers. Defending the school psychologist, the guidance expert, music or art specialist, helping teacher, visiting teacher, and the like against the sharp axes of those who begrudge funds for education to begin with is a rough job. When cutting back does begin, it is always those who do not cover classes who go first. The addition of lower-skill persons attracts attack, not praise for economy. The "let teacher cover the classroom" philosophy is familiar and easy to understand. Modern concepts of cost accounting are Greek to most of those citizens interested in school affairs. So long as we have a classroom setup, this primitive and terribly wasteful way of looking at school costs will slow progress. When finally the classroom walls begin to crumble, we will become freer to staff our school on a functional basis, as we staff a factory, a store, an office, a hospital, a church, or even a PTA.

Second, and also potent, is the opposition of the classroom teacher. While some will welcome help eagerly, we may expect more to resist — humans being human. Those who have long regarded their classrooms as their private walled castles actively resent the intrusion of another, and possibly critical, adult. However unobtrusive and compliant an aide, the teacher is no longer alone with children behind a firmly closed door.

Emotionally, the change for some may be intolerable. "I just can't stand having anyone in my classroom watching me all the time!"

Even when no such emotional barrier exists, the teacher may be wholly untrained and unskilled at using the services of assistants effectively. The classroom offers minimum opportunity for learning how to. The situation is opposite from that in which an executive trainee in a large corporation finds himself. He may know little about how to use the help of others either, but he has only to look about him to see how older hands manage it. Shut away in a classroom with children, and in effect barred from other classrooms, the teacher has no way to acquire skill in the tricky and subtle technique of using assistance wisely and happily. Feeling uneasy and unprepared, the teacher fights off the proffered help.

Outside pressures often work best to bring about division of labor within the classroom system. If classes have swollen to outrageous size, or if teachers for some other reason are collapsing under the load, aides may be introduced; or an intolerable clerical load may bring clerks into the picture. But such situations may make what is actually a long step forward, in theory at least, seem no more than an emergency measure, to be resisted anew when the pressure lessens.

Sometimes the very people who profess to be most anxious that schools be improved stand unwittingly in the way of progress. PTA officials, for example, often keep a watchdog surveillance on class size. To be sure, increasing class size without any other change is a favorite way of holding down school expense. But for many well-meaning persons, class size has become something of a fetish. We can readily understand why: in the morass of dubious fact and suspect axiom that is education today, class size seems to be a reassuringly solid and simple reference point. Such research as there is on class size is distressingly reluctant to confirm the rule that the smaller the class the better the results. Research findings sometimes come out the other way. But few lay persons leave the comfortably "obvious" to muddle into research. And few stop to realize that to lay great stress on this single factor in a complicated situation is to fall into the trap of vigorously supporting the cornerstone of the whole obsolete system—the fixed class. Lacking understanding of the theory of division of labor, PTA leaders may regard introduction of aides, clerks, and other low-cost help as no more than a devious way to junk the "standards" they have so long fought for.

To break the barriers against change, the classroom system and its accumulated evils must be understood on a theoretical level by at least a majority of leaders in the community. Until then, the forward-looking board or administrator must expect brickbats and abuse from all directions if it seeks any real change. But once the classroom concept is vigorously attacked and the ancient barrier to progress is broken, the way is smoother. A sweeping change, accomplished at a proper pace, is easier to win support for than painful tinkering. When there are no classes in the old sense, there can be no arguments about class size. No longer can the budget divide into "classroom teachers" (essential) and "others" (frills). Instead, there is only the category "staff."

When the teacher is let out of the solitary confinement of the classroom and permitted to work like other people as a member of a functional team, there no longer can be the fear of classroom "interlopers." Teachers understand the principle of division of labor, but they have never been given enough opportunity to experience it. A period of adjustment must be expected; but we may feel confident that the teacher who finds boring and distasteful jobs stripped away, and more time allowed for use of highest skills, will usually not take long to become a supporter of the new system that makes his or her work easier, more rewarding, and more professional.

In Part II, we will get at least a glimpse of what it will be like to teach and learn in schools freed of the grip of that stultifying institution, the classroom.

PART II

"Even though literature in the field of education reflects considerable concern over change in American education, the writers reflect little understanding of both the processes and consequences of change. In fact, it is only very recently that serious consideration has been given to the idea of carefully planned change."

Roy A. Larmee in *Nongraded Schools in Action,* edited by David W. Beggs III and Edward G. Buffie, published by Indiana University Press

13

THE TECHNIQUE OF CHANGE

No proposal for change is of much use unless there is some practical means for getting from where we are to where it might be well to be. In this part of this book, the object is to consider *how* our obsolete class-and-grade system can be shucked off.

The execution of change is very much a human problem. Irwin Edman has summarized John Dewey's view: "The enemy of life (and its opposite) is rigidity and blind resistance to change. The function of intelligence is to be alertly critical of outmoded methods in society, in government, in feeling, in thought." Besides intelligence, however, there is also sloth, egotism, confusion, fear. There is the tendency of parents, especially mothers, to speak of "education" and "our schools" when they have in mind only what is happening to their own offspring at the moment. Any administrator groans before he issues an announcement of change of any kind—he knows it will bring a freshet of calls protesting in purely individual terms. Sometimes it seems that intelligence is the least of the factors involved.

Let me then create a fictional community and school system, and a Dr. Thomas Morrow to be our guide and mentor
as we explore the process of change and where it could take us.

Dr. Morrow, I fear, may appear a bit wiser in this account
than some of his counterparts in reality, and the successes
of his New Lea system and Isaac Newton School to have come
about with less emotional bloodshed than seems completely
convincing. But that will be because he is looking backwards,
while we of solider flesh must look forwards, where the view
is seldom as clear. But Dr. Morrow is intended nonetheless
to be not the special case that every school system actually
is so much as a summary of many. Though there may be no
schools precisely like that he conducts us through, there is
hardly an aspect discussed that we could not find, long in operation, in many schools. The Appendix will help bear this out.
And the picture he gives us of schools that have escaped from
the clutch of the class-and-grade system may, I hope, give us
a sense of what the new kind of school will be like, better
than any number of case histories.

*   *   *

Just inside the door of Isaac Newton School Dr. Morrow
met us and shook hands. "We can begin," he said. "The others
are here." He led us down the corridor, a tallish man with
standard equipment of pleasant manner, a scholarly air,
sparse brown hair, and heavy black glasses. Attitude and appearance suggested the typical long-suffering, tightrope-
walking school administrator; but it was to become evident
Dr. Morrow was both less conformist and more rugged than he
looked.

He ushered us into the Faculty Room, which appeared to be
several cuts above the usual dreary teachers' retreat. The
lighting was good, the furniture comfortable and in good repair,
the decor almost that of a reading room in a tolerable club.
Telephones were available, on tables, and in a booth. Periodicals covered a long counter, and books the shelves above.
Sound equipment and television occupied one corner. What
appeared to be a closed-circuit monitor stood across the room.

Several original paintings graced the walls. The carpet under-
foot felt almost luxurious.

"Please don't be taken aback," commented the observant
Dr. Morrow. "We try to keep up to the level minor executives might enjoy in a corporation office. Besides, we use
this room a good deal for meetings and conferences — this tonight, for example. I hope, too, you won't be shocked to know
this room is for both male and female teachers. We figure that
if both sexes of children can meet, maybe our adults can
handle it, too. Not that it came about without a few hassles,
though."

Introductions followed. It was evident that when a school
system moves ahead, it acquires the burden of informing
those who would like to follow. Those present represented
a dozen communities; and we knew meetings such as this were
held with some frequency. We settled down, and Dr. Morrow
began.

Better education [he said] is something most people are
"for," even as they are for freedom, peace, democracy, and
prosperity for all. But let's not kid ourselves: better schools
in a community don't come about just because many people
are for them. It takes more than that. Often the people who
want the schools improved most aren't willing to face what it
does take. They may insist on the importance of education,
and cry for money to be poured out as needed; but I doubt
that often gets results. They are right, of course. But it isn't
enough to be right — you have to have a method that can get
you where you want to go.

Stop and think. Schools are supported by public funds
that must come from taxes. Nobody likes taxes. In a typical
community, you add up the taxpayers who don't have children,
or have children too young or too old for school, or who
send them to private or parochial schools, or who just don't
care deeply about the quality of education their offspring get,
and all told you have a sizeable group that is at best lukewarm
toward better schools if they are going to cost more. Will they
really be better because they cost more? Who says? And will
they be better enough to matter? Just how is the money to be

spent? What new-fangled frills and nonsense will be brought in? What good, old-fashioned, stern teachers will be bounced out?

You can hear the chorus of grumbling I'm speaking of, I'm sure. Trying to get somewhere through this resistance is rough. And bear in mind, in many places costs must go up year by year even if no improvement in quality is sought, so there may be a history of raised taxes with nothing to show for the ever-increasing bill.

To my mind, to get better schools you have to think of these reluctant taxpayers, and offer something of more direct interest to them than just "better education." You have to get the support of people this conservative element will respect and listen to. At the same time, I think, you may need to put your target higher than just "better" schools; and if you can get some emotional factors into the picture, so much the better. Often that is a matter of luck and timing, plus a bit of skillful stage-managing. One thing is certain: you don't just drift into better schools.

With that introduction, let me tell you what happened here. About five years ago, this city, fairly typical of many between fifty and a hundred thousand, had suffered a series of blows. One of our oldest and biggest industries had just closed its plants here. Our biggest retail store had been gutted by fire and had decided to rebuild in a shopping center out of town. City finances were in poor shape, some of our politicians under indictment, and our tax rates had just gone up—again.

This led three of our most important citizens to commence meeting at lunch. One was a retired man, owner of a good deal of real estate here, a patron of the arts, and a very respected member of various committees and boards. Another was a tax lawyer, who works for some of the largest concerns around. The third is the town's leading jeweler, once mayor, and active in his religion. I should point out that all three were eminently respectable and hardly open to instant attack as dreamers, subversives, do-gooders, or spenders. Like some of their counterparts around 1776, they were the ideal men to sponsor a revolution.

Not that they met for that purpose. I'm told they were not at first thinking about our schools at all. They *were* afraid a shrinking tax base would bring further tax increases, and that in turn would make it harder to bring new business and industry. Having more homes go up for sale would tend to depress real estate values and make the spiral worse. Education crept into their talks primarily as one important factor bearing on attracting new employers.

Let me dwell on this point a moment. I'm an educator, not a tax man; but it's a mixed-up educator who forgets that money is the first step in the educational process. To have adequate funds for education today, a community has to have a firm tax base. Usually that means substantial business and industry to carry a good share of the load. Before these concerns will move in, I'm told, they usually take a hard look at the educational resources. The reason is simple — to attract and keep the executives and key specialists they need, they have to offer not only good jobs but good living conditions. And good schools are an essential. For many such concerns, a continuing supply of well-educated young people is important, too. They look ahead. Not only must the prospective town offer a good school system, but it must be moving ahead, not rusticating or sliding off. Of course, the same principle applies to individual families considering buying a house. If the schools are weak, that may end their interest, period.

The committee of three got a larger committee formed to attract new taxpayers. Twice they got desirable businesses interested, only to end choosing another town. In each case the committee found our unimpressive school system was the deciding reason for not coming here. Meanwhile, of course, we had a lot of citizens unhappy with our schools. That is hardly unusual. Some of the loudest voices, I'm afraid, were regarded by many people, including our Board of Education, as cranks or nuisances. We also had the usual organizations variously concerned with education. Some were dormant, some tiresomely ground the same axe forever, and some, including our PTA's, were led by persons more interested in office-holding than meaningful results. All were ineffective, and scarcely any two groups pulled the same way.

Then, in that mysterious way such things happen, public

support began to coalesce. A "segregation" incident involving a principal brought an investigation, and a lot of talk and heat. It was blown up out of all proportion, but it made the schools news. Then three well respected high school teachers resigned in a body, protesting an administrative measure. And behind the scenes the committee to attract new businesses was having some pointed words with the Board. The pressure mounted. Next spring, we had some new Board members and a new superintendent of schools.

I was a principal then. I'd tried a few experiments in my school, but they hadn't gone far. I didn't have much support for them or time to give them, not to mention money. And at this point, such are the fortuities of life, my own brother-in-law played a part. He visited us—he was nearby because his corporation was installing a new computer-controlled communications system. What impressed me was that he had been taken off his regular job and put in charge of this change, with no other duties and with a staff to help him. He planted the thought with me that to bring about any major change, you've got to do something of the kind. Change means work, and a lot of close attention. You have to have people so assigned.

Talking with some of the Board members, I passed this thought along. To my surprise, a couple of months later our new superintendent was passing it back to me. Would I care to head up such a program, to concentrate on new ideas and techniques for our system? There would be a budget and a new title of Assistant Superintendent. I said I would.

Looking back, I think this arrangement was the key to what success we have had. Try to bring about changes when each change means an additional load on everybody concerned, and you obviously put a big handicap on the program. Soon "change" becomes a dirty word. But provide funds and people assigned to change, and you both lessen the burden and avoid much opposition. A school system is mighty complicated. One like ours that was in trouble and sliding off is especially likely to be full of trouble spots ready to explode. I just don't believe a school system can make important changes of the scale needed today without acute pain, dislocations, and possibly near-disasters, unless it organizes for it along the general lines we used here, and that business and other large organizations employ as a matter of course.

If there is one thought more than any other I'd like you to take away tonight, that's it.

Now let me tell you how we went about things and what we did.

Dr. Morrow paused for a drink. A lady inquired:

"Dr. Morrow, what do you do if you don't seem to have more than a handful of people interested in improving the schools, and a lot fussing about high taxes?"

"I suspect you don't get change when only a few people without special influence want change," said Dr. Morrow. "On the other hand, if you wait until everybody, or even most people, want major change, you'll likely wait forever. I've thought about this a bit as groups have come here, and I'd say these are the elements you need.

"First, change has to be change *to* something. At least a good nucleus of people have to have a fairly clear concept of practical, better alternatives, that can be reached by practical steps.

"Second, there has to be some reason for commencing change *now*. That can be a crisis of some kind, some new or intensified pressures, some incidents that emotionalize pressures existing, or something of the kind. Or, there can be a tradition that invites change. In profit business and military matters, competition does it. But the tradition is awfully weak in education, I'm afraid.

"Third, there must be a few people, sometimes very few, who can start the revolution moving. I don't mean idea people or specialists. I mean persons who are above all *respectable*. Those thought of as solid, sober citizens, not revolutionaries. They may not be the prime thinkers, but they are the prime movers. Once they give their blessing, a crackpot demand suddenly metamorphoses into a sound plan.

"Fourth, it's very helpful to have examples of similar problems being solved elsewhere. Which brings us back to what we did here."

"We'll be moving around the school," said a pleasant young teacher in the rear, "so perhaps you'd like some coffee now."

The editor . . . is not the first to suggest that the domain of education—both its practice and its study—constitutes a kind of anachronistic folk subculture . . . in the midst of an otherwise rationalized world. Intelligence does have its uses; the theory and practice of educational innovation may well turn out to be one of them. At least, let us hope so.

Matthew B. Miles in *Innovation in Education*

14

HOW TO KNOW
WHAT YOU'RE DOING

While you're having some refreshment [Dr. Morrow said], let me fill you in on our research program. As we move about the school and discuss some of our methods, I'd like you to keep thinking of this program as something behind the scenes. It's a program that extends a long way in time, too, reaching out to explore the future like an insect's long antennae, checking on the present like a cash register, and looking back on what has happened to see where we have been like the famous dumdum bird. Please pardon my metaphors — but this program is our pride and joy. It's where progress begins.

It's odd that while research is taken for granted as a necessity in business, industry, the military, medicine, and so on, in education it is almost a curiosity. For example, an ordinarily prudent investor won't buy the stock of a big company without likely asking, "How much money are they putting into research?" He's used to seeing annual statements in which companies lay stress on their research expenditures, which prove they are worrying about what may lie over the horizon in new products, new methods, new markets. The head of research in a company is typically a key official whose ability is regarded as vital to the company's continued existence over a period. Business knows all too well that with change as rapid as it is today, failure to look ahead and keep ahead means falling by the wayside. In education we spend billions each year, yet only a trickle of that, for many years, went for research; and only a tiny part of that trickle went for what can be called projective research — finding out how to do things better in the future.

Although research plays a tremendous role in every phase to life today, many people never come directly in touch with any research activity. I may mention now, if you're a teacher or student in a New Lea school, you do! So forgive me if I point out three kinds of research. Suppose you're going to buy a new car. A wise step might be to compile a lot of *available* information that may guide your choice. Now, say, you have your car, and you want to decide whether to run it on regular or premium gas. So you set up a test, or *experiment.* You try one for awhile, then the other. You have to measure, keep accurate records, of course, to learn anything from this test. Then, you might go further — you might actually work out a modification of the engine, putting in new cams or valves, or a supercharger. You might call this a *creative* experiment. It goes beyond a simple test and obviously it requires a depth of knowledge and a much greater effort.

So with research in practical terms. If someone has already found out what you want to know, and you can find out that they have found out, that's the easiest way — presumably. Actually, so much research in all fields has been done now that a major effort is being made to find ways to use computers to locate research findings when they are needed. A vast amount of scientific research is redone and redone because the information can't be found readily. If you can't find what you want to know, you may want to run a test, or get into a creative experiment. In any event, good research is scientific in spirit even if it doesn't deal with science. You have to check and recheck your facts, your methods, your conclusions. And your research should also be done a standard, professional way, so that other researchers can check up on and evaluate what you've done or found. In a word, research is nothing for amateurs, any more than brain surgery or bridge building. You need trained people, and not long ago about the last thing you found in any school system was a trained researcher. There still aren't many, but the idea is catching on.

When Dr. Barth, our new superintendent, took over, he announced a program of improving our schools through the usual channels—better staffing, better functioning. I was named head of a Research and Utilization Committee. My job was to find out how to do everything better. I didn't just get a title. I got an office, an assistant, a secretary, and a fund for expenses. For the first year the total cost came to around $30,000. A lot? Well, our system was spending over $10 million a year. So this meant devoting about one-third of one percent to finding out how best to spend it. Many a profit-seeking corporation spends two, five, seven percent or more for research without a whimper! Why? Clearly, because research more than pays its way, just on a pure money basis. After five years, we've got our research ration up close to one percent. Two months ago the Board actually *urged* me to try to find good ways to spend more research money!

Let me present Mr. Sidney Piner now. I'm not a trained research man. He is. Sidney?

Mr. Piner, a heavy-set young man with a hairy head and a highly enthusiastic manner, took the floor.

"Laymen are apt to think," he said, "that information bearing on education should be very easy to get. After all, there are big government offices in Washington, and in each state capital. There are universities, colleges, teachers' colleges, the professional press, learned fraternities, funds for this and that, foundations, associations, and committees. The fact is, organization overall is very poor, and valid, useful data hard to come by. The government offices often get too little money, and too little of that goes for finding things out. A postcard will get you books of facts on vacations in our national parks, or diseases of chickens; but try to get something reliable on the best way to teach math in the early years, or the best ways to use clerks in schools! As Dr. Morrow said, you have to check,

check everything. In the field of education, it has long been recognized that much research is so bad it is either laughable or maddening, depending on your mood at the moment. Much is done by students working for degrees. The quality is often abominable. One favorite kind of project is to collect the opinions or impressions of an assortment of teachers, administrators, or so-called researchers, and write a report on that basis. I need hardly point out that a summary of a lot of opinion is even less reliable than the opinions themselves. A thousand opinions don't make one scientific fact.

"Even statistics can't be relied on. Many are patently pulled out of somebody's hat, or sloppily interpreted, or politically slanted.

"But what is worse are the deserts — the vast areas in which it is hard to find the scantiest valid research. When you get to the middle elementary years, for example, there is incredibly little available. To make matters worse, the channels of communications are poor. First, everything is fractionated into elementary, junior high, and high school levels. There is little communication between them; and almost nobody is interested in education as a continuous process.

"In a word, it's a jungle — wild, tangled, and uncultivated. You have to cut your own paths, and it grows over so fast the next fellow has to cut his. Fortunately, things are rapidly improving. But there is an awful long way to go. So much of my time goes in hunting down information on what other schools have done, or basic research on learning and teaching methods, mostly in the colleges, and in working out our own experiments. At first most of this we had to do alone, but now that some nearby systems have research specialists too, we work more and more together. Also, we work closely with two of the universities. Through them, an experiment may be run in several places at once, with rapid exchange of information. That helps greatly, especially in speeding development of techniques and materials. I think one does not have to be much of a prophet to foresee that the day is coming when this informal sort of cooperation will grow into a well organized network of research centers across the country, much of it conducted by colleges and aided by government funds as a matter of course. The Education Act of 1965 has made a big difference, with the new ERIC facilities beginning the network, and many localized Title III centers helping.

"Before I was hired, Dr. Barth used to be asked why he couldn't visit other systems and keep up with the literature. I'll give you an idea. To keep tabs on one exploratory development in teaching science in another state, I have so far paid three visits this year to each of two schools, two hundred miles apart, and two to the university which is assisting. I also visited another school, still further away, that has a comparable program. On my last visit, I stayed three days, sat in on classes, talked with a dozen people, made seven rolls of tape, took eighty pictures, and came back with an armful of literature, workbooks, reports, and texts. Just to write up my report, with the aid of an undergraduate assistant, took over two full days. Obviously superintendents and principals can't afford to work at this depth, on top of their other duties. Even with part-time assistance and some good volunteer help to visit schools far away, I can barely keep up with projects that interest us keenly. Survey reading, of course, goes on all the time. My office puts out a précis of significant research reports and other literature, for the use of all the faculty and administration. We think it saves everybody a great deal of time and helps them locate and read what is most important for their needs."

Mr. Piner sat down, looking more enthusiastic than when he had begun.

"I should mention," resumed Dr. Morrow, "that after we got our research program rolling, we ran into the problem of getting information to our Board of Education. Our Board, like most, gets pretty well tied up in immediate matters at regular meetings. The future tended to get shunted aside. We persuaded the Board to hold a special meeting devoted wholly to our work. They loved it. One member said to me afterwards, 'That's the first time I've got my nose above tomorrow in three years!' At first, much we reported seemed far afield or even wild; but gradually the fact that all of these things were real, were being done, and could be useful to our system, took hold. You can get used to what first seems a wild notion pretty fast, if you work at it a bit. Some members, of course, stayed aloof, skeptical. But they weren't antagonistic, once they began to think in terms of replacing an old, broken-down system with a new, more practical one. What we had to combat most was a desire some people had to tinker and patch rather than *replace*. Once the idea got across that we were seeking sweeping changes that added up to a new concept, not isolated fiddling with this or that, we could focus on what the sweeping changes should be. A lot of people demanded convincing evidence we were headed the right way. We dug it out for them.

"Now a word about Utilization, the other half of the committee's title. We use the term to mean the way we use, and how well we use, personnel, plant, equipment of all kinds, and techniques of teaching, learning, and child development. You can say the question is twofold: how are we using what we have, and what should we get?

"This is obviously a big field. We can divide it more or less into *organization,* or how we set things up, and *operation.* We avoid getting into what should be taught and why, unless we are asked to. That's not the Committee's prime concern. Of course, sometimes the decision on what to teach hinges on how you might teach it. We have found, though, that old arguments about curriculum have tended to diminish as our programs have become more flexible and give each student more individual freedom.

"Now I'd like you to meet Miss Lois Calper. Like Mr. Piner, she is a research specialist, and soon will join him in admitting to a doctoral degree, if you corner them."

Miss Calper, lithe of figure and crisp in black and white, seemed closer to a fashion model than a researcher, but less so as she spoke with calm authority.

"My job," said Miss Calper, "is to measure. If we are going to experiment to see whether a new way to accomplish something is better, I first set up a base, or control, so we can compare. Then I check to see that the test is fair—that it is really testing what it is supposed to, with other factors offset or excluded as far as possible. I observe it as it progresses, and figure out ways to evaluate results. Then I report them. Sometimes this process may run years, other times just weeks. I also do time studies and interviewing intended to develop basic facts. For example, we may study how a team of teachers actually divide their time, or how much writing certain students do within a certain period. As I said, I measure."

Dr. Morrow took over once more. "One of Miss Calper's virtues is brevity. She makes it all sound simple; but we at times fight some bloody battles over evaluations. I can't stress too much how important this phase of research is. It's all too common to find experiments being run which then can't be properly evaluated because no base was set up first, and no allowance made for the parts enthusiasm, personalities, and circumstance may play. You are probably aware, too, of what is called the Hawthorne effect—a tendency to get better than normal results from people because your experiment makes them the center of attention for a while. And overall there is the risk of personal involvement producing a bias in judgment or even in observation. You can see what you want to see. Miss Calper needs all her degrees and prestige to face down critics, pouters, and dissidents. She's tough. Without her, I'm afraid, we'd have a lot more argument and a good deal less progress.

"So I hope you begin to see how we work here. All the people you have met so far can earn their pay only by showing the way to improvements in organizing and operating our schools. Working with Dr. Barth and the Board, we select the most promising ideas and program them. We set up, if we possibly can, careful provisions for measuring and evaluating results. But we also take risks and some part-guesses. Waiting for 'certainty' or 'proof' makes rapid change almost impossible. If we score a success, we put it into wider use and try to improve on it by refining the details. Sometimes what seems a good idea doesn't work out. If so, we admit it. Usually the damage is minor—a loss of time and effort is the major cost. And even a failure, if properly studied and reported, can give us useful information and deeper understanding. Our schools here, after five years of this kind of improvement, are very, very different from the conventional schools they were when we began this plan. And I feel confident you'll agree we've moved the right way, as we now make our tour. On—to the kindergarten!"

❝ *Kindergarten and first grade years are strategic, not only in what a child learns in knowledge and the basic skills, but also in the inner feelings and attitudes he acquires about himself as a learner.* **❞**

Roma Gans in *Common Sense in Teaching Reading,* copyright © 1963 by The Bobbs-Merrill Company, Inc., reprinted by permission of the publishers.

15

THE CRITICAL DAYS

Sit down—at your own risk," invited Dr. Morrow. "You may find the tables more comfortable than the chairs."

We had already inspected the small kindergarten room, with its one-way mirror and observation booth behind. This room we were in was much larger, at first glance a typical kindergarten but for two television receivers, and a row of three typewriters on a long desk.

"This is where our children begin school," continued Dr. Morrow. "But we don't think of it that way. Let me quote briefly from this book, *Education in the Elementary School*, by Hollis L. Caswell and Arthur W. Foshay:

> The importance of the group to the child entering it can scarcely be overestimated. Entrance to a new group is a profound emotional experience; the child may face it with fear, or eager anticipation, or some combination of these— but we can be sure that only a very rare child faces it with indifference.

We agree. Who can disagree? Yet the conventional way is to bring twenty, thirty, forty children into a room like this, all for

their first experience of something called 'school.' Some are
healthy and strong, some small and frail; some bold and outgoing, others timid; some from literate homes and academically well along, others totally unprepared. And some feel secure among friends, others know they are strangers in a strange
place. To start a group off this way, often under teachers who
have very limited experience, is much like throwing them all
into deep water to learn to swim. Some don't make it. Some begin under serious handicap. As Daniel Prescott long since
pointed out after thousands of studies of individual children,
the school itself often creates the maladjusted child.

"Our state laws are a bit sticky about admissions. In spite of
all we know about the differences among children, date of
birth is still the one usual consideration. Tommy born Monday
must be taken in, Johnny born the next day can't be admitted.
Fortunately, the legal language in our case is a little loose. We
hope to get the law amended; meanwhile, no one is protesting
our interpretation that we can choose an admission date if the
parent agrees. Most parents go along, so we are able to admit
children a few at a time.

"Now it is time to present one of our most liked teachers,
Mrs. Emily Portal. She is our admissions officer. She'll explain
what that title means."

Mrs. Portal came forward and flashed a warm smile. She
was a very large woman, almost six feet tall, Negro, along in
years. You felt you could see swarms of grandchildren happily
clamoring to crawl into her lap, even as she folded her hands
and waited quietly for silence.

"My job is easily stated, too," she began. "It is to help bring
children into school situations so that they get off to a good
start and feel they belong. I do that not only for this kindergarten, but for any child who may transfer into Isaac Newton;
and also for each child who transfers out to another school in
our system. Just as we don't believe in dumping a group into
kindergarten, we don't favor dumping a class all at once into
junior high, or into high school. Each child moves on his own,
when ready. And many of our students, while still attending
here, will go for some work to the junior high, or even the high
school. If students move to a new school all at once, there ob-

viously is a lockstep system that pretends they are all alike. We've thrown out the old lockstep system. So when any of the children I handle are ready to move, I'm consulted, and also for each new child entering.

"We commence in May each year to canvass the new children eligible to start school. For this we form a task force, under my direction. If the children have siblings in school, we know something about the home. We'll try to visit it in any case, and observe the new child there — as well as make friends. The child and mother are invited to visit school for a party. We hold a series of such small parties. As we gather information and impressions, we get the data to the Evaluator's office. In September, we get a physical and health record set up on each child. Then we begin admitting them, just a few at a time. Each new child tours the school, meets specially selected teachers, aides, and also students. If the new child gets the impression this is a nice place to be, a friendly place, full of pleasant wonders, that is no accident. He sees many children well behaved, working away, and enjoying it. If the child is from a minority, or for any reason may feel inferior or strange, we take special steps. We get some Puerto Rican children now, for example. You can be sure they meet teachers who speak fluent Spanish and who have been to Puerto Rico just for this purpose.

"At first, this new group of six to ten children gathers in the small room you saw. As they play and talk, they are studied by a panel behind the mirror. Each one is observed, several times during the first week. During this period our teachers, who are experienced and highly trained for this work, join the panels and evaluate each child. We give a battery of tests during this week, too. Now, what I am going to say next may sound boastful, but I think it is fact: we know more about each child at the end of that week than the ordinary school ever knows in twelve years. And we know it *fast*. If a child can read, we know it. If a child is deaf, has a seeing defect, is undernourished, we know it. If there is an emotional problem, we spot it. There is no such thing in Newton as discovering that the reason a nine-year-old is so retiring is a speech defect. Here we'd know that by the first Wednesday.

"By the second week at latest, we have planned a tentative program for each child, and we are observing how the child is reacting to it—a check on our evaluations. If remedial help of some kind is needed, it has been begun, too. A child who can read is reading. A child talented in any direction is given free rein. The bolder children move into larger groups, the timid ones get more attention and reassurance. Where work in the home is indicated, our specialists have been given the assignment.

"Now the next group is admitted, and we repeat the process. Before two months are up, admissions are largely completed. We do advise some mothers to delay longer for special reasons; but if so we usually arrange meetings with the mother to help speed the day when the child can enter.

"Our panels during this period include teachers who specialize in this early identification work, two doctors who now are very expert at it, a psychologist, and our evaluators. If they need to consult a psychiatrist, a speech expert, or a linguist, that is provided for. And of course there is experienced clerical help available too.

"All of us who work with entering children feel very strongly about this—the first two weeks are a crucial period. If the child is disappointed, frustrated, frightened, embarrassed, or made to feel unwelcome, the effect may last for years. Coming to school is often the child's greatest experience up to that time. We feel the school must look on it as a great experience, too, and strain every resource to make it a success.

"The other admissions I deal with are less critical, but the difference is only in degree. Basically there is always the same need to orient and accept the student. Do we coddle them? I don't believe so. Remember that each student here is far more a free agent, is more mobile, works with many more adults than in a classroom school. He gets much more actual experience in adjusting to situations, including some he may not care for. It is the 'crippling' situation we work hard to prevent— the one in which the child feels confused or out of place, and yearns to escape. Prevent those, and the doors of learning open wider and wider."

"Before you begin asking questions of Mrs. Portal," Dr. Morrow said, "I greatly fear I must unfurl my balance sheet and play the auditor again. I can practically hear some of you wondering how we can afford this program Mrs. Portal has described. It does cost a tidy bit, to be sure, as against just putting a low-bracket young teacher in charge of the whole operation. But what we really are doing is preventing a host of problems that would otherwise show up later and continuing vexing us all for years. As any teacher or any administrator will agree, it is the *problems* that eat into time and energy, that frustrate, and sometimes seem to make a mockery of the whole proceedings . . . for example, when you find a number of your junior high students can't read or do simple arithmetic, as you begin to discuss the Constitution or the physics of motion. Under the old system, the cost of such problems is largely hidden — it shows up only when it becomes desirable to add teachers to cope with them. As long as a classroom teacher can struggle through somehow, sort of sweeping the educational dirt under the rug, no one is supposed to notice. But to deny that the cost is there is rather foolish. The school is paying teachers to teach, but they can't teach because of these problems diverting their time and energy.

"But even on an open and honest bookkeeping system, one of the main advantages of our early identification plan might not show up in a classroom setup. It does in ours. For we can see more clearly that it costs so much per year to keep each student in our schools. If a certain student gets through in ten years instead of twelve, we have saved more than a thousand dollars. The student we want to get through faster is the outstanding one, who can get to college sooner. Realize this: today more students are getting advanced and professional degrees, as a percentage of the whole, than used to even enter college about three generations back. Many a highly trained person is nearing thirty now before he or she can really take hold professionally. The more we can telescope the years of training, while maintaining quality, the better off the student is — and yet the less his education has cost him and the community. At the other end, we want to avoid the dropouts, those who leave school as soon as the law permits, only to find they land the poorest sort of jobs, if any at all. Early identification plays a major part in speeding the academically able student through, perhaps to early entrance to college, or to entrance with advanced standing, and at the same time, helps reduce the social waste of dropouts. When we tote up the accounts on this, we find here that we more than offset the cost of retaining the dropouts. Even though in five years the full effect of our early identification is far from evident, we could make out a pretty good case that it reduces costs overall, even on an out-of-pocket basis. The savings in human and educational terms, of course, is enormous. I don't know how you can measure it, though we certainly can observe it.

"In converting from a conventional school to a modern system, we put our major effort into working from the youngest students up. Curiously, that is just the reverse of the usual: many people working for this sort of change are locked into the secondary level, so the high school is where you'll find the new developments. We've made changes at all levels; but our concept is of a wave of 'new children' moving up the system. They are children who never have known the old class-and-grade arrangement. They'd be struck dumb at the notion of spending most of their time in one classroom with the same group and the same teacher."

A stream of questions almost overwhelmed Mrs. Portal, and it was some time before Dr. Morrow could break in.

"Our publications will answer some of your detailed queries," he said. "Now we must show you a circus. Just let me add, to give you perspective, that this kindergarten is a sorting-out pool. Some children may stay here up to a year, but most remain a good deal less. We move students out of here day by day, as they seem ready. Because we know so much more about each child, and have perhaps five times as much expertise to bring to bear, we get our children adjusted and ready, even eager, for school work a lot faster in most cases. The more we experiment and learn, the less stock we put in the conventional 'readiness' concepts. That is one reason you see typewriters here. Certain children who show no 'reading readiness' by ordinary standards will nevertheless become fascinated with these electric machines. Others who seem to have only the shortest attention spans sometimes show dramatic change when some of the handicaps they are under are recognized and dealt with. Still others who seem very shy and immature will also blossom when, among the five or six faculty people who work here part-time, they find one they can be responsive to, rather than having to relate to just one or two teachers. Some children require a man, for instance, to put them at ease — and where have you seen a male teacher in a kindergarten?

"In a word, our policy here is active. We don't push any child; but neither do we just baby-sit while he gets older. The school begins here. Our methods begin here."

Severe behavior problems have disappeared when children have been allowed to study independently. Nonreaders have become good readers; nonachievers have become outstanding achievers; social isolates and rejectees have become accepted, productive group members; and apathetic, reluctant learners have become eager and excited about learning.

E. Paul Torrance in *Theory into Practice*, December 1966

16

ESCAPE FROM THE
CLASSROOM

Our group moved upstairs and gathered in the corridor. Two large display cases on opposite walls caught our attention. Divided into sections, they exhibited student work of many kinds: compositions, some in printed form, drawings, models, scientific devices, illustrated reports, maps, sculpture, musical compositions, photographs. Dr. Morrow smiled as he rejoined us.

"I can't blame you for looking at those," he said. "Some of them are quite wonderful. This is part of our incentive program —at any one time, we have at least 50 achievements like these on exhibit about the school. We also have 40 or so of the best from all the schools on display around the town, in banks, stores, City Hall, and so on. It's hard to tell whether the students or the parents get the bigger bang out of this kind of recognition. Getting a project into an exhibit is a success every student in the school recognizes."

But [continued Dr. Morrow], we're up here to look at a "circus," a more basic part of our operations. When they hear that word some of our children expect animals at first, but of course it simply means a place designed for traffic to circulate. Some other schools use the term "cluster," which seems to us less apt.

As you saw on entering, this is an old school, typical of thousands of other "eggcrate" structures. We had classrooms, an auditorium, an undersized gymnasium, and little else. Our newest elementary school, now being built, has been completely designed for the new system; but here we make do. First, we knocked out a lot of walls, to get some flexible space. We also tore down the rear wall of the school for about 40 feet, and built a new wall some 14 feet further out. That gave us room for our two theatres, and a little extra footage we needed anyway, since the school was crowded. For the rest, we have had to improvise rooms and areas of various sizes in spite of the original egg-crate plans. We make do, not too badly; but let's hope no more public funds go into building schools that are monuments to the past, not machines for the future. I've seen some brand new ones that are glossy, but about as modern as a muzzle-loading cannon.

Broadly speaking, we have three kinds of space: for large-group, medium-group, and small-group activity. Those rooms on your left, for example, look much like the old classrooms — though I assure you they aren't used that way. That one has been made longer. It now provides working space for up to 40 students. This smaller one is equipped as a language lab, or the "drill lab," as we call it, since it is used for many repetition purposes. You'll notice these rooms are carpeted, as most of our rooms are. That isn't luxury. Carpeting, as quite a few schools have discovered, brings some savings and helps sound-proof. It also affects behavior favorably. A dropped book, for example, doesn't sound like an explosion and interrupt every-body, perhaps cause laughter and embarrassment. Since in a workroom, as we call our medium areas, many students are doing different work simultaneously, sound control and a non-raucous atmosphere are important.

Now, you will notice our drill lab has, instead of tables and chairs, fixed positions. Each provides earphones and a microphone. The teacher can listen in on each child by flicking a switch, and offer a correction or comment that the others do not hear. Or a tape can be fed to the earphones—any one of eight tape sources to any pair of earphones. Since each child hears only his own voice, it's a quiet room to him regardless of how it would sound if you walked it. Much of the time, all the children here will be drilling together. But at other times, especially when there are fewer children here, they may be doing quite different work, from the tape sources or with one or more teachers or operators. We believe in drill, for vocabulary, arithmetical tables, speech, certain factual matter, and of course foreign languages. The headphones and shielded microphones here, plus the sources, give us a room that is about 20 times as efficient in use of space and time as a plain room.

I should add that while we use drill a good deal, we always use it briskly, vigorously, and for quite brief periods at a time. Most children like drill this way. They don't waste time here drilling on things they know—a guaranteed source of boredom. They can see their own progress. Every day, there will be children in here on off-schedule hours, using tapes on their own initiative. Of course, there will be an adult present to help. You see why we can move a student ahead from one drill unit to the next so easily—just by hooking him up to it.

When we are doing group drill and a child feels he has mastered the material and no longer needs the drill, he tells us so. A teacher "checks him out." If he is correct, he is excused, until the schedule permits bringing him in for the next unit. When he is excused, he is instead on "non-sked" time, which he can use to follow his own interests or work on projects, as you'll see. *No child is bound to a group:* he is always an individual learning as an individual, and his progress in any drill program is recorded and controlled from his own card in that large rotary file on the desk. Incidentally, if a child is lagging in progress in drills, that fact becomes apparent very soon, and we investigate quickly to find out why. If he is too eager to drill, that too may be symptomatic. So this busy room serves in an additional way.

Now, let's cross the corridor. Here is a small-group area. As you see, we have knocked out walls to get a large room.

Those glassed-in cubicles around the far walls are the offices of the members of this teaching team. Each has a desk, a telephone, private files, a book case; and typewriters and dictation machines are available. We don't let teachers waste time not teaching—we have clerks and every machine that can pay its way in saving clerical work. On that score alone, three of our teachers do more *professional* work than four used to do, so we think offices, machines, and clerks are pretty good investments.

The work tables in the center are for the students. Those low dividers on the tables are movable, and help cut down noise and limit distraction. Here students can work on their own, or in groups of two or three, under the observation of teachers, and with teachers available to consult. Taking 30 students from an old-style classroom and putting them in here to work this way might create some behavior difficulties— though I don't expect as many as you might think. But remember that the students we put in here have never been in a classroom. They have been "brought up" in this new atmosphere. Working without constant "tell-me-what-to-do-now" supervision is normal for them. In general, they accept it, respond to it, and don't even think about it. For generations the classroom system has taught children quite effectively that teacher is there to keep them in order, and that therefore order comes from the teacher, not from them. Occasional lectures to the contrary don't offset the example. With some classes, the ordinary teacher doesn't dare leave the room. With others, leaving is done with the fingers crossed. The poor temporary substitute teacher expects and usually gets a rough reception. Here, we teach them from the beginning that *they* must be orderly and responsible, and that the teacher is there to teach and help them learn. It is not really a new approach: the Montessori people have been using it in their schools for many years. It's amusing to note that they even put rather fragile furniture in their schools, deliberately, rather than try to provide iron-clad pieces children *can't* destroy. Quite a difference in approach!

But please—don't jump to any false conclusions. We have

no interest here in the overdone "progressive" approach by which the child, in effect, bosses or overrules the teacher. We have not revived that monster in a new skin. Here there is never any doubt who is steering and guiding—not the child, but the faculty. What is required to be done or learned must be accomplished—and thoroughly. But if you go back to John Dewey directly, you may agree we are applying principles he might have approved. We put the child in a real-life situation: not the mock-life of playing store and such, but the reality of individual work to be accomplished under varying levels of supervision. Teachers coming here remark that all the children seem more mature. It is not that they are any less children, I assure you. They simply have been allowed and encouraged to assume responsibility in a normal way, instead of being taught to go with the class, lockstep, and do nothing till teacher says what to do.

Let me give an example that came to my attention recently. Three boys, one twelve and two older, decided entirely on their own to build a log cabin, in the country, and spent all summer on it. They read up on the subject, drew plans, sought out an old man who had built many, and found a source of suitable logs. Then they rented a chain saw, dragged their logs with an old car, and rigged a derrick to place them. They had the walls up and roofing begun by the time they went back to school. What did they do there? In shop, they made tie-racks. The rest of the time they spent in classes where some teacher told them what to do, minute by minute. Is the contrast painful? It is equally so with younger children. Have you seen them put together a complicated model in a few hours? In their school, the equivalent accomplishment would become a unit stretching over perhaps three weeks, each step made ponderous by the attempt to pull a whole class of assorted children along together.

Here we are able to let our children *go*. They are never in groupings that hold them back, nor any that try to hurry them along. In our small-group areas, like this one, children may work alone, writing a paper or report, or carrying out some project. You will notice the reference library over in that corner. You see the telephone there. With permission, a student may use it to get information: we teach them how to use the telephone to get information and facilitate work, much as we teach them how to exploit a library. Most of the time our children prefer to work in groups or teams of two or more often three, an arrangement that definitely keeps interest high, and almost invariably leads to each child learning something from the others. For the most part they form their own teams, which keep changing. We don't let them get frozen.

In their offices, the teachers can conveniently meet with student teams, or with individuals. Usually there will be such a meeting to launch a project, another to check its progress, and a third to review it when completed; but there is no rigid schedule of this kind—the teachers simply stimulate, guide, and criticize as each situation demands. Conferences are often quite short, just five minutes or so, with longer ones at intervals. Since any one child may meet with the various teachers he has four to six times a week, each teacher's opportunity to get to know and understand the child is enormously greater than under classroom conditions. We require that some of the conferences, on a fairly regular schedule, be with only one child. These are the main basis of reporting on the child's progress as the teacher sees it—reporting that is far more penetrating and meaningful than the mechanical recording of daily marks or grades, nonsense we dispense with entirely.

You see, then, why this room is set up this way. Students can work here while the teachers confer with one group, or individual, after another. Notice the little windows in the teachers' offices. When the window is open, any student may go up and ask a question. When it is closed, the teacher is not to be interrupted. I wish you could see all these rooms in action by coming in the daytime; but you will understand that we have to limit observers. A fair hubbub goes on here, but the children learn to keep their voices down, and the carpeting and sound-proofing also help. A reasonable background noise level seems to foster concentration rather than hurt.

Will you follow me please into this small room? It is specially equipped to supplement the teaching of reading. Schools have

been teaching reading for generations. It is one of their oldest
key tasks. You might think that research would be rich in conclusions on the best ways to do it. But amazingly, when we
first launched this experimental school, we could find only
scraps of valid research to help us, amid a forest of claims.
Now there is a bit more, and we keep refining our methods and
techniques as we can.

Our premise is simple: every child must learn to read well
and fairly early if he is to get a normal education. Except
for children with serious defects or emotional disabilities, every
student here does learn. We feel there is nothing more cruel,
more disgraceful in the conventional classroom system than
the pushing along, grade by grade, of children who can't really
read. Then, perhaps when the child gets to junior high school
and increasingly difficult work, there may be an attempt at what
is blithely called "remedial" reading. Pity the child who day after
day goes to school, knowing he is doomed to public failure
because he will be asked to do things that depend on reading
—and he can't read. While others in the class are answering
a quiz, he is trying to grasp the instructions. When others are
discussing a book or article, he must pretend he has read it
too, or sit on the sidelines. A word problem in arithmetic is
beyond him, even if he knows the mathematics it involves.
Year after year this fiendish torture is continued . . . then a
few hours of remedial reading may be scheduled, if the budget
permits a remedial teacher, and one can be found.

Of course, if the child is "held back," not promoted, because he can't read, the damage may be as great. To be left
behind, publicly shamed, put in with smaller children, branded
a failure at the tender age of eight or nine . . . but let's waste
no time detailing these miseries. When you scrap the classroom
system, you scrap these tortures too.

We use this room to help most of our children; but its
special purpose is to aid those who are slow to learn to read.
With our early identification system, of course, we know reading
abilities pretty well by the time a child has been in our school
a day or two at most. The children who can read when they
come, or soon learn to, may never see this room. Others are

obviously handicapped by the home they come from, by language, by the strata of society they live in. Let me offer a quick example. Try to teach such words as "throw" or "sidewalk" or "pajama" to a child who has never heard these words used. You might as well teach them to him in a foreign tongue! But if you did, you'd be aware they were foreign to him. You'd explain them. But in a typical first-grade classroom, a teacher who may be a good deal less than expert in teaching reading, or even a beginner, can be quite unaware that certain children before her never heard these words. The vocabularies children bring to the school vary enormously in nature and range — but only the expert realizes how much and why.

Motivations vary, too. One child is "bustin'" to read. Another expects reading to unfold fascinating wonders forthwith. At the other extreme, a child from a non-literate home may be quite unable to comprehend why other children are so eager to read. When he observes that the school appears to side with them, and puts great stress on an activity that has no role in the life he knows, he may well conclude he is in the wrong place, or he may feel inferior and handicapped. Resistance to learning to read can be built up instead of desire.

Even books themselves may appear quite different to the child who has been given books since infancy, who has learned to expect pleasure from this object, and to the child who has perhaps never had a book, and has had no such association. It can become for him an object that connotes humiliation and failure. And when reading and the use of books is constantly made a public affair, as a classroom activity, the embarrassment is painfully multiplied.

So we don't teach reading, as such, in classes. We don't even teach beginners in groups, except for those who are clearly going to become very good readers. We do work on learning letters and sounds, on word recognition and word building, in groups, sometimes using the drill lab for the purpose. But when it comes to the early actual attempts to read, most of our children work either alone with a teacher, or in teams of two or three. Some of the work is done in this room, which is equipped with machines for the purpose. There are now many kinds of machines available—this is one we are using now with some success. It projects a card, as you see, on this small screen. The operator can show a picture on the card, the word, or both, by wiggling this little lever. We now have six of the machines in use. Each child, or team, of those getting intensive work here has a special tray of cards. At first it holds much of the child's normal vocabulary. Then it is built up steadily—a constant measure of progress. In ten minutes here, a child will run through some 200 cards. Ten sessions a week mean 2,000 learning opportunities, with errors forestalled or at once corrected, and right responses continually reinforced. We often let the child typewrite as a reward. Effective as it is, this machine is only one tool of many. We have no cut-and-dried or official way of teaching reading: since we don't teach classes and do use experts, we don't need any. We use whatever combination of approaches and devices works best with the individual child. We put some in small teams that let the abler readers help and encourage the less able or younger.

In a word, we let nothing stand in the way of learning to read. We use everything that will help. That includes motivating and stimulating the child, which we do constantly in large groupings and small. It is a rare child indeed who does not want to read, once the pressure is taken off and success is assured by the personal attention of a teacher.

Now you are wondering how we can possibly staff this program. First note that we don't expend much effort on the able reader, who doesn't require it, and will in fact only be bored and held back by routine attention. We don't neglect them. We check on their progress, and help where necessary. We insist they learn the alphabet and proper spelling. But they learn fast and need little help. Our system lets us transfer time from them to those who need more work.

Second, remember here we don't go by the semester or year. We give many children intensive work, but perhaps for only two or three months. And we give this intensive work when it is needed, not to all at once. Other children may need four months, which we estimate is about equal to three years of routine classroom teaching of reading. Very few need more.

Our reading experts devote all their time to the reading program, and we use them very efficiently.

Third, we supplement our professionals with non-expert help, as I'll explain when we return downstairs. And perhaps I should add a fourth point: since we are willing to do whatever is needed to get a child reading early in his school career, we don't have to spend money later for "remedial" patchwork, nor do we carry the deadweight burden of non-readers right through high school. No, teaching reading as if you meant it has its economical side, too.

Now, while we go to the theatre over here, where large-group instruction is done, let me talk some about organization. In round numbers, this school has a population of about 550. Take out the kindergarten group, which fluctuates constantly, and certain special students, and we have roughly 500. We divide this into Lower School and Upper School, so now we have 250. This we divide once more into A and B circus groups, 125 or so each. Please avoid thinking of these numbers as parallel to classroom groupings: they are not nearly so rigid, and mean little in the instance of any one student. For example, one might be at times in Upper and at times in Lower School. I am giving you just the broad administrative framework.

The technique of organizing team teaching has been well worked out in many schools. Arrangements vary a good deal, but the basic idea is the division of students into parallel A and B groups. While the A half is in large-group functions, the B half is in medium- or small-group functions. Then they change around: the B unit uses the large-group facilities, while the A half moves into smaller groups.

Here we are now in one of our large-group facilities. This theatre serves the Lower School primarily. We call whatever goes on here "presentation." For most presentation, we need only one teacher and an aide. For some, such as a movie that does not call for teacher participation, there may be only an aide present. She can, if need be, call assistance quickly. This room accommodates up to 140 students. Normally we don't have more than 125. In a classroom school, we'd need four or five teachers to "cover" this many students. So you see this large grouping frees three or four teachers to meet with small groups, or with individuals, in the workrooms or small-group areas. Since students spend almost a third of their time in the theatre, we gain an important amount of teacher time this way.

As you'll note, this room is fixed up in theater style, with the rear seats rising on platforms so all can see well. There are four television receivers along the walls, used both for closed-circuit within the room, and for programs from outside or broadcast sources. Thus everyone in the room can see the tiniest object on the lecture desk, if the teacher points the camera at it. You'll observe that the desk is equipped for science work, with water, compressed air, and gas on tap. And this section of the desk swings back easily, to leave room for a small stage: we use dramatics a good deal. On the end you see an overhead projector. On this control panel are buttons which, as you see, lower or raise the louvered blinds on the windows, to darken the theatre to any degree wanted in daytime. Other switches here control or dim the overhead lights and the spotlights. I even have dials which show the room temperature and controls to regulate the ventilation.

I have more wonders for you. This button raises this screen behind me, to reveal a rear-projection screen. We can show anything from a slide to a film on it, without needing to darken the room more than slightly. This means that the teacher, in the midst of a lecture, can introduce a few minutes of film, or a sequence of slides, without fuss or interruption. Everything visual that can help him is at his command.

The same is true for sound. There are three tape machines behind there, in the projection room, all of which can be run from this console here, or the teacher can use this cue signal device, or he can talk directly to the operator through a mike. There are also a record player and a radio to pick up news events. And there is one tape console to record and play television programs. We hope to have several soon, as the cost of recorded television drops a bit more.

We have operators who service this equipment and set it up for presentations. For some, they stand by; for others they aren't needed. They are part-time workers, usually from the neighborhood, or parent volunteers whom we train.

In this corner closet over here is a second television camera, and some lighting equipment. And in this corner, you see, there is a glassed-in booth where a teacher may sit and work while keeping an eye on the presentation, if she is not active in it for a period.

All this sounds very elaborate, I'm sure. You can see why the children find this room a pretty exciting place to come to. But the cost of all the special equipment in this theatre, after taking advantages of discounts, some help from local business people and skilled volunteers, and some federal government grants, is under $8,000. Not only does this room permit enormously better instruction, but it saves thousands of dollars worth of teachers' time each year. Expensive? You answer that question.

The assumptions that underlie many present grouping practices, many extant teaching procedures, segmented vertical progression through prepackaged graded materials, promotion and non-promotion policies, and a host of other activities are fundamentally at odds with the assumptions that seem critically significant concerning behavior and the way in which youngsters live, learn, and grow.

Maurie Hillson in *The Non-Graded School,* edited by Richard I. Miller

17

THE IDEA OF AN OPEN SCHOOL

We took our seats again in the Faculty Room, with fresh appreciation of their adult size. Dr. Morrow perched himself on the long table on which literature was displayed, and resumed:

Now, you have seen a circus. In contrast to the "self-contained" classroom of the conventional school, it permits each individual child to *move*. Not just to another classroom, like a sheep going from one pen to another, but to a different situation, a different function; and not with a fixed group of other sheep, but fundamentally on his own, to serve his own needs as they arise—that is the idea I want to focus on now. It's the concept of an "open" school, one in which the fences have been knocked down: the fences of fixed grouping, of fixed facilities, of fixed time periods, of fixed subjects, of fixed sequences of learning.

So far we have just wet our toes. Put on your life jackets, please—we're going in deep now. But first let me mention those facilities we haven't time tonight to visit.

The auditorium and the gymnasium are not remarkable,

and still are about what you would expect in a school this old. Our library is more remarkable. First, of course, let me note that we *have* a library. A great many elementary schools don't, or have only an excuse for one. We take ours very seriously. We have a consulting professional librarian who serves all our elementary schools. Then we draw help from each of our teaching teams, and from some of our school clerks. There is also a student staff, which does a great deal of work, and finally we have some volunteers, mothers who work in the library on a regular schedule. We need a lot of help because the library gets heavy use, and we keep it open from eight-thirty in the morning to five o'clock at night, and Saturday mornings. It's also open a good deal on special schedule during vacations.

I pause to ask a question. Isn't it rather absurd to use public funds and facilities to set up a learning center, and then chase the children home when a bell rings at three? To shut the children away from our facilities during vacations, when they have the most free time? Perhaps absurd is not strong enough a word.

We not only keep the library open, but also other rooms. There is a craft and art room, a music room, a shop, and a lab. I must admit that the facilities are far less than ideal: we've stolen space wherever we could, and improvised a good deal. But the rooms are there, and the children use them. There is no compulsion to, in general, but most want to. To the children from less favored homes they can be particularly important, for almost everything in them is something that cannot be had at home, besides the freedom to work, and interested and skilled help and counsel at hand, much of it provided by volunteers, including some retired men who love to help. This is a community school—the community helps operate it. It is fascinating to see how the IQ barrier crumbles for some children when they are led into this new world of opportunity. Those who may have sat like vegetables now begin to request help and information. Their spans of attention grow rapidly. Often their achievements, when taken home, win praise from parents, and neighborhood attention. Once we have a child interested in something, *anything!*, and we know

what that something is, we have a starting point to spiral out
from. In the classroom system, a teacher can easily fail to
learn of such an interest, especially in the case of a student who
is shy, resentful, or distrustful. Here we dig for these key interests, help create them, and exploit them to the fullest. In some
instances the results are spectacular.

The benefits, of course, are not limited to this disadvantaged group. There is no telling, we find, which students will
suddenly blossom in this atmosphere. Perhaps you noticed some
of those fine photographs upstairs in the display cases. They
are the work of a ten-year-old boy, who develops and prints
them himself in the lab. He has now taught three other boys to
assist him, and they have quite a little business. To my amazement, they gave the lab a new enlarger last month, bought with
money they have earned and a prize one photo brought. This
boy is not outstanding in any other area—if he did not have
this opportunity, he'd be set down as average in ability and
below average in motivation and energy. A girl whose home life
is about as distressing as you could find is doing wonderfully
on the violin. Another boy, a Japanese, carries on the family
skill by raising flowers experimentally. You may have noticed
some around the various rooms. He has quite a respectable
grasp of Mendelian principles, as well as a great deal of skill.
These are some remarkable examples, but let's not undervalue
those that are less striking.

If you're wondering whether our teachers work longer
hours, they do. It's small wonder teachers in a classroom school
sigh deeply when the last bell rings, and hope to escape to
calmer, less frustrating scenes quickly. They still have a lot
of correcting to do, probably, and lessons and lesson plans to
prepare, as well as records to complete and reports to file.
Here, a teacher's life is considerably different. Clerks do the
clerical work, not teachers. Much of the correcting is done during the day, since immediate correction has so much more
value. Aides take care of arrangements, such as getting the
equipment that will be needed, or scheduling. Such lesson
plans as there are become a team problem, not a job each teacher
has to do for herself; and as you will see, there is no regular

planning for tomorrow's class because the class doesn't exist. So our teachers work a full day, and half also work through each of the vacations during the school year.

Our students don't hurry home, either. We keep a bus running, on a circular route, until after five. You'll often see it bringing students *back* to school, after they have gone home for some reason at the end of scheduled time. A school where you can grow your own way, and be successful, and never be bored, is a place a lot of children want to be.

So far, the differences between our school and the usual classroom type have been rather easy to see. But the core of the difference, the heart of it, is not something you can see. Let me approach it with a bit of our history.

When we first decided to experiment vigorously in our system, we chose this Isaac Newton School because it seemed rather typical, or median. After a summer of preparation, we dove right in, on as large a scale as we thought we might handle. Among other tests, we set up three teaching teams, drawing on the experience of many other schools. One team took in the fifth and sixth grades, another served the third grade, and another the first- and second-year students, who were non-graded.

Results varied. The fifth-sixth team got off to a fast start, and after some strain and crises along the way was adjudged a clear success by the end of the first semester. The third grade hit more troubles, and almost foundered from personality difficulties until some changes were made. Then it did fairly well. But the third team had the roughest going. It tried hard, and we gave it additional help. But the combination of the team method and non-grading soon had the team haggard, trying to meet all the problems of handling groups of several sizes and still letting individuals move freely. As in systems that have used non-grading for years, we still had classes, though a child might be moved from one to another working at a more advanced level at any time thought wise. We also had the usual subjects, a curriculum divided into fixed segments, and the segments in the usual fixed sequence. All of this we simply retained from past practice. Our teams and non-grading took so much of our attention that we felt we had radically changed from our old classroom system. In fact, we hadn't.

Each day we seemed to solve ten problems only to have twenty arise. We labored far into the night again and again trying to keep up with administrative needs, and to choose or create materials. For awhile we seemed close to admitting failure and scrambling back to where we had been. But by luck, a board member offered us a chance to arrange a three-day holiday conference at a nearby resort. A selected group of ten of us attended. For three days, we talked, argued, thought out loud, and got even more confused. But the seed was planted: some weeks later the session bore fruit, as we became able to see and at least state the underlying problem.

The nub of it was that we were trying to keep our groups, whether large, medium, or small, composed of students who were more or less at the same stage of progress in the subject — the familiar classroom approach. In the higher grades this did not create too many new problems. But combined with non-grading it spawned dozens. We had no way of advancing children except in large jumps. Had we not expected too much from non-grading we could have been content that we had improved over classroom annual jumps; but we had set our sights high, and the beginnings of our early identification program made us want much more room to handle children individually than the operation gave us.

The solution began to emerge. At first it seemed too bizarre and outrageous to consider. But as new ideas will, it became less horrifying as we got familiar with it. And as also will happen, as we got familiar with it, it turned out to be rather less new than it seemed at first. In fact, it began to look like an old and welcome friend in new surroundings. We simply observed that at least some of the time *there appeared to be no great reason why all in the group had to be at about the same stage of progress.*

For example, after a couple of automobile accident scares we arranged for two special safety lectures. How many groupings did we need? We had a very engaging safety expert available, a local man we had used before, and a film. It seemed clear that the lectures could be given to the entire school.

Soon after this, the third-grade team of teachers prepared a large-group presentation on water supply. On an impulse, we had them give it also to the fifth-sixth groups, and then, still unchanged, to the youngest group. In each case it went over well, except that the youngest group found it too long. We checked up on how much had been learned. The youngest students missed some ideas completely; but on the whole they seemed to grasp many of the basic concepts, and a good deal of information. There wasn't much difference between the two older groups. All three groups seemed to benefit amply from the time expended.

So we tested again. We selected a random group of sixth graders and third graders and some advanced first graders, and had a gifted mathematics teacher give them, separately, three sessions on graphs, graphing equations, and curves. This was new material to all of them, and it was presented to all in much the same way. Most members of all three groups grasped the basic ideas and procedures satisfactorily.

These findings, of course, should not have surprised us: there is plenty of research and experience to show that the conventional curriculum has little close relationship to what children *can* learn. But these instances opened our eyes to the solution of our problem.

Let me digress a bit now, for a little mind-loosening. Pardon me—but my experience tells me it's necessary. We are all so steeped in the class-and-grade system that we are not aware how conditioned we are. We went through this system as children. Then again as parents. Some of us work in the system. None of us, I believe, can have had much contact with the class-and-grade system without frequently becoming aware of its shortcomings. But such weaknesses can be experienced and even suffered without insight or understanding— without even attributing them to their source. The system is so pervasive, so established, that it scarcely occurs to us, except under strong prodding, to even for a moment consider the possibility that there may be alternatives. And when we do, we do not view the alternative and the old systems from an *external* point of view. Rather, we view the new system *from* the old, and often it is hard for us to realize that is what we are doing. We are like the trolley-driver who is made a bus driver: he is at first aghast that he has to steer, something he never did on the trolley. He has the feeling only because he is looking at the bus from the viewpoint of the trolley. Had he been driving a truck he would not give a second thought to having to steer. Do I make my point?

Mentally we may let go our grasp on one phase of the old class-and-grade system, not realizing that to compensate we are holding firmer than ever at several other places. Indulge me in another analogy. Suppose you had been a clerk in an old, service-type food store for many years. The store is closed, and now you work in a large self-service supermarket. You feel a great wrench. Again and again you have to give up old ways, old habits of thought, because they make no sense and have no place in a self-service concept. You will feel just this kind of wrench, the same sense of floundering, the same irritating necessity to change and adjust again and again, as you move from the old class-and-grade system, rigidly oriented toward administration, to the new system, freely oriented toward the student. They are polar opposites. You can't get from one to the other timidly, inch by inch. Nor can anyone make the mental switch without some mental sweat.

The class-and-grade system was not in use long before the falsity and human cost of its lockstep approach became evident. There is a long history of attempts to change it or modify it, to rectify its painfully obvious shortcomings. One of the earliest introductions of the classroom system was in the Quincy Grammar School in Boston in 1848. It was quite a few years before the classroom idea took wide hold and became the prevailing system. But the various "plans" were being advocated and tried well before that.

In 1862 there was interest in the St. Louis Plan of quarterly promotion. A few years later there was the Pueblo Plan, which called for "homogeneous" smaller groups. The "track" idea was introduced around 1893 in the Cambridge Plan. The Elizabeth Plan called for free promotion any time of year. The idea of fixed requirements to be completed to govern pupil movement was embodied as early as 1898 in the North Denver Plan, and later emerged as the famous Dalton Plan, around 1919, and the Winnetka Plan, about as old. The "platoon" idea dates from 1900 in Bluffton, Indiana, and 1908 in Gary. This by no means covers all the "plans"—but you see how far back the efforts to "do something" about the system go. Even today you can hear administrators talking about "track" systems and some form of checkpoint advancement as if those ideas were not old and ragged.

Most of the plans I have mentioned got a good deal of attention in their day, but none got far in solving the problem. We can see better now why they didn't: they changed one or two elements, instead of changing the basic theoretical approach. You might say they were attempts to put a steering wheel on the trolley, while still leaving it on the tracks.

Now let me spell out what is fundamental to the class-and-grade system. Think of it in its early state, to make the principles clearer. The system is still with us, however much compromised and complicated.

First, the lockstep system forced the students into *groups,* fixed groups. Not for educational reasons, note, but for administrative convenience, including economy and good use of what teachers were available.

Second, it chopped up education (then elementary education) into neat, equal *segments,* like wedges of a pumpkin pie. This process has run on so far that today even our great universities give you a bachelor degree not when you prove understanding or accomplishment, but when you have a sufficient number of "points"—exactly as you ladies can get a coffee percolator when you have saved up enough trading stamps. The sheepskin dispensers don't even bother to blush as they solemnly affix the learned institution's seal.

Third, the class-and-grade system set these segments in a fixed time sequence, with segments coming one after another as undeviatingly as the vertebrae of a snake. There are still a great many people who accept without the slightest challenge the time sequences they are familiar with, and the idea that there must be a fixed time sequence. "School" is thought of *as* a time sequence, in which subject follows subject, course follows course, and grade follows grade.

Groups, segments, sequence — none of these concepts is from the tablets Moses brought down the mount. None is in any way fundamental to education. None is valid for today's needs. *All three ideas have to be swept away to break the hold of the classroom system.* Realistically, children can't be forced into groups that will permit their being treated as alike, or even as similar. Individual differences and variances are just too great. What we call "education" can't be parceled up neatly into unit segments, unless we are willing to stretch pretense past the breaking point. Nor is there any one or ten fixed sequences of study that are best or inevitable or true for a variety of students. Let us not be deceived by this administrative claptrap a day longer, however well it may be accepted in some surprisingly high places. Not if we genuinely regard the individual as important, and his individual education!

I see from your faces that some of you are baffled. You are thinking: how can you operate a public school without these devices? How can it be structured, how can it be afforded? Let me clarify.

I'm not saying don't group. There is nothing wrong with grouping per se. A school where each child always worked alone, and never shared the excitement and interchange of a group would be dull beyond description, and would deprive the child of an important share of essential preparation for living. I'm saying simply, don't group for administrative reasons, but for educational reasons. And don't have fixed groups, because no child stays fixed. A fixed group is automatically administrative.

Nor am I objecting to one thing coming after another. You can't do everything at once. I am just saying that we have to recognize, unless we are blinded by conventions and habit, that the sequences on which we build subjects and courses are largely arbitrary. They don't have to be the same for each child. They don't have to be rigid, fixed. There doesn't even have to be just one sequence operating at a time. You can conceive, perhaps vaguely for the moment, that in our circus there could be one sequence for presentations, another for the workrooms, and still another for small-group. Besides that, there might be one for the student's non-sked time.

Consider the way a boy learns baseball in his neighborhood. He learns to throw, to catch, to bat, to field, the rules of the game; but of ten children, no two will learn these in quite the same sequence. If baseball were a subject being taught in a classroom, however, the normal effort would be to construct a fixed sequence, and try to make each child follow it. And after a time this sequence would be taken very seriously, and possibly become the topic of furious debates as to whether this or that minor alteration in it should be made. I submit the fixed sequence is an attack on the natural way of learning.

But what about the teaching machine and programmed learning, which seems to prove so effective? Isn't this a fixed sequence in the greatest detail? Yes and no. First note that the writer of a program would be the first to admit that it is only *one* possible program for the purpose. Ten other writers would turn out ten other programs, all of which might be effective. Second, note that ten students using one of these programs will follow ten different sequences of learning, as they make errors or fail to grasp points, and are sent back at various points. But more important, programming is by nature most suitable for small, rather sharply defined blocks of "hard" learning. The sequences I am discussing are on a much larger scale—for the moment I will have to call them sequences of subjects and courses. Here again I say: if you find these sequences frozen, or relatively inflexible from kindergarten on, you should suspect administrative reasons and convenience, not educational motives. To chop up education into neat units and set them in neat order is tidy. Tidiness is a fine middle-class virtue. But in education it must be highly suspect. Human beings have refused to fall into neat packages for many thousands of years.

Perhaps it will help us think this through if we change the scene. Forget schools for the moment. Imagine, if you will, that you have been given charge of the education of a prince, one in no danger of becoming a ruler. But money, privileges, all facilities, are available. You are assured charge until the boy is seventeen or more. You are required only to give him the best education for *him*, one that will develop him to his fullest, even while it prepares him to live in the modern world.

This fiction, you see, puts administration out of the picture. You are concerned only with education. What do you do now? Do you put your prince in a class with 20 boys and insist they progress in lockstep fashion—however modified or disguised? Of course not. Do you select ten youngsters as closely matched to your prince as possible, and operate a "homogeneous" class? I doubt very much you would try anything so artificial.

What about segments and sequences? Would you now sit down, and labor over a curriculum for 12 years ahead, plotting just how much time would be allotted to each, just when each would begin and end? Or would you say, "We shall begin with a loose, broad plan. We shall expose the boy to many learning opportunities . . . and see which way *he* moves!" Dealing with one boy, you are aware plainly enough that he may show a flair for languages, or for mathematics, or for music—or prove a dunce in any one. What use is a detailed plan until you know? You might well see, too, that in a field such as history it is hardly pressing to decide that Recent European will be studied when he is ten, Ancient History at eleven, and American History at twelve. Any such ruling is obviously arbitrary. Might it not be wiser to decide that all three should be covered, but that the order is best dictated by his interests at a particular time? If he wants to learn all about America after a visit there, will you tell him, no, the subject is scheduled for two years hence? In science, will you insist he study Chemistry if he shows a growing interest in Biology? If for any reason he gets deeply fascinated by Geometry, will you tell him that Algebra must come first?

To let him roam from subject to subject and end up with a hodge-podge, with painful gaps showing, would be regrettable, true. To choke off his interests when they are keenest in order to hold to an arbitrary schedule and sequence is equally so, and stupid to boot. There is nothing a teacher can hope for so much as interest in what she is teaching, when she is teaching it. The proper aim must lie in between: to utilize the student's interests fully, yet guide him to a final result, a formal education suited to him, and to the world he will live in, so far as we can manage.

We arrive at the conclusion that the curriculum and sequence of study had better be adapted to our prince, not he to it. But where should we begin? What should he or must he learn first? We can agree, I suspect, that he needs certain *skills* first, because these are the tools he will use to learn further. Of skills, reading is by far the most important and urgent. It will be obviously helpful that he learn to write and spell. He must attain a minimum facility in mathematics, and also in manual dexterity, in arts or crafts, and in larger muscle coordination, if he can.

That is a good start. Over a longer period we can add skill in expressing himself orally and in writing, in communicating; skill in listening, to follow instructions, to grasp meaning. He should learn how to read books for content, for information, for enjoyment; how to use a library; how to evaluate what he reads or hears; how to organize a task, utilize data and research, put ideas in order, assemble evidence. Certainly we want him in this age to have a deep understanding of the scientific approach and method. And enough general academic skill to follow a discipline, not just skim it. Overall, we want to be sure he has the key skill of applying himself to a job or course of action and carrying it through. These are the skills that count; but you find few listed in the ordinary curriculum, which isn't conceived in these terms at all, but only in terms *convenient* for the lockstep segment and sequence system of the classroom school.

If our prince achieves these skills to a reasonable degree, we can feel reasonably confident of his achieving a respectable education. We do not need to worry too much about "content," or factual information. Unless we lock him in a tower cell, he will acquire an ample store — and know how to supplement it quickly as needed. Of course, the more we expose him to, the more we may expect him to pick up. What we do have to check is his store of basic ideas, or *concepts*. He will not go far in mathematics if he has not grasped, for example, the structure of the decimal system, the idea of equation, of negative numbers. He could know a miscellany of facts in history, yet miss the key concepts. In every field there are these key concepts: ideas, relationships, sometimes devices. Understanding them is the hallmark of the educated man, and the basis of communication among specialists. They form a structure on which information can be hung, and which will support further moves higher into any discipline or field of knowledge.

Skills, content, concepts. To think in these terms about our prince's education can be far more fruitful than to think in terms of subjects in a fixed sequence.

We see, too, that we cannot educate our prince in isolation. We can hardly pretend he is prepared for the world he must live in unless he has experience in groups of many sizes. He needs the stimulation, and even the frustrations, of working with others — one or two others, several others, many others. He needs social experiences, to give and get esteem, to succeed and fail alone and in the sight of others, if he is to build a proper estimate of himself, and confidence. If these are not academic aspects of his education, it is still wise, surely, to offer opportunity for this experience if we can. And we see that even though we *can* give our prince purely individual attention and instruction, we scarcely want to all the time. Shall we have him drill in a language alone, when it is more stimulating and interesting to do it in a group? Shall we have a visiting lecturer speak to him alone, when an audience of 200 would make it a better lecture? If a group of ten would permit a lively discussion, shall we deny him the right sized group? I think we could only conclude that he will be best off in the group that is best *educationally* for the function of the moment.

So much for our prince. Now let's try to organize a school for 500 princes. We may have to do some tailoring to fit our commoner purse; but we can still take the same approach: educational desirability, not administrative convenience. We can organize not to treat each child as alike, but as different. If to do so we have to sweep away such rusty devices as fixed grouping, fixed subject, fixed sequence, then out they must go. Here, they've gone!

❝*Every learner says in effect, 'I am ready and eager to learn, but what you have to offer must be personally significant to me, appropriate to my present level of growth, and related to my goals for the future.'*❞

H. Gerthon Morgan in *NEA Journal,* November 1959

18

SKILLS, CONCEPTS, CONTENT

An owlish-looking man, with heavy black eyeglasses, red hair, and an engaging smile opened the door tentatively, and was waved inside by Dr. Morrow. "Just in good time," said Dr. Morrow. "This is our Evaluator, Mr. McMurray, who tells us how each child is doing—and hence how *we* are doing. He does a lot of work at night, so I'm glad he could join us. Catch your breath, Lloyd, and we'll call on you shortly."

You are eager, I'm sure [went on Dr. Morrow], for me to come down to cases, to tell you how we do operate. I'm more than willing; but as I have said, we have all been brought up in the classroom system, and it is something like that octopus of underwater fiction that keeps laying on new tentacles as the previous ones are cut off. One reason is that our educational vocabulary stems from the classroom system, and when we use the old words we drag along the old ideas. We find it necessary to develop new words and new meanings, to operate our new system. So I can't just describe—I have to explain, too.

Let's consider a boy. We'll call him Joey, and he's in our Lower School, and just seven. Joey comes to school in the morning and reports to a regular place. Here he joins a "unit," a group of six or seven students. The unit is a flexible, rather temporary grouping for administrative purposes, and often will include some children from the same neighborhood, though the makeup of a unit is a casual and pretty random matter. Each unit has a student chairman and a secretary, offices which rotate every few weeks. The officers check attendance, convey any announcements or changes of plans, see if all members feel well, handle any other unit matters, and then report to a faculty member who comes by. All this takes just a few minutes.

Perhaps there is a new child up from kindergarten this morning. He is introduced to the unit, which takes him under the wing — pompously, but effectively. All members keep an eye out for him as they move around the circus and sit next to him if he is in the same room. The newly "up" child wears a pin and ribbon, presented as an "award." All the students are trained to be helpful and friendly when they see the ribbon, and they do a good job. Faculty, too, greet the new student. If all this makes him feel very welcome and important, that is precisely what we intend.

Joey's schedule calls for theatre next. He learned his schedule when he first came "up." It has since been altered and modified many times, but since the changes come one at a time, Joey knows where to go as well as he knows his way around his own home. To a new child, we give a card which serves as a guide for the first few days. It is color-coded, to match the doors of the rooms, so he can figure it out himself, or he can ask an older child to read it for him. Rarely does this cause any problem: by the time a child is sent up he can manage himself this way quite readily, if he is allowed to and expected to. Joey, an old hand, goes to the theatre with anticipation. Like most of the children, he finds the shows there "better than television," and seldom if ever has he been bored there. He is very curious to know what the program will be today.

If Joey is progressing well, he may go to the theatre as many as ten times a week. If he is having trouble of any kind, he may be diverted to another room for special work. He will miss some presentations, but as you will see that is not of much concern in the overall picture. You can see that this continuing series of presentations, each done expertly, with every aid that will help, and each checked and rechecked for value and effectiveness, is tremendously stimulating. The children pick up great gobs of information. They develop interests, and ambitions. Perhaps best, they acquire a thirst to know more.

Now, you have seen the theatre, and you gather *how* we work in it, but now I must explain what we are trying to do there. So let's leave Joey, his eyes big as they move from screen to master teacher and back, laughing one moment, frowning with hard thought the next. We'll come back to him.

We had to scrap the word "subject." Doesn't "subject" call up vividly a certain class, a certain teacher, a certain year? So we use "phase." We speak of the science phase, or the English phase, or spelling phase. It does *not* mean subject in the old sense: it means a particular field of learning without beginning or end or walls. Because we have dumped the "subjects" of the old system. We consider any phase in terms of *skills, concepts,* and *content.*

So let's take a look at four old-system "subjects" in the light of this division into skills, concepts, and content.

Reading is almost wholly a skill. What is read, at this early level, is usually diverse and of minor importance: while the child is acquiring skill in reading, the main concern should be interest and reward. We are not really worrying that he learn the content or factual material. Please don't think by that that we favor texts of the "See the man run, why does the man run" variety. We think whatever he reads should be worth reading. But we are a long way from McGuffey days, when a year might be spent plowing through an assortment of pious selections. Then the content of the selections was thought very important, in part because it was considered to have great moral values, and in part because there wasn't much else around to read. Today we are trying to enable our children to wolf down 50 books a year, plus magazines and newspapers, not to mention comics, cereal boxes, and bubble gum wrappers. In reading, then, skill is almost everything, and content is minor. The same is true for concepts. Much later, our students may find language itself fascinating for concepts; but right now we think the skill must be given all the attention.

Now contrast *mathematics*. Here we have concepts, right from the start, if the phase is properly taught. Content? You might call the tables that, and some skill is involved in using them, and the algorithms or procedures. You can see that the real mathematics teacher will begin with concepts right off, while the teachers who dislike and fear the subject will tend to go heavily for the tables and algorithms, avoiding concepts if they can. (Incidentally, note that when we analyze by skills, concepts, and content, we get new insight into teachers' strengths and weaknesses.) The further we move along in mathematics, the more concerned we must be with concepts and skills in using them. Content, or factual information, remains a minor factor.

Consider *science*. It is no secret to you, I'm sure, that some scientists are outraged at the way science is taught at the lower levels. Many concepts *can* be taught, right from the start; but again, to teach them it is helpful to understand them, and far too many elementary teachers simply don't. So they bring content to the fore, instead. Students are told a lot *about* science. They are shown demonstrations that are labelled "experiments," although they are not experiments at all. And usually, no skills are taught. Here at Newton, we feel information is only miscellany unless it is tied to concepts. We begin science with concepts, just as in mathematics. Students conduct genuine experiments, conceiving them, executing them, and evaluating results. And since we see that skills are needed more and more as one gets deeper and deeper into a science, we begin teaching them at the outset, too. It may startle you to see Joey peering into a microscope or weighing out chemicals on a balance he has built, but why not? Science demands sure, accurate techniques, careful observation, and creative ingenuity. Here science is not taught by young ladies who wish they could somehow get out of teaching it. It is taught solidly. Analysis by concept, content, and skills helps us do so from the outset.

Now, think about *social studies* — beginning to rival science for unhappiness over the way it is taught. A lot of the usual syllabus goes back to a 1916 committee report, so it is barely possible that things *are* a bit out of date. As I've said, once these sequences are set up, they tend to become sacred mummies, not to be profaned by feeling for a pulse. In this field, too, what should be *concepts* are often converted into *content,* mostly because the teaching of concept isn't adequate. Teaching content always seems so much easier! The child is *told* that there is a police department, or that daddy gets paid for his labor, but the underlying concepts don't get across. In time, the concepts that should stand out in shining clarity in history, civics, geography, and other social study areas are apt to be buried under a rubble of fact. *Skills* usually are passed over: how many high school graduates, for example, can really read maps?

In this school we regard concepts as the basic structure. Facts clothe the concepts, as a building's walls and floors and roof are attached to its steel framework. So concepts and facts must be taught together. Consider such concepts as "world," "city," "trade," "navigation," "climate," "history." You do not get those across to a seven-year-old in a hurry. But we want to get them across as soon as possible, so other concepts can be meshed with them, and facts attached to them. We can *aim* to accomplish this; and since we are clear on objectives we can *measure* how much understanding is achieved. Not by using true-false quizzes, I might add. The "objective" type of test is tied to content-teaching.

Before going further, I should stress that there are, of course, other advanced school systems which are trying to accomplish the same results we are after here, and they approach the problem in various ways. I don't mean at any time to suggest that our arrangements are the only possible ones, or the best for all time, or the outcome of inevitable logic. If we have something of a solution here, it is only one of many possible. But this we would submit: that *however a school is structured, to be highly effective it must have a clear notion of what it is teaching— skills, concepts, content—at any particular moment.* Once you begin to think in these terms (whatever actual words you may use), you begin to see what you are really trying to do. You get rid of the hodgepodge that seems more respectable when it is called "subject." Curriculum ceases to be so many one-pound, heat-sealed packets of hamburger, and becomes instead a rational, interconnected structure, not artificial or arbitrary, but attuned to the way real, live human beings learn.

Here let me mention in passing what I think are a couple of gilded entrances to blind alleys. One is the notion that if you subdivide the packets of hamburger again and again, until finally you have them bite-size, you have somehow made progress. Sorry, it is still packaged hamburger. This avenue has been tried again and again with negative results. It looks like a change, but fundamentally it is only a complication. There is no change in thinking. The same is true of fractionating grades, or using "track" systems. All you end up with is a more complicated version of a false premise. None of these moves brings you in harmony with how humans learn and grow — *not* in an orderly way, *not* in equal increments, *not* in a neat sequence.

The other notion is that human beings are large pigeons. A clever experimental psychologist can teach a pigeon to dance in a figure-eight in a few minutes by "reinforcement." The principle is highly useful when applied to programmed instruction, which unquestionably can teach with sometimes astonishing effectiveness and efficiency. But while you can get a highly trained pigeon, I doubt the world will ever see an educated one. *We think here of an educated person as one who has an interconnected structure, a web, a fabric, of concepts, information, and skills.* You can use the reinforcement method to help teach a man to operate a milling machine. But the educated man's understanding of the machine rests on a broad base, perhaps on a conglomeration of physics, economics, human relations, business administration, European history, and so forth. His understanding of the machine draws from all these areas. To understand the Renaissance, or Shakespeare, or the Civil War, you must draw on a variety of concepts, a mass of information or content, and use a complex of skills. Here you are far beyond the scope of simple "reinforcement."

The ability to put together, to compare, to relate, is what is important. The resemblance between the human brain and our new giant computers has been well noted: but the human brain has almost infinite capacity, can store ideas as readily as data, and its owner can combine and utilize concepts, content and skills in marvelous variety. It's only human, perhaps, to forget how human we are—but it *is* a mistake.

One further thought must chasten an educator. The children we are educating in this school will live in a world we have never seen and cannot foretell. We can't prepare them *for* it in any strict sense, but only to live in it—to meet whatever conditions and problems they have to—by drawing on the educational preparation we have given them.

Now let's get back to Joey. I know that to think of a school stripped of the familiar "subject" courses is not easy. As we follow Joey and his peers, and see how our large groups, medium groups and small groups facilitate teaching skills, content, and concepts, I think you will gradually build your understanding of the new kind of school. Remember please: when you are talking "subject" and "course," "hours," "points," "credits," you are talking *administration*. When you talk skills, content, concepts, you are talking *education*.

Let's continue speaking of large groups. The prime function of our presentations is to build *comprehension of concepts*. The theatre is next to useless for developing skills; and while the students do pick up a sometimes astonishing amount of content there, we do not rely on it for that purpose. You have likely noticed that before children read, they tend to pick up bits of information visually and aurally with great ease. As they learn to read, they seem to shift over rapidly to the printed word as their source. For children from culturally less favored homes, who may learn to read later than others, our presentations do have important content value. If Joey is from such a home, he feels no sense of handicap as he sits in the theatre. Once he becomes used to the situation, which may overstimulate or overwhelm him to some degree the first time or two, he is apt to enjoy it hugely. He is relaxed—no one is going to call on him, or make him stand up, or go to the chalk board. For two or three weeks, we find, he may refuse to talk about the presentations. Then it may be hard to turn off his talking! The continuing function of the theatre presentations is to expand the *conceptual* world of each student, and we find it highly successful for this purpose right through high school. It is most effective during these earliest years, and especially so with the less privileged children, because it bypasses reading and all other prerequisites. So it has the important incidental function of giving the lowest 20% to 40%, depending on the school, a vital "break" that lets them get started in school on much more even terms than under the classroom system.

When we first launched this program, we invited all concerned to submit lists of concepts it should include. The raw list ran above 400. We worked it over, culling out those we didn't feel were concepts, combining others, until we had 280. Since then, we have dropped some, added others. Our Lower School list is now fairly stable, with a "hard" group of 210 concepts, plus a "soft" list of 82. By "soft" we mean those that are important, but not necessarily so to every child. The "hard" group concepts are those we want every student to have a firm grasp of.

Please understand that a presentation is *not* planned or given like a class lesson. Presentations are a new concept. They don't run any set time. They may last 20 to 35 minutes for the younger children, up to an hour in high school. Sitting in on some, you might find it hard to say what "subject" was being taught, or what the main point or object was. In the earlier years, particularly, they tend to be discursive; as students advance, the presentations become tighter in construction, and go deeper into a topic, rather than relate horizontally. But for Joey and his peers, we are not trying to slam over a single concept each time, but to stimulate his thinking and give him material to think *with*. Presentations are also planned so that missing a few does not leave a hole, a gap.

Please remember again that here we do not believe in trying to teach a group of children a group of ideas or facts in a set, arbitrary sequence. We know that such an attempt is fighting nature: *different children learn in different sequences — no power on earth can force them to learn successfully in somebody else's sequence.* So instead of taking a concept and building a presentation for it, which implies a fixed sequence, we use a "weaving" approach. You will find me using that simile again and again, because it is basic to our thinking. We will try to bring several concepts into a presentation; then, a bit later, approach some of these same concepts from a completely different point of view; and so continue to combine.

The reason is simple, and every classroom teacher knows it from experience. Let us say we are trying to explain a concept. For it to be really grasped, it must "hook on" to concepts and information, perhaps experiences too, that the child already has. (You will remember William James on the subject.) Now, if we had some sort of mental X-ray and turned it on each child, we would find that each had a different assortment of concepts, information, and experience—a different set of hooks. Only in the case of identical twins, equally healthy and brought up together, might you find a similar set of hooks. So if you are fortunate enough to have found an excellent way to explain your concept, perhaps as many as 80 out of 125 children may grasp it. Their assortment of hooks are adequate. That leaves 45 not yet reached. Try another way to explain it, reaching for a different set of hooks, and you may add 25 to those who understand. A third way may add another batch. Of course, each time you explain the concept a new way, you also strengthen understanding in those who grasped it before. So we routinely present concepts in several different ways, in different contexts.

Let me illustrate. Today Joey may be listening to a talk about automobiles and how they are made, illustrated with pictures and movies and perhaps a model car examined via closed circuit television. The key concepts involved may be "trade," "cities," and "change-sequence," or development. "Trade" is dealt with in terms of what must be bought to make cars and how the cars are marketed. "Cities" come in through discussion of where cars are made and the need for plants to be located near where workers live. A review of old cars and of their gradual change from horse-and-buggy inspiration to modern design conveys the idea of "change-sequence"—a concept we consider of top importance, because it is essential to understand both history of any kind and the frantically changing world we now live in.

Two weeks from now, Joey may be rapt over a presentation on ancient history and archeology. He will hear of cities built and destroyed time and again, of trade over great distances by sea and land, as men sought metals for weapons and dyes for ornament, and of the slowness of sequence-change in those times. Still another presentation may deal with the oceans, yet these same three concepts may be woven into the topic, along with others. You are ahead of me, I am sure, in grasping that by this program we not only avoid much fractionating of knowledge to make it fit an arbitrary syllabus, but positively integrate right from the outset.

In three years, chances are Joey will sit in on about 900 presentations. Each one, remember, has been expertly conceived, thoroughly prepared, and given with skill and every possible technical aid. Further, each has been checked and re-checked for effectiveness. Do you wonder Joey may know a great deal, and grasp a great deal, before he is ten? We, of course, will not have to wonder: we will know. For periodically we will check on Joey's progress, by tests, by what he writes and says, and by what he reads—all reliably and systematically evaluated. If gaps in his knowledge and understanding show up, we move to fill them.

Now you may be questioning how we can assemble this huge number of presentations. Is it really so big? Consider: at present, in a conventional classroom school, any fourth grade teacher is actually making about as many "presentations" in a single school year! Of course, she may not realize it, and she has little time and less help for preparation, and not much in the way of technical aids; but it is probably a rare day that she does not, half a dozen times, go into fairly lengthy explanations or discourses on various subjects, more or less tied to the subjects she teaches. It is not news that teachers do a great deal of talking, nor that they are not always too well prepared to talk. Under the demands of the classroom system, no teacher can be—at least, not by our standards here.

We have a team to prepare each of our presentations, and it can and does draw on our entire system faculty plus outside resource people. And bear in mind that we do not keep creating hundreds of new presentations. Many are, in whole or part,

recorded. Others are in script form, with all needed supple-
mentary materials listed. Then, too, we repeat quite a number,
at intervals of several months or more. Some are so often re-
quested by the children that we run them in non-sked time.

As we refine and polish, we find a growing list that can be
shown over a surprisingly wide age range. Joey may watch a
presentation and respond to it quite differently from Helen,
twice his age; but both enjoy it and profit. We all know this can
be so from home television. Certain programs are for certain
ages, others interest the whole family. Because the adults watch
with a different context of knowledge and experience from that
of the children, you might in a sense say they are seeing different programs. Surely you have had the experience, too, of re-
reading a childhood book as an adult, and discovering in it
new or greatly altered meanings. Just so, as we repeat presentations, children draw new understandings from the same material, and deepen their perceptions.

We have no set form for presentations. Each new one is
assigned to a committee of three or four. After discussion,
someone is named to rough out an outline. Resources are then
examined, and the outline may be modified to make better use
of known resources, or there may be a further hunt for resources, such as pictures, films, an informed person or specialist who is available. At some point the question of "presenter"
arises: perhaps a particular person is called for, perhaps not.

We have a cross-index file on every member of the faculty
and one on resource people in or near the community who can
be called on. If they are personable and excellent speakers,
and willing, we may use them directly. If not, we pick their
brains, and one of our master teachers becomes the presenter.
For example, not long ago we had a high school science teacher,
an expert on certain aspects of sound, make an Upper School
presentation. Feedback, which is our broad term for reaction
which may influence the presentation, showed areas of weakness. We had sound-taped the presentation, so we had a version to begin improving. We asked the teacher to redo one part,
and put that on film. We had students design and build some
better equipment for demonstrations. The second version,

with a new presenter doing much of it, did better. Some "bugs" showed up in the demonstrations, however, and one section ran too long. The third version is much smoother. And it is now in such "set" form that the presentation can be given any time, with little new effort. The presenter need only play a tape to refresh his memory, and order the demonstration devices and recorded portions readied.

You can see why presentations actually save our teachers a great deal of time. They don't have to do the same work over and over, as in a classroom situation. Most of their effort can go into creating and improving—and checking on results. I should add that we are opportunistic, too. We buy or borrow some materials. We keep a close eye on news events and on our neighboring big cities. Last year we used a baseball World Series as a springboard for a myriad of projects. We snared three Bolivian Indians, a rocket scientist, a diplomat of some note, and a young female Olympic swimming champion—among others. We like to use the flexibility of the presentation program to help make school a pretty exciting place to come to.

I hope I have made clear our approach to the presentation. You see that it is quite a long way from merely being a large class, nor has it much in common with the "survey" type of course. There is hardly a trace of the fixed sequence approach. Rather, there is a deliberately random sequence, with each concept coming up again and again. The total effect for any half-year is anything but random: it works out very close to what we intend. We think this program is in harmony with the way people naturally learn concepts. It both permits and encourages the integration of knowledge, even more strongly than the "subject" approach tends to fractionate it. It gives the children from less advantaged backgrounds an enormous lift, again in contrast to the classroom approach which multiplies their handicaps.

Above all, it allows each child to advance at his own pace, in his own way. And shall I add, as icing on the cake, that our presentations are, with rare exceptions, what the children like best in a school where they like a great deal? I think I shall.

The educational system provides the young person with a sense of what society expects of him in the way of performance. If it is lax in its demands, then he will believe that such are the expectations of his society. If much is expected of him, the chances are that he will expect much of himself.

John W. Gardner in *Self-Renewal: The Individual and the Innovative Society*

19

NEW STANDARDS FOR OLD

Let's get back to our friend Joey [continued Dr. Morrow], at the end of that morning large-group presentation. Normally the students go to recess after the theatre—they're ready to work off some energy. But perhaps today Joey first joins those who filter down to the front of the theatre to ask the presenter a question or two, look more closely at the exhibits, or just listen to the discussion that usually goes on. This session, purely voluntary, is valuable to the presenter for feedback, and also because it may reveal a student interest sparked by the presentation. As I've said, we all watch for these interests because the school can "ride" them.

For example, Joey one day became fascinated with a guitar, played during a presentation that touched on Spain and Spanish culture. The fact was observed, noted on an Interest Card, which circulated to several teachers. Joey was informed he could handle a guitar when he went to Music. During a teacher conference, Joey was also assigned, as a project, to really *look* at a guitar, draw it, and be able to describe it in detail. We like these opportunities to build skill in observation and in communication. Presentations help create them.

At first, we felt that any presentation should be promptly followed up by a session in which the student would review what he had learned from it and be active rather than passive. Many educators worry about passivity when team teaching first creates these large-group situations. We have come to realize, however, that such efforts partially destroy the learning situation advantages of presentations. Joey is at ease because he knows that he does *not* have to participate, or report, or prove he paid attention or remembered. He is free to abstract from the materials presented that information and those concepts which meet his current intellectual needs, without any of the strain or fear or restriction that the need to look for "right answers" would cause. Preoccupation with right answers is the curse of the classroom! As our students advance, they are more and more guided into discussion groups related to recent presentations, but these do not examine the student to make sure he paid attention in the old classroom sense. We are not trying to effect thought-control, not trying to make every student think down the same path at the same time.

Today, after a bit, Joey goes off to recess. Remember, we don't have bells ringing all through the day, commanding that one activity stop, perhaps in the middle of a sentence, and another begin. We don't march armies of excited children through the halls en masse. The student takes himself where he should go. Few problems arise. If a student does goof off, as they put it, we want to know why—it can signal something wrong. As a sort of punishment, we may require a child to report more rigidly: it is quite an effective withdrawal of privilege and status. But we seldom need it—we make good behavior quite attractive.

Recess is supervised by an aide, who will move Joey along with a reminder if necessary, if games run too long. His schedule may call for the Skills Room of his circus as his next stop. He reports to it, a teacher there checks his record of progress if necessary, and he goes to work, perhaps on reading or writing. There is no "class" as such: he works on his own or with another student. He may spend time at one of the reading machines, under a watchful eye.

Or it may be that Joey can use some work on listening, on

following instructions, or on verbal expression. He goes to that skills area, participates in a small group discussion, or maybe puts on earphones and works with taped materials. This is small-group instruction, which can become one-to-one instruction for a short period, in which case instruction is by a specialist rather than an all-purpose follow-up teacher. All this can be called drill or practice. It doesn't bore Joey because it is personalized. He need not strive to keep up with those faster than he, nor suffer waiting for those slower, nor do work he personally doesn't need. His skills work is scheduled, not for a term, but for exactly as long as necessary.

Now let's say he goes to his Math Room. Presentations cover many of the math concepts—the aim is to make them familiar as early as possible. Some presentations are overtly on the subject, or phase. For instance, one is on "Zero." In part it uses a film made by students in our High School, combining live action and animation (we have animation equipment there, about $10,000 worth, that has long since paid for itself), and it is really quite amusing. It covers a lot of zero situations, such as no runs scored, being out of gas, zero and below zero—our students, you will find, grasp the concept of negative values at a tender age, instead of being baffled by it in ninth grade. Another film lays the basis for understanding multiplication without overtly talking about it. It shows some youngsters trying to drill like a marching band, with the problem of arranging ranks. You may wonder whether this is "sugar coating." Not quite. However palatable, these presentations are dealing with solid intellectual concepts, often far in advance of those children might otherwise be exposed to. We are never afraid, at any level, to invite the child into the world of *ideas*. The invitation is often attractive, but we do not water down the concept.

Joey's math teacher, most of the time, does not conduct a class. Rather the students work on their own, usually with a partner. This gives the teacher ample opportunity to work with Joey for several minutes at a time and to see whether he has really grasped the concepts he has been exposed to. Only when she is sure Joey does understand, because he can explain to her or to a partner, does the emphasis shift to algorithms and practice—what we call repetition. This is the skill aspect, and it helps set Joey's understanding and convince him of his grasp. In many schools, the teacher is upset if parents or others show their students some variation on an algorithm, for fear it will confuse them. On the contrary, we deliberately explore other ways, including the use of adding machines and calculators right from the start. "How else could you get the answer?" is a frequent question. Of course, we also are adamant that the content involved be thoroughly learned: multiplication tables, signs, formulas, procedures, and so on. They are taught by rote and drill and practice, and no bones about it. We may use simple or electronic devices to help speed this learning, but it must be done.

As I've emphasized, we usually let our students work with one or more others, not necessarily at the same stage of progress. There has long been evidence that children learn fast and easily this way—it is, of course, the way they learn *outside* school. As parents well know, children love to instruct one another, and the teacher seems to learn along with the pupil. They may also suddenly reverse roles! Besides, this forces them to talk, to put thoughts and ideas in words, and by the same token to listen. Children have a great and obvious need to verbalize ideas, and this may be the reason this method works so effectively. It's hard to use, of course, in the rigid classroom. *Our* rooms are equipped and designed for it.

I should state that we don't tolerate loafing or "fooling around" or any slackness in this kind of session. These are working periods, and the children accept them as such. Indeed, they often seem to a visitor to be dreadfully serious about their work—the Montessori people have long had the same experience. A deeply interested child frowns and seems to worry; but you'll also see ear-wide grins when triumphs are achieved. But we do not push. We have no treadmill timetable to hold to, so we can be relaxed. If a child seems distracted or unhappy, we don't yell at him to pay attention: we send him on to something else. Tomorrow will be another day.

Here we come to a very important point I must pause to cover: what we call *completion*. In the classroom system, time is fixed, and completion is the variable. That is, a certain gob of work is supposed to be covered by the class in a set period, usually a semester or school year. Some students do master this work within the period, while others master only fragments, and there are all degrees in between. Yet most of these "pass," and go on, despite the fact there may be great gaps and weaknesses in their preparation. They have put in the fixed time, so they move. Parents assume they pick up in the next grade where they left off — a very large assumption indeed. This whole arrangement is essentially a farce, though the results aren't amusing.

We use exactly the reverse plan. We make *completion* the fixed factor, and time the variable. This is so plainly sensible that I am embarrassed to state it. In each phase, we predetermine what *must* be learned, including basic concepts. How long it takes we don't really care, so long as the delay is not caused by some negligence or failure of the school. We don't tolerate any "65%, pass," merely because the term has ended. We insist on mastery of all fundamentals and "foundation" learning — in effect, every child has to score 100%. The effect of this policy shows up more and more, year after year. We don't have nonreaders; or students who are "lost" in math; or who can't write a clear, correct paragraph at age twelve. Nor do we have children the school has labelled "failures" or "left-backs," convinced by a brutal system that they are stupid and inept, and who therefore continue to fail as expected of them.

Back to Joey. After lunch, he usually will have another presentation. Then there may be a gap before he has science, which we handle from the outset as a workshop, laboratory, or small-group session. In our High School, Joey will have to pass some standard examinations, and "take some subjects," so we will have a record of the conventional kind to send to a college or elsewhere. But by the time he takes Chemistry or Physics this way, he will already have a sure grasp of most of the concepts, all of the math involved, and most of the laboratory techniques, besides a great deal of the content. If he is an average student, he'll complete the year's course in a couple of months, and pass the exam with ease. These gaps in the schedule help, too, because they allow Joey to go, as he wishes, to the

library and resource center, or his work room (you remember
that large room with the teachers' offices around it — he'll probably go there if he has a project to complete), or the gym or
outdoor athletics, or any of the non-sked rooms set up for art,
crafts, mechanics, shop, or lab work. They are supervised, but
any student has a lot of room to do what interests him. At
Joey's age, interests may run to "binges." In Joey's home, he
may have little chance to use tools, let us say. Here, within wide
limits, we'll let him work with tools to his heart's content. Next
he may go on a basketball binge. We'll let him. It's quite possible
he'll read half a dozen books on basketball. But also, he'll learn
what it is to develop skill, to keep at an objective. In a classroom
school, effort is constantly directed by the teacher, and fragmented by period bells. Students are quite literally taught,
year after year, *not* to maintain an interest or effort more than
forty minutes or so, at most. This effectively helps convert
able students into "underachievers," whose fragmented efforts
the school then piously deplores.

Isn't it curious how most elementary schools go to great
trouble to take children on trips, but bar them from interests
close at hand? A group will be shepherded for a quick look at
a newspaper plant, but will any of them be allowed to print anything in school? They tour a factory to learn about machinery,
but should a lad bring his bicycle in for help in fixing it, he'd
get cold stares and short shrift! We fix a lot of bikes here, or at
least a teacher and students will take a good look at one — and
get some introduction to the mechanics and physics involved.
A newspaper plant can be a lot more meaningful after you've
run an offset machine or miniature letterpress. It's truly amazing how the classroom school typically beats down or closes the
door to the child's eager interests, but hardly surprising that
the child soon learns to suppress or conceal them in school.
By about fifth grade most children won't tell most teachers anything about themselves or their interests. They wear masks.

Let me say in passing — it's a big subject — that we don't
think of all our students as "academic." We're aware of the
creative type, the artist, the athlete, the child with hand skills,
the performer, the socializer. Such aptitudes and leanings may
become evident quite early; but the average lockstep school

does a good job of squashing them into the standard mold if possible, or suppressing them at least. A child with a flair for writing, or art, is likely to spend several years with nice young women who would probably react negatively if they recognized the talent at all, and who would not have the competence to encourage it themselves, if they did. Only by great good luck will a child have classroom teachers who welcome patterns well outside the usual academic conformity. Our students can seek out a teacher who will respond.

I hope I have given you some picture of how Joey spends his time in school. You'll note the variety of groupings he gets into; the freedom he has even while he positively achieves completion of each stage; and the many opportunities he has to really talk with teachers, and they with him. He also talks with other students—that's perhaps the most striking contrast with classroom schools, where "stop talking!" is the most frequent injunction heard during instruction. The child *needs* to talk, must talk and talk well if he is to learn, and develop the basic communication skills. And please also note how much we have taken the *fear* of the classroom school out of ours, along with the constant direction and regimentation.

As Joey progresses, there will be some gradual shifts in emphasis. In skills, for example, we will later on teach Joey how *not* to read: how to use an index, how to skim material to find what he wants quickly, and how on inspection to separate opinion and folklore from fact and research. We will strongly stress ability to communicate in writing. Joey will become quite sophisticated, compared to classroom children, in observing. He will increasingly grasp the organization of the world around him and gain an idea of how he and his parents relate to it, interact, and have some degree of control.

The presentations will bit by bit become less general and discursive, and their intellectual rigor and level will rise. In them, Joey will see, hear, and possibly meet several dozen persons of some distinction. Some presentations may take several days to complete; but even while many grow more specific and detailed, others will continue to weave the fabric of knowledge, tying together different fields. Joey will acquire a sense of history, development, and change-sequence far beyond that of the classroom student.

Anytime about the age of ten to twelve, Joey may be so advanced in one or more fields that he will begin spending part of his time at what we still call the Junior High School. Or he may even go to the High School on certain days, for a session or conference with a teacher there. Just as we don't transfer students as a class, so we don't send them en bloc to another school. They go when their progress dictates, and to some degree to suit our convenience, since there is nothing critical about making the shift now or two months from now. This helps us keep our facilities more evenly in use.

Our High School uses the Trump Plan now. This plan for secondary schools, as you may know, is in quite wide use with much success. It is named for Dr. J. Lloyd Trump who headed a commission on staff utilization, and involves the use of full team teaching with large groupings, small groupings, and about a third of the student's time allotted to individual work, alone or with one or two other students and not under direct teacher supervision. It also calls for a staff having many titles and assignments, rather than just "teacher." Dr. Trump described it in a pamphlet called "Images of the Future" published in 1959 and surely a landmark in American education. Incidentally, there seems to be no reason why the plan wasn't offered for use in lower grades except that the commission was composed of secondary school people who therefore talked in secondary terms! The approach is gaining a foothold in elementary schools. We here go beyond it. By the time our "new type" students reach age sixteen or so, they will be even more on their own, doing at least half their work without any teacher directly supervising. Those that go to college should find the transition easy, instead of the rude jolt that scuttles nearly half of most freshman classes.

You've been wondering, I'm sure, how we can offer so much individualization and yet keep close track of each student's progress. And our evaluator here has been wondering when he was ever going to get a chance to tell you.

“Continuing assessment of the product of the schools . . . is necessary. This means the development of principles and techniques for critically judging the worth of whatever the schools teach and the effectiveness and efficiency of their methods of instruction.”

From *Innovation in Education: New Directions for the American School,* statement by the Research and Policy Committee of the Committee for Economic Development

20

HOW TO KNOW THE SCORE

Happily, tonight I can present Mr. McMurray to speak for himself. He was our first evaluator, and so the best one to tell you about this new and important office. I'll say only this, that the work he and his colleagues do is so important that I doubt we could operate as we do without them. Lloyd?"

"My job is simply stated," said Mr. McMurray. "It is to keep tabs on the progress of some 1,250 students month by month and year by year. My load includes all of this school, another elementary school, and part of a junior high. It's a little too large, actually, and we will try to reduce it some in time. To help me I have a young and able psychologist, Miss Praag, and a good stenographer. I can get more help at times from the pool of clerks. If this sounds like a rather elaborate and expensive setup, let me say at once that the cost per student works out at a bit over $25 per year. By no means is this all extra cost. We relieve teachers of a huge amount of clerical work and report-card writing, as well as most parent calls and interviews. We take a similar load off the principals, and some off the school office clerks. We also make each counselor many times as effective. All this shows up in actual payroll savings. Some people are kind enough to think my office breaks about even. Others are still more kind—they think evaluators worth $25 even if it were pure expense."

Under the classroom system [continued Mr. McMurray], no one checked systematically on the progress of each child. That may sound startling when said so baldly; but I think you will agree it is substantially the fact. Those that ran into trouble in some way, or obviously needed special handling, came to the attention of the principal. In some schools, teachers might consult the principal about certain students. We did now and then have an extraordinary principal who knew something about each child—quite a feat, but essentially a tour de force rather than a systematic, thorough follow-up. Much more usually, the "non-deviant" child was assumed to be doing all right. Much of our principals' time went to the special cases, to disciplinary efforts, and to dealing with parents, especially disgruntled parents.

Teachers, of course, evaluated the student's progress for each school year. The problems of such evaluating and reporting are familiar—and painful. We have long known that teachers' evaluations vary a great deal, and can be inaccurate and inconsistent for a long list of reasons. But the prime difficulty is that the teacher usually has each child only for a period, not continuously. And even during this period, the teacher is of necessity herself involved in the evaluation, for how well the student progressed must be to considerable degree a reflection of how well the teacher, too, has performed.

In the higher grades, the teacher becomes limited to one course. Guidance people may take over to some extent here, but then we get into other shortcomings. Often there are not enough guidance counselors, so again the deviants get most of the attention, and that on a crisis rather than continuing basis. I may say, too, that persons less than well qualified are often pressed into guidance work, and guidance may be in large part concerned with vocational work and college placement.

So, instead of a continuous evaluation of how well each child is doing, systematic, automatic, and expertly done, we had intermittent evaluation on many different levels—and no one person clearly charged with responsibility. Our situation was typical of most school systems, I believe. We simply did not know what the score was for most pupils, except that they seemed to be "getting along." True, we ran ability and achievement tests; but again, no one systematically and expertly made use of the findings.

When a few years ago I was made an evaluator, very little about the office was clear. But one thing was very clear—I had better not walk down dark alleys. Few educators have ever become so unpopular so quickly. Compared to me, the dourest of baseball umpires was a warmly beloved character. I'm happy to report that now I am better accepted. If few send flowers and kind notes, at least I seldom have to duck a pop bottle.

My function, you see, is to evaluate the progress of each child, whether deviant or non-deviant, whether genius, dolt, average, teachers' pet, cut-up, grind, diligent, or delinquent. I must gather all that is known about each one, and judge his progress in the light of it. And I am under positive orders to report on each one, periodically and in writing, to the principal. I'm not a teacher, not a principal, not responsible to any one but the Superintendent. I am never in the position, in evaluating student progress, of rating or defending my own work. On the contrary, I am ordered and paid, and I am supposed to be trained, to be utterly cold-blooded, efficient, and impartial. I'm worse than the umpire, you see, because his calls are forgotten the next day, but mine are a matter of record. My evaluations, in some form, get to the student, the parents, the teachers, the principals, and in summary to the Superintendent. This is something new, you see—knowing the score, all the time, for each pupil, accurately and impartially.

The process is not too intricate, although naturally it has taken us some years to develop it, and we continue to make improvements. Each teacher receives cards from my office with the student's name, and certain information. We call these "contact cards." When the teacher has a "contact" with the child that can be a basis for evaluation, a card is filled in and routed to us. You'll understand that we are not interested in recitation marks, homework grades and such trivia. In fact, such grading is severely discouraged as a time-wasting annoyance to everybody concerned. Rather, contact reports are based on a private session with the student, on a major paper or report or project, or on a scheduled written or oral exam. Contact reports also come in when a student completes a unit of work. Unusual incidents or significant achievements or failures may be reported. The teacher can report by check marks on scales provided, or by comment, or both. Usually comment is brief, in writing.

We process these cards on a punch machine, then send them to a firm downtown that has a computer and allows us time on it for a modest fee. In minutes hundreds of cards put data into the machine, and it prints out master cards completely up to date whenever we need them. It summarizes all the reports, compares them with those previously processed, and calls our attention to changes in trend and achievement levels. It will also signal changes in emotional control, health, diligence of work, and interests. There is a limit to how far even one of these EDP monsters can go, however, and that is where we take over. Regularly, each student's progress is reviewed in detail.

I might remark in passing that many schools keep a lot of records. The trouble is they often take so much time and effort to compile that there is none left to make use of them. They disappear into filing cabinets and usually nobody ever looks at them again. Our records are boiled down and streamlined; but invariably they are *used*.

To begin with, we systematically interview each student. Simple, isn't it? Yet a most valuable way of keeping tabs. Out of the school year, we earmark 120 days for interviewing. Many student interviews take only five minutes—enough to verify what our records show, that everything is going well. And to remind the student that we have a personal interest in how he does. It also gives him a chance to speak up if there is something on his mind. Of course, when we suspect a longer interview may turn up something, we don't terminate it in five minutes. Once in a while what begins as a five-minute session runs half an hour.

Please bear in mind that the function of these interviews

is evaluating, not correcting. If a problem turns up, that's something else, to be handled according to its nature and our resources. My office is charged with *noting* problems as they are reflected in progress or lack of it. But I must repeat, we are just as concerned with the child who doesn't show any trace of a personal problem. And the only kind of problem we are likely to tackle directly is one that clearly involves the process of evaluation per se. Some children are hard to evaluate. For them, we may schedule more frequent interviews. In general, a student is apt to have two interviews a year, and we often manage thirty or so a day, along with other duties.

In the old classroom system, teachers often disagreed sharply on how children were doing, and on their capabilities. Teachers aren't computers: they respond both favorably and unfavorably to the various individuals they teach. Even when they agreed, they were often wrong in their judgments. Teachers still disagree in our new system, and they still make errors of judgment. But now we do something about it. When my office spots disagreements among teachers, or between information we have and what they think, we often get together to thrash the matter out. At first, such sessions were rugged. The air crackled even before a word was said. Now our faculty people are used to the procedure, and it is taken a lot less personally — not that things don't get tense now and then. We have a technique for these meetings: Each party concerned listens to the others. The cards are reviewed. A report from a doctor, parent, psychologist may be introduced. Usually each party to a disagreement goes away a bit more thoughtful and less positive about the child, and agreement is often reached later.

Then there are the parent interviews. In this job, you must expect to work nights. We have "open school" nights when we talk with parents in groups. Otherwise, we arrange conferences only if they or we especially want to. Three times a year, for each student, the computer issues a card, addressed and ready to mail, that gives a report on many phases of the child's progress. It carries marks or grades only for special examinations and projects, and is very little like conventional report cards.

First, it is a running report on the student as a person, as the school sees him. It points out the areas he is strong in and weak, where he has progressed and where he hasn't. The intent here is primarily to let the parents know what is going on. We never use reports punitively—that is, to suggest that the parents better do something to get him on the ball. A situation of that kind we always handle by conference or by a letter or telephone call.

Second, we think of the report as a report on how the school is doing, too. If he isn't doing as well as he should, maybe we are to blame. A duplicate of every card that suggests possible school failure is routed to the Superintendent, and it is then up to the faculty to show action to correct the difficulty, one way or another. Only by having an independent evaluator's office, of course, is such an approach possible.

Long ago, the report card was pretty much a judgment from the throne. For many children, it was an ordeal, a prelude to a beating, punishment or scolding, or embarrassment. In more recent time it has been fancied up in innumerable ways, but much of the old attitudes still prevail. In the heyday of progressivism, of course, there was a swing the other way— it took a swami to figure out what the teachers' pretty phrases really meant. Just because we use computers, please don't think our approach is mechanical. The computer simply does the chores, the clerical work. We're able to give the parent much more specific information. For example, we report on major projects accomplished, often quoting a teacher. We always give a physical profile. We can show what interests are growing stronger and which are diminishing. We can spot and report problems arising from emotional strain, lack of sleep, eye troubles, and the like, particularly if there is a sudden onset. The combination of observation by several teachers, in various situations, frequent and continuous reporting, skilled supervision of reporting, and use of machines to eliminate clerical work means reporting far more accurate and comprehensive than could be even attempted in a classroom school.

Incidentally, we long ago ditched the notion that report cards have to be given out to all children simultaneously, or at any special time. We spread the load over much of the year.

We also make much use of what we call "School Notes." These are brief, small leaflets covering many special topics, written for the information of parents. If a child makes a major move, for example, to a new grouping, or program, or phase of work, we send the appropriate note explaining just what it means. Incidentally, many of these are written by the students, as projects, and they run them off, too. Others discuss some of the behavior patterns that may be expected at various ages, and how to cope with some frequent problems. Some of these a classroom teacher might hesitate to send, for fear of causing offense; but coming from our impersonal office they seem to be quite acceptable. They save a very considerable amount of time and trouble, too, we think.

All told, my office does some 3,500 interviews of all kinds a year, and we send out more than 5,000 reports of all kinds on our 1,250 workload. I think we can fairly say that we know how each child is doing; the school knows; and the parent knows.

And now, if I may, I'd like to head home.

Mr. McMurray grinned, and Dr. Morrow waved his hand. "Excused."

Dr. Morrow resumed as Lloyd McMurray vanished through the door. "His job requires a patient, devoted and tactful man. He has done some fine pioneering for us."

When we first began our evaluating system [he continued], the going was rough. We had little experience to steer by, and every detail had to be worked out, tested, and revised. I can admit now that teacher enthusiasm for it was about nil. Those who had long reigned over a classroom were particularly bitter about having some one say how *they* were doing, as well as their charges. I suppose evaluating could be introduced in a classroom school—but I'd hate to be the one to do it. As it was, we had enough trouble. But we felt we *had* to "know the score" for each child.

What swung sentiment over, as much as anything, was the clerical part. We not only took the burden of reporting off the teachers, we also cut out the constant giving of marks and grades, and all the bookkeeping that went with it. Soon many of our people were appreciating the relief from clerical work. Not all — two teachers had to be transferred because they could not give up using grades punitively. Others who had been now came to realize what they had been doing and agreed that the new atmosphere was better.

A few dramatic and far from typical instances helped us, too. In one case, a husky-looking boy considered difficult and lazy was spotted, through evaluating, as possibly ill. He was found to have tuberculosis. It was caught and cured. In another case, a child who had offended several teachers and had a ferocious reputation turned into a brilliant success when a couple of minor problems were seen, dealt with, and resolved. In several cases, children thought to be very "slow" turned out to be quite able. A child considered quiet and likeable turned out to be psychopathic and in need of urgent treatment. In fact, after a couple of years almost every teacher knew at first hand of some instance in which our new evaluation methods produced startling results. But I must emphasize that these exceptional cases were exceptional. The greatest value of our far more accurate and thorough follow-up has been with more run of the mill students, simply because there are a lot more of them. Sensitive, continuing evaluation permits us to use our very individualized methods, with confidence that we can catch and correct mistakes quickly, and find and encourage interests and abilities that usually stay submerged in the class-room school.

How did the children like our move to independent evaluation? I think I can state they loved it. But actually, the changes came about so gradually from their point of view that many are scarcely aware of a shift. How they feel shows up in the way they behave.

That brings me to discipline. When now our people visit a conventional system, we find ourselves amazed at how much faculty energy goes into "discipline." We're reminded that study after study shows it is the biggest worry of the newer teachers. In larger schools, an assistant principal will often devote time to little else. In most schools, principals find discipline their most wearing problem. It used to be that way in our system too, but now it is a matter of minor concern and interest.

You have seen one big reason: our entrance arrangements

and early identification program. By far the worst discipline problems are badly disturbed children. We get as many as most schools; but we know a great deal more about each disturbed child, usually before he even sets foot in the kindergarten. There is no such thing here as discovering that a child has serious emotional troubles only after he becomes intolerable, say in sixth grade. Our program to deal with emotional disturbance is in effect when the child enters. If it occurs later, our evaluation system detects it in short order. We do what we can as a school, and enlist other community agencies to do what a school can't. True, with a few of the more severe situations, we don't get very far. But with half or more, and especially with the milder cases, we do ameliorate the problem a good deal. Guided by the evaluator's reports, these children are carefully observed. Everybody on the staff who deals with them knows the score. I may add that our teachers who handle entering classes are not sweet, willing but beginning teachers who may never have seen a disturbed child before. They are carefully picked and trained and they have still more expert help to back them up. The first few weeks are the most critical—and we staff to reflect that fact.

Our organization helps greatly in day to day dealing with this problem. In an ordinary class, one disturbed child can give a teacher fits, and take a third or more of her time. She can deal with him *or* the class—but often not both. In our setup there is always more than one adult present or quickly available. If a child causes a disturbance, the proceedings don't come to a halt amid chaos. The child is simply removed. With many disruptive children, this works almost magically. The effort for attention gets response, but of a kind the child usually finds unrewarding. The larger groupings also have a social-pressure effect: in the theatre, for example, a child who causes a disturbance is likely to respond to the annoyance and displeasure of his peers. In small groups, the attention of an adult is easily obtained. There is little of the competition for attention we find commonly in the conventional classroom. So there is no need to create a disturbance to get noticed.

But let me go further: the classroom school, many educators now realize, can be said to be *designed* to aggravate the behavior problems of the disturbed child. It restricts movement and talk, constantly flaunts authority, and bathes the insecure child in fear and anxiety. Small wonder it produces aggression, disruption, aversion, withdrawal. Many teachers who have struggled with unruly children in classrooms cannot believe how differently these pupils behave in our open school. Feeling secure, allowed to do what deeply interests them, and free to relate to adults of their choice privately and intimately when they wish, they usually behave like angels. You would have a hard time picking out most of our disturbed children by observation!

For the adolescent who has "authority" problems with his parents, the conventional school represents one form of oppressive authority piled upon another. He may seethe with frustrations and suppressed hatred, and vent his emotions in a variety of socially undesirable ways. Adolescence is a time of insecurities for most children. The school can easily accentuate them, rather than relieve them, by permitting and then emphasizing failure. The child can be all too readily persuaded to accept the school's evaluation. The institution charged with educating and developing the student instead chops him down, heightens his self-doubts, even helps drive him to suicide in too many cases. The open school, by organization and approach, builds more confident children—and you have few behavior or discipline problems with youngsters who have come to know and trust their own abilities and who feel secure and unthreatened.

Because, like most schools that have broken away from the classroom, we have almost no discipline problems, our teaching staff can far more easily detect emotional problems as they arise: the child who is too quiet, too good, the terrified, the rejected, the hungry, those stupefied by lack of sleep, family turmoil, or brutal punishment, those from other environments and cultures who feel bewildered and among strangers, and those already sliding toward the deeper silences of psychosis. Free of the wearing burden of maintaining "classroom discipline," our staff can observe, relate, help, and get help.

Though emotional disturbance is a prime cause of disciplinary strain, there are others. Boredom is one, particularly affecting the bright and more energetic child. Failure is another, weighing heaviest on the less academically able or handicapped child. And perhaps the feeling of being out of place, of not belonging, of being held prisoner and denied status that might be obtainable elsewhere is as potent a cause of trouble as any, and more so as the student grows older.

We hunt out boredom as a good housekeeper goes after cobwebs. I wish you could see our children here in the daytime. They go into a session expecting it to be *good*—absorbing, challenging, fast-moving, wonderful in the core sense of that word. Usually, they are not disappointed.

We hold failure down to proper levels, mainly through our early identification and reading programs—and from there on through evaluation. When a child begins to "slide," we spot it, soon, and find out why. Youngsters are like adults: a little failure is a challenge, too much brings avoidance. And anybody can cope better with failure if they have a solid feeling of success in some area. We look for those success areas in each child, and provide the facilities and encouragement that is needed. Here, every student "belongs."

We search out and throw out middle-classism. For example, we don't stress neatness, a middle-class moral value—we demand *order*, an intellectual value. We don't assume middle-class motivations—we build motivation in each child's own terms. We don't teach "work is good" to children who have already observed that work their parents must do is dull, dirty, and discouraging. We try to prove that some work can be rewarding, and that education can open new doors to opportunity.

Wishing, and good intentions, however, can be a large jump from reality. It is splendid, you may agree, to have hundreds of children who love their school, because each can grow and develop in his own fashion. It could also be an awful mess, a chaotic scramble in which noble words obscure failure. There is enough of that in the conventional school. Here, we often say a prayer for Lloyd McMurray, a hard-minded evaluator, armed with computer, who can tell us how any student is really doing, at any time, and how we, the faculty and administration are doing, too.

Suddenly we have realized that our institutions of learning are the chief foundations of our national progress in a complex and highly technical world.

Alvin C. Eurich in *American Education Today*

21

THE ROLE OF TECHNOLOGY

The clock tells me," resumed Dr. Morrow, "that I had better conclude. I must, however, say a word on the subject of technology. You have seen some of our equipment on your tour. Each year we put more to work. By next year we expect to have our own computer installation, which can in time be extended to serve all our elementary schools. It will take over, among other tasks, a good part of the drilling and repetition of children, on an individualized basis. You understand it will not treat them alike; rather, the child and the computer will in each instance 'talk' back and forth in a responsive way. It is amazing that we can set up a machine that can actually give children more individual attention than the best classroom teacher can, but that's the fact. The greatest virtue of the computer, however, is its bottomless patience. The one we have on order is guaranteed never to get cross with a student, no matter what."

I say that in jest [he continued], but at the risk of being hooted out of my profession, I'll add that there is truth in it. We keep hearing people say, "No machine can take the place of a real, live teacher," but nobody goes on to tell us why not. To be sure, a computer can't put its arm around an upset child. But it may not upset the child in the first place. For at least certain functions, a child may be more at ease with a machine.

The hardest thing for any teacher is to refrain from directing a child. It can be done even unconsciously, even by the situation alone. The child responds emotionally, and learning may be impeded. The machine can be impersonal. I'm not suggesting schools where the child works only with machines, of course. But very definitely machines can replace the live, present teacher, and there can be important advantages all around, including freeing the teachers of some drudgery.

Quite obviously, the schools are just beginning to get their educational feet wet in the application of technology to instruction. They are no strangers to technology per se. We have buses, and machines to cut grass and shovel snow, and IBM monsters to print out schedules and report cards, and advanced bookkeeping machines in the business office, and horrendous public address systems capable of instant mass interruption. But when it comes to instruction, what have we? Only in the last few years, since Federal money first began to trickle in under the "defense" guise, has there been much visible movement toward using technology. By and large, our classroom schools have been no more dependent on the use of machines and electronics than those of Lincoln's era. This is a strange contrast to the world all around the schools. I think we should understand that here again the classroom system is to blame.

Consider a typical classroom teacher who decides to show her class a film. She requests the movie in advance, hoping that it will arrive in time to tie in with her subject. She reserves the projector. On the day scheduled, perhaps two weeks later, all she need do is somehow get the machine into her room, set it up, place and connect the speaker, plug in the power cord, thread the film, put up the screen, try to darken the room, focus, pray the film won't snarl or break and the bulb won't expire, and proceed. Afterwards, she has to get the machine back together, pack the film for return, return both, and fill out a report or two. The machine has served usefully (assuming the film turned out to be suitable) for twenty minutes: it brought the visual and sound resources of motion pictures to the class. But the poor teacher feels as if she has been through a wearying battle.

Something is wrong. Machines are supposed to reduce work and cost. But this one added to her labors and stress. And it occasioned specific extra costs, clearly chargeable to her. Even while the machine was in use, she was not freed for other work for a moment.

For contrast, compare what happens in our non-classroom school here. The machine is not brought in: the students go to a fully equipped theatre. At a signal, a technician runs it, expertly. If the teacher has seen it, she can go elsewhere, or slip into a soundproof glass booth and do some other work. At the end, she has no extra duties to perform. No specific expenses are involved, since film, machine, and operator are all present and available as a normal school resource. Note, too, that the film will usually be shown to large groups, not just one class of thirty or so.

I think the principle involved becomes pretty clear. So long as we think in terms of a teacher "covering" a class, it is pretty hard to get the school system to pay for giving her a lot of equipment—movie projector, overhead projector, slide projector, tape recorder, radio, record player, typewriter, duplicator, copying machine, demonstration equipment, and so forth. It is all looked on as "extra" expense—it does not "save labor" because we still need sixteen teachers to cover sixteen classrooms. Of course, we can suggest that with the equipment the teachers can teach better. But that is arguable, while the cost is undeniable.

Further, the teacher usually won't want the equipment, won't ask for it, and frequently won't use it even if provided. Her experience with equipment has very likely been on the discouraging side. She has found it a struggle to use. For example, a teacher may try employing a simple and increasingly popular device, the overhead projector. She discovers it requires transparencies. Many are available ready to use, but it can take up to a year and a half to have the purchase approved and the sheets delivered! She can prepare her own, directly or by using special acetate sheets and an office copier. But she may have no idea how to do this, or where or how to get the sheets, or where there is a suitable copier, or how to run that. Some schools do have competent audio-visual consultants she can go to, but most do not. In any case, each step is likely to involve effort, favors, and red tape – plus delay. And maintenance service may become an even greater problem. If a device stops working, it may require another struggle and weeks to get it fixed and back in use.

Incidentally, the teacher who does use modern equipment may find herself criticized for it, on the grounds that she shows films because "she is too lazy to teach," or uses devices to "entertain" the children, thus spoiling them for teachers who sternly and righteously cling to ancient, ineffective, and boring ways. Can you picture an office manager saying to a secretary, "If you weren't so shiftless, you wouldn't type those letters, you'd write them out in beautiful Spencerian hand"?

It's pretty obvious, isn't it, that putting duplicate equipment in each classroom, where it may be little used, is wasteful. Nor does it seem sensible to attempt to train all teachers to use all machines, especially since many teachers are quite resistant to learning – an attitude they deplore in their students, but manage to tolerate in themselves.

How is it done outside the schools, where full use of the newest in technology is pretty much taken for granted? Suppose a factory manager is considering installing some new machines. Can you really imagine him ordering them without first planning in detail how they will be put to use, what changes in procedure and organization must be made to use them effectively, and how his people are to be trained and emotionally prepared to take full advantage of them? Everybody concerned understands that new machines demand *changes* – often complicated and far-reaching changes that require broad-scale planning to accommodate. But this is where the classroom system pinches. Classrooms fragment the school. Within wide limits each teacher does as he or she pleases. The principal is by no means the manager the factory director is: he has nowhere near the same effective authority or freedom to alter the arrangements. He cannot plan for the school as a unit, but only classroom by classroom – and in each he has to cope with a teacher who regards her classroom as her private property.

On the economic side, the classroom organization provides

the same pinch. The schools, of course, often sneer at any cost-accounting approach, even while they plead "no money" as an excuse for clinging to outmoded methods. But outside the schools, every competent manager understands the basic economics of the machine—a trade of *operating expense* for *capital investment*. For example, if $100,000 invested in a machine will permit an annual saving in labor and other expense of $25,000, it can be a good trade. Interest, depreciation and other costs may total only $20,000. So the organization has the use of a $100,000 machine that does work faster and better, and saves $5,000 a year into the bargain. The machine is better than "free"! In schools, instructional salary is by far the biggest expense. Even a small saving in this area will pay for a large investment in equipment. For example, if machines can help teach reading faster, they free teachers for other work. But this advantage can't be realized within the classroom system, because we will still need sixteen teachers for sixteen classrooms, no matter what. Only in an open, flexible school is the way clear to introduce technology, to effect better learning, better use of teacher skills, and economic benefits in addition.

When any suggestion is made out loud that by using proper equipment a school can require fewer teachers, there is often a reaction of shock and horror. Why? Haven't we a shortage of teachers—and a much greater one of good teachers? Are we running schools to make jobs, or to educate our children? Let me make clear that the use of technology is not likely to put competent present teachers out of work. We are constantly expanding our standards of how much education is desirable. It is rather absurd to worry about having a teacher surplus in the foreseeable future.

Machines aren't going to squeeze humans out of the schools any more than they wipe people out of offices or hospitals. But I think it childish not to recognize the role of machines. Nothing the best teacher can do can equate a good color film. No teacher can show a child how he pronounces words as a tape recorder does. No teacher can give a child the calm, personal attention a computerized teaching device always does. Not to see how machines and people can work together is to bury one's head in the sand. For teachers not to realize that proper use of equipment can make their work both far more effective and easier is, in my view, rather stupid, primitive, and stubborn. Let me applaud the growing number who are quite eager to use helpful devices, if only the school will show them how to and provide the back-up services.

We should all really remember that the schools have long relied very heavily on one of the greatest achievements of technology, the printed book. To a large extent (too large, in my view) instruction is built around it. Times have changed: other media are now important, as Marshall McLuhan and others have so vividly pointed out. When we hear educators howl about new technology entering the schools, let us remember that howls just as loud greeted the introduction of our now worshiped book. The notion that it is fine for children to read books freely is quite a recent one in the history of education. Most people are so used to the book in education that to refer to it as "technology" startles them.

If we stand back a bit, it is quite clear that the many newer forms of technology useful in education *are* going to come into general use in the schools. Some people in education will fight a rearguard action and sabotage as they can. Others will think it a good idea for the schools to enter the twentieth century along with everybody else. But it seems clear enough that *the classroom system and technology are natural enemies.* As this absurd system goes out, technology can come in—to the enormous advantage of our children, who are going to live in a far more technological world than even we inhabit.

"And now I thank you for coming, and bid you goodnight," concluded Dr. Morrow.

❝*The young student today grows up in an electronically configured world. It is a world not of wheels but of circuits, not of fragments but of integral patterns. . . . At school, however, he encounters a situation organized by means of classified information. The subjects are unrelated. They are visually conceived in terms of a blueprint. The student can find no possible means of involvement for himself, nor can he discover how the educational scene relates to the 'mythic' world of electronically processed data and experience he takes for granted. As one IBM executive puts it, 'My children had lived several lifetimes compared to their grandparents when they began grade one.'*❞

Marshall McLuhan in *Understanding Media*. Copyright © by Marshall McLuhan. Used by permission of McGraw-Hill Book Co.

22

TO BROAD NEW PATTERNS

Our visit to imaginary Isaac Newton School and the New Lea system was intended to suggest the "feel" and the far less rigid organization of the new, "open" school—so called because the prison-like classroom walls that have stood for a century have at last been broken through.

Let me emphasize at once that this was no attempt to describe *the* new organization. Certainly not the least benefit of the open approach is that it can be, and should be—and let us hope, will be—highly pluralistic, permitting and encouraging a variety of solutions. One of the oddest aspects of the "system" we have is that many salaams are offered to the great god Local Control; yet in organization schools tend to be conventionally class-and-grade in structure, which leaves only trivial room for variations. Mighty battles are fought over whether the high school in a community should operate on a three-year or four-year plan, although only the bravest educator would attempt to prove that it makes any educational difference. And the pattern used in a conventional upper-middle-class suburban school is likely to be found in attempted use in a ghetto school a few miles away, with perhaps a militant local group insisting that their school be made still *more* like the suburb's.

The Establishment, too, lays heavy hands on those who might stray from the conventional. The State Department of Education, in a perhaps well-meant effort to pull up the low end in rural areas, in most states relies more on certificate, quasi-legal regulation, and tape-measure than on idea, test, and research. Both federal and state funds filter through sieves of approvals that pass the conventional far more readily. But the severity of the education disaster can no longer be concealed or ignored: the riots; the unemployed; the hippies and runaways and drug users; the restless, angry students; the ruthless teacher strikes; the defeated budgets and referenda; the ever-louder chorus of complaint—these are among the more evident aspects of pressing need for and tolerance of change—change we had better achieve before anarchistic radicals bent on disruption beat us to it.

The school we have inspected does not exist; but the reader well informed on recent developments will have small difficulty in recognizing a synthesis of "experiments" firmly fleshed with actuality. Not a few of the practices and approaches at our Isaac Newton School have been in use, in various advanced schools or systems, for some five to fifteen years or even longer. The number of schools with experience in their use runs into the hundreds.

It is a mistake, as a rule, to call these "experiments." They represent, with a few exceptions, the usual slow, painful, creeping, trial-and-error efforts of bolder educators "feeling their way"—as they will often freely confess. In most cases the innovations on examination prove fragmentary, unconnected by any sharp, generalized theory that could provide direction and illumine the results achieved. Nonetheless, there exists already a large fund of experience from which the underpinnings of an adequate theory can be extracted.

Theoretically, the open school is a great distance removed from the class-and-grade type, but this may not be easy to see. The new school, especially if making shift in an old building, *looks* not too dissimilar. One still finds rooms, halls, students,

teachers, books, many of the old trappings. The children leave
home and return to report on a quarrel, a lost glove, and a role
in a play. Though sizable changes may have been made, the
sense of continuity remains strong. We have apparently altered
the old homestead, knocked off the porch, and painted the shut-
ters, but the address is the same.

Not so with the open school! *It cannot be thought of as a modification or improvement of the class-and-grade school* — to do so is to
compromise and cripple it at the outset. The open school is not a
renovation, but a *replacement*. We can get from the class-and-
grade organization to a true open school only by a group of
"quantum jumps."

The term derives, of course, from atomic physics; but it
is now used by scientists, engineers, managers, and others to
mean any relatively sudden, large, and *dis*continuous advance.
For example, the automobile since its beginnings has been
greatly improved by a long series of modifications; but no
amount of gradual change will make an automobile into an airplane. At some point we have to say, "We are going to design
not a car but a plane." If a modification produces a 5% advance,
we are apt to be very pleased. In contrast, a true quantum jump
may produce an advance of 1,000% — our plane can go 600
miles an hour against 50 for the cruising automobile.

The old school is our automobile, the new open school our
airplane. I do not believe we can modify one into the other —
they are different systems, based on *opposing* objectives and
theoretical bases. There is no bridge from one to the other,
anymore than from the doctrine of spontaneous generation to
that of evolution; or from the devil theory of disease causation
to that of infection; or from the decimal base of an adding machine to the binary base of a computer. One must *jump*, discard-
ing the old and accepting the new.

Unfortunately, to working educators the quantum jump
looms as a strange and frightening threat, an unfamiliar experience. It rests, with rare exception, on application of a sound
body of theory. Though successful innovators often begin with
a lucky or accidental observation, they do not bumble or cut-
and-patch to a quantum jump: the knowledge of *why* something

new may work much better is there before the details of *how* to put the parts together. As we have seen, education is sadly lacking in valid and useful theory, and most of the "knowledge" of how to arrange and conduct education turns out, on realistic examination, to be folklore, pure dogma, or nonsense. And to make matters worse, most educators *think* in terms of modification. Even when they do, by some chance, make some change that approaches a quantum jump, they are apt to miss the significance of their own act, and gradually pull the jump back to the "safer" aspects of one more modification. (This, I believe, is why many "bold experiments" in the schools tend to peter out in a few years.)

The last quantum jump in our public schools was the one that gave us the class-and-grade system—a sharp break from approaches used before, and a far better solution for the needs and aims of the Civil War era. Since, we have extended the system and modified it ad nauseam; but it is still the same thing and instantly recognizable. Modifications will no longer serve: at best, they produce only small gains, and we are desperately in need of very large gains.

We need a new, and grand, quantum jump. It can hardly be expected from working educators, save in rare instances, for the reasons just given. Nor can much help be expected from boards of education, and still less from the PTA ladies, to whom pecking-order is real and "theory" vague. In broad, the energy and drive and imagination must come from those *not* enmeshed in the antique world of education or with a stake in the tottering status quo. And, we might add, from those who believe that public education can be *enormously* better.

The "modifiers," of course, argue that one must proceed cautiously, that is, change slowly, and that "our children must not be guinea pigs." It is a strange argument, although hardly one that surprises. Let us suppose we discovered a highly contagious disease spreading through a school. Would we argue for slow, careful change—or for urgent action? Suppose we hear that children are being whipped in a certain school (Boston will come to mind). Do we suggest that the administration "taper off"—or should we demand a stop? It makes no more sense to be patient with the brutal shortcomings of our present schools. To claim that we "make guinea pigs" of our children when we free them abruptly from torture and frustration and imprisonment is to express fear of change itself. But to some extent we *do* make guinea pigs of children when we subject them to modifications which cannot conceivably achieve the degree of change needed for relief.

Lest quantum jumps sound too alarming, let us note that they can be modest *quantitatively*. A system doesn't have to change over all its schools at once. It may be possible to alter even a half, or a third, of a large school. In practice, it is usually far wiser to perfect the new pattern in a "lead" or "pilot" school, using it also to train personnel and develop suitable materials. But the quantum jump itself cannot be qualitatively compromised. One cannot jump across a chasm by small stages or halfway. Nor can the jump be successful, likely, if it is not understood by those making it to be a jump, not a modification.

If I perhaps belabor the point, it may be because so few, even among reform leaders, enunciate it. We constantly hear, "We need better schools." "Better," I fear, suggests modification. We need *different* schools!

Let us look at some of the group of quantum jumps required to get them.

1. FROM "TEACHING" TO "LEARNING"

Few myths in education are more mischievous than the notion that "teaching" and "learning" are directly linked—that one is the obverse of the other. This innocent misconception leads some parents, and others who should know better, to urge "teach harder" when the apparent learning accomplished or the grades on the report card are less than pleasing. Usually well-intentioned persons will arise in public meetings to urge more old-fashioned, no-nonsense teaching, more homework, hard study and fewer "frills," and tighter discipline—even a touch of the whip to "make them pay attention." (Some who can find little to admire in most Europeans surprisingly sing praises to their often more rigid schools!)

Behind such approaches one is apt to discover the "empty vessel" concept of education. The function of the teacher is to pour learning into the child, like coffee into a cup. If for some reason the vessel stubbornly refuses to fill, the teacher simply pours more and harder. Maybe a good rap on the vessel will persuade it to accept and retain more readily!

In far simpler days, this now quaint approach had some practical validity—the aim was to transfer a limited amount of information, elementary skills, and moral precepts from the old generation, represented by the teacher, to the new, in the form of the children in the group. The material was mostly "hard," meaning that it was little subject to argument, varied interpretation, or vague boundaries. It was also fixed, in that what was taught at the beginning and end of a decade would show little difference. Most of the teaching was by rote, which made evaluation of results easy. A child could spell so many given words correctly, name so many capitals, recite so many rules or principles verbatim, whether grasped or not.

Learning of this kind, if it occurred, likely happened in the school, not outside it, and was the result of the teaching effort. The child *was* usually pretty much an empty vessel so far as the "education" attempted by the school was concerned. A sharp line divided "book learning" from everyday experience. The child might learn a good deal about nature, or the operation of a farm or blacksmith shop, or home and kitchen chores, but most of this had little overlap with what went on in school. School was where one learned to read, and write, and do sums, and to memorize some poems, names of presidents, and a smattering of other facts.

This is the root of our present tendency to assume that "education" takes place mainly or largely in the schools, and that what the schools "teach" will become nearly the total of what our children know and understand and can do. Plainly this is no longer so: *today the schools play a minor role in education.* It is still an important role, because education has become so much more essential that a minor role now can be much greater than the whole role a century ago.

As the scope of the education attempted by the school has

broadened and deepened manyfold, the line between "in school" and "outside school" learning has largely disappeared, except (as we shall consider) for the ghetto child. The overlap is now great. And in "inputs," the situation for most children has changed to a staggering degree and with astounding speed.

The education of today's parents is on the whole far above the average for even fifty years ago. Census figures from 1940 to 1960 suggest the rapidity of the shift: from 26% with full high school or college, to 43% two decades later, for whites. For non-whites, the figures jumped from 8% to 22%. Since 1960 the trend has operated still faster. For whites, illiteracy among those under 35 now is well below one percent, and for non-whites is put at about 5%. Quite obviously, the educational level of parents has a profound effect on the child's input both before and after he goes to school.

The most striking change has been in the mass media — with television, of course, setting the pace. As recently as 1955, about two thirds of homes had television. The figure today is well over 90%. Today the child *entering* first grade has probably had 3,000 or more hours of television watching — or more time than he may spend in instruction in school for the next four years. Even allowing for a large share of dross, the input of information, ideas, impressions, experiences, adds up to a dizzying total. Criticizing the "quality" of television programs ranks as a major indoor preoccupation, but we should not let this conceal the reality of "input." Viewing television, the child gets literally millions of "bits" of input, which are the raw material of learning. Moral and taste considerations are besides the point.

To television, add radio, records, and tape; the astronomic increase in the quantity, technical quality, and variety of books, magazines, newspapers, and other publications; an astonishing variety of playthings, craft and hobby supplies; photography and motion pictures; and even such factors as the enormously greater number of packages in the home (has any Ph.D. candidate studied the influence of cereal packages on early reading?). Today's child is exposed to articles, pictures, images, reading matter, music, talk, sounds, as well as facts, ideas, opinions, and behavior on the order of *perhaps a thousand times the input of the child of Lincoln's era* — when our school system took shape.

Besides these inputs inside the home, we still have to add today's child's far greater mobility and involvement in his community. A child of seven today may well have gone more miles, on short trips and long ones, than a 1900 adult went in a normal lifetime. A child of twelve may very well have participated in a dozen or more structured activities such as a nursery or play group, Cub Scouts, organized summer camps or leagues, a church group, and various private or group programs wholly or partly instructional, in music, art, dance, chess, astronomy, religious history, electronics, rock-hounding, hog-raising, on down an interminable list.

This is still only a partial list of inputs to which children in general are exposed. To regard them as "empty vessels" in the old sense seems patently absurd; to assume that the school is the most important educational input is to move even further from the obvious facts. Marshall McLuhan has suggested, in his waspish and provocative fashion, that the child "interrupts" his education when he attends school, and that when he enters its doors he moves from a higher to a lower level of input.

One effect of this "input revolution," of course, is to still further accentuate the differences among children. *The quality of the input, for educational purposes, and to some extent the quantity, will reflect the home and the community* — and so will be influenced greatly by income. The child from a higher income home is likely to have more books, publications, records, playthings, craft supplies, more travel exposure, more involvements in camps, clubs, courses, and the like. His input is also likely to overlap the school's areas of interest more. The ghetto child may know and understand a great deal about his community; but when he enters the classroom of a prim, middle-class teacher he learns quickly enough that a chasm exists between his real world and that of the school. Much of his input does not overlap.

But even if we look only at the middle range of children, we can quickly see that any effort to "teach" them is going to run into trouble very rapidly. The whole concept of teaching a group is based on the empty vessel principle: how can you teach a *group* who vary enormously in what they know, what they think they know, and what they know that isn't so? The only approach that offers much promise is to ignore what they know, and teach as if they were blank slates. The twin results are insufferable boredom and waste. *Huge amounts of school money are spent "teaching" pupils what they already know.*

In an unusual published case study of a transition, *The Non-graded Primary School* by Lillian Glogau and Murray Fessel, the minutes of teachers' discussion report finding increasing evidence that much of what is taught to the children "they already know before they get to us, or they are retaught too many times." Rarely does it occur to teachers to find out what their pupils/do know before they launch into a unit or program. In *Learning and the Educative Process,* edited by J. D. Krumboltz and published in 1965, researcher Robert Gagné does report on a series of tests given to students *before* various lessons. Half the children, it turned out, were able to complete the tests nearly perfectly!

A large study of the effectiveness of courses in civics, made by the Michigan Survey Research Center, compared the knowledge and understanding of students who had taken such courses with that of those who hadn't. They found only "trivial" differences: the giving of such courses (compulsory in many states) is apparently pure ritual and total waste. (On the hypothesis that Negroes might have less exposure outside of school, a smaller study was made. It proved out. These students did learn something.)

Evidence that "teaching" is staggeringly inefficient abounds, and has for many years. But there has been little realization that *most of the learning (apart from rote) that the school blandly takes credit for rests on inputs received outside the school.* The school provides only a small part of the total learning process; almost none of this derives from "teaching"—that is, planned and sequentially arranged instruction, intended to oblige the class or group to cover certain material in a predetermined order.

Mathematics gives us some view of the efficiency of the school in an area where outside inputs are apt to be weakest.

Nearly every child studies mathematics through most of his elementary and secondary schooling. What are the results? Common observation tells us that a lot of adults seem extremely ill at ease with even such problems as balancing a checkbook — some banks kindly provide "automatic" forms that avoid any thinking. The massive Project Talent study of our high schools gives us more precise information in its 1964 publication, *The American High School Student,* edited by John C. Flanagan. It shows that in arithmetical reasoning, ninth graders on the average could answer only seven of 16 problems — all of which dealt with "how" rather than actual computations, and most of them at a level of difficulty that should not have troubled a bright elementary school child at all. In grade twelve the score rose to 10 of 16 for boys, and under nine for girls. When we put the endless hours of teaching against these findings, we must indeed wonder. If a student has not mastered simple arithmetical reasoning, what *has* he learned?

Because of the grade system, schools are likely to assume that if a student has passed an examination, he then "knows" the material. The record *says* he knows it. Few longitudinal studies have been made to discover what is retained. Where there is evidence on what the *school* has "taught," it is usually as disheartening as that above. And because teaching implies "subjects," we find teachers, particularly in the upper grades, forced to take a "not my table" attitude. If the science teacher finds the students shockingly ignorant of basic historical concepts, what is he to do? Stop teaching his subject and teach another? Shall he complain to the principal that the social studies teachers did a poor job? Unless he is eager for trouble, he will shake his head and resume instruction in *his* subject. The interweaving of "subjects," which *is* both education and the basis of retention, is actively discouraged by the school's organization.

The traditional view that "teaching" and "learning" are merely opposite sides of the same process derives in large measure, it would seem, from the large body of psychological experiments of the classic "rat in a box" laboratory type. An animal is put into a totally unnatural situation, kept confined, starved so it will seek the reward of food, and perhaps electrically shocked as punishment if it responds in certain ways. By brute force, it is compelled to take certain actions, and this is measured as "learning."

Let us translate this. Suppose a madman gets you in his power. Pointing a gun at you, he demands that you grovel and recite the alphabet backwards each time he whistles. If you wish to survive, you comply. Can we conceivably call your behavior "learning" in any sense connected with education? Totalitarian states developed this technique into "brainwashing," producing certain responses through terror and threat. Can we say the victim has "learned"? In a strict technical sense, perhaps; in any educational sense, no.

A classroom, "teaching" school is patterned directly upon this brutal laboratory approach, a fact examined at some length as long ago as 1952 by the eminent Dr. James L. Mursell of Columbia University, in *Psychology for Modern Education*. Dr. Mursell noted the unfortunate close parallel between test animals confined to boxes and children confined to classrooms. What both wanted most, he suggested, was *out*, and there lay the root cause of discipline problems.

Professor B. F. Skinner, the even more eminent Harvard experimental psychologist, has expressed a similar point of view. In an October 1965 article in *Saturday Review*, he noted the heavy reliance of teachers on coercion and "aversive control" and its effect:

> The student who works mainly to escape aversive stimulation discovers other ways of escaping. He is tardy — "creeping like snail unwillingly to school." He stays away from school altogether. . . . There are subtler forms of escape. Though physically present and looking at teacher or text, the student does not pay attention. He is hysterically deaf. His mind wanders. He daydreams. "Mental fatigue" is usually not a state of exhaustion but an uncontrollable disposition to escape. . . . The periods into which the school day is broken measure the limits of successful aversive control rather than the capacity for sustained attention.

One of the easiest forms of escape, he adds, is simply to forget all that has been learned — a path to freedom hard to block.

It is shocking to reflect on how much of the school's energy goes into *making* children do things. When compulsion enters, joy flies out. A vicious circle develops: those parents who remember their schooling as a dull, grinding submission to raw authority are none too likely to pack their children off to school with the expectation that they will find learning a shining, enjoyable, rewarding experience. Rather, the parents are prepared to drive the child through school, so that in due course he may have "educated" stamped upon his forehead. A school where children learn willingly and joyfully may, at least at first, be regarded with suspicion. Doesn't the child need "discipline" to prepare him for a grim world? Must he not suffer as his parents did? Can anything he enjoys be good for him? Education is seen as a penalty a child must pay for the privilege of growing old enough to escape from it, the privilege of never again having to read a book or educate himself further except as his job may demand. The classroom is often a bitter experience not easily forgotten.

Here we can pause to sympathize with the classroom teacher. After all, she did not create the situation—she is forced into it quite as much as are the children. She may well demand, "How else can I handle a class? I must have them under control—that is the first demand the school makes of me. I must direct what shall be done, and who shall speak, and about what; and I must have attention when *I* speak. Otherwise how can I possibly get this class over all the work they have to cover?"

So long as we tolerate the classroom as the educational situation, there is no easy answer.

We may note that teachers not unnaturally deceive themselves enormously as a rule. It is the *other* teachers who are at fault! A teacher really *must* believe he or she is "teaching" the children, helping them, benefitting them, to retain mental health. The strict, blatantly directive teacher, the warm, gentle, persuasive teacher, and the cold, distant, authoritative teacher, all will insist on the validity of their approach.

In truth, they have a point; for it makes only a modest difference whether a child is driven or led, and whether he is led by personality, by Socratic questioning, or even by planned "discovery." He is being forced, like the white rat, to go the way the teacher wants him to go—to arrive at "the right answer." The teacher desperately wants the right answer, because it is cue and permission to proceed to the next material to be covered. The better and kinder teachers may lead; but few children are so stupid that they do not early realize they must suffer themselves to be led. Any resistance, any deviation, will draw on the student the displeasure of the teacher, and if necessary the full tyrannical force of the school.

Because we think of education as automatically "good," and because success in school (on report cards and records) is deemed essential, we tend to blind ourselves to the true nature of the classroom school—the more so if the principal has a kindly twinkle in his eye and some gray at the temples, and the teacher is a cute young thing with nice blue eyes and a soft voice.

But the structure of the school is a design for tyranny, and the constant operating force is fear. The class-and-grade school *directs* the pupil, from first grade through twelfth, within an inch of his life. Each day, each hour, each minute he is *told* what to do, how to behave, and frequently what to think (the child who is stubbornly honest about his thinking and slow to give the "right answer" even when he knows it inspires exasperation in most teachers). He is literally an *inmate* of the school, imprisoned, constantly under authority from which there is little practical appeal. The story is told of the young boy who was sent to the school yard to gather some dirt for a flower pot. "You know, Mother," he reported later, "I could have escaped!"

Typically, the student has minimal liberty in terms of what he, individually, shall do—except as he acquires increasing skill in evading or partially defying the pervasive authority. *Most of the time, he cannot even talk—not a word—without risking punishment.* When he may talk, he is expected to say what the teacher wants to hear. All of this stems from the effort to *teach,* to force certain, predetermined "learning" upon the child—and worse, to force it upon a *group* of children in brash defiance of their differences and the variations of input materials they bring to the situation. Despite efforts at "modern" teaching, the classroom teacher still indisputably is trying to teach groups of inmates the same thing at the same time in much the same way. It doesn't work. And it is a form of torture, carried on systematically for years.

In *How Children Fail,* teacher John Holt, who worked with small classes in a private school, reports:

> The valiant and resolute band of travelers I thought I was leading towards a much-hoped-for destination turned out instead to be more like convicts in a chain gang, forced under threat of punishment to move along a rough path leading nobody knew where and down which they could see hardly more than a few steps ahead. School feels like this to children: it is a place where *they* make you go and where *they* tell you to do things and where *they* try to make your life unpleasant if you don't do them or don't do them right.

Children come to school accustomed to adult domination and continual, detailed direction ("Go brush your teeth!" "Sit up at table!" "Be careful!" "Don't scuff your new shoes!"); but direction in the school is so incessant that they are apt to be baffled. Dr. Jerome S. Bruner observes in *Toward A Theory of Instruction:* "Young children in school expend extraordinary time and effort figuring out what it is the teacher wants—and usually come to the conclusion that she or he wants tidiness or remembering or doing things at a certain time in a certain way."

It is significant that Dr. Bruner, a psychologist at Harvard and one of the most noted leaders in this area of investigation, titled his book not *A Theory of Instruction* or *Notes on A Theory of Instruction* but *Toward A Theory of Instruction.* Only in the last several years has it dawned on educators—and still on only a small minority—that the schools, despite their numbers and experience and the billions they spend, *have built almost no theory of instruction.* They know a good deal about "normative" teaching—that is, what is done, in a descriptive sense. But the testing of alternatives is largely a post-Sputnik phenomenon. Limited as the findings are, they are shattering in implication.

Stuck in the deadly rut of the "teaching" approach, the schools have fallen further and further behind reality, to and past the disaster point.

We should bear in mind that the "teaching" approach, based on fear, force, and brutal disrespect (aside from lip-service) for individual differences, does not simply fail to accomplish all the learning desired. It frequently, perhaps usually, has a negative effect: *it discourages, impedes, and belittles genuine learning.* The more the class-and-grade structure is adhered to, the greater this effect. There are few parents of a high school graduate who have not witnessed it, first hand, in the distress of the child caught in this common situation.

Clearly what the schools need is a quantum jump from the present atmosphere of imprisonment, direction, compulsion, and punishment, to one in which the individual child is enabled and encouraged, from the outset, to take on much of the responsibility for his own learning. That children can do so is indisputable. A child not yet two responds to an inner urge to learn to walk. No one "teaches" him how. Fortunately, he is so young that it seldom occurs to parents to tell him: "Now, Johnny, put your left foot forward. No, Johnny, your *left* foot! Here, I'll do it for you. Now, shift your weight to that leg. Johnny, you're not paying attention! No, you can't have a drink of water—our walking lesson has fifteen minutes to go. Now, you're on your left leg—shift your weight to the right one, meanwhile swinging your arms the opposite way. Johnny, you fell down. You're not cooperating with me. I'm afraid I'll have to give you a zero." Even without such invaluable teaching, Johnny amazingly learns to walk—the faster if the parents encourage and applaud in relaxed fashion and offer assistance *when it is asked for.* Having learned to walk, the child rapidly improves his skill.

At about the same tender age the child begins acquiring skill in the far more difficult art of speech. He learns to articulate sounds that are intelligible; he grasps the amazing idea that words relate to things and even motions and abstractions; he builds a vocabulary; and in some mysterious way develops his own private syntax (not learned from his parents), from which he goes to the conventional syntax he is exposed to. Again, he does best if he has relaxed encouragement and help *when he asks for it.* Let the parents try to push, or teach, or correct, and the child may become a lifelong stutterer.

In the book referred to, Dr. Bruner comments: "Learning is so deeply ingrained in man that it is almost involuntary, and thoughtful students of human behavior have even speculated that our specialization as a species is a specialization for learning." With today's inputs, children in ordinarily good surroundings and good health learn spectacularly — until they hit school.

The jump from "teaching" to "learning" essentially involves getting the teacher, however "good" or kindly or lovable or well-intentioned, off the child's back and out of his way. Children cannot learn effectively at the same speed and the same time and in the same way. *Each child must proceed from the point his inputs have brought him to at any given moment.* Since, even if we teach him alone we cannot be sure (except in the case of the simpler, measurable skills) what this point is, we must make radical changes in organization: from fixed grouping to individual progress, and from sequential to random instruction. These quantum jumps, plus leaping from "teaching" to a largely self-directed, "random" learning approach, will bring us to the open school.

"Today's learner . . . is one to whom things are done rather than one who does. If he becomes too active or gives way to self-expression, and especially if he deviates, he will run the risk of the teacher's condemnation, assignment to the detention room, failure, and even expulsion."

William C. Kvaraceus in *Educational Leadership*, April 1967

23

MORE QUANTUM JUMPS

2. FROM GROUP TO INDIVIDUAL

The class-and-grade system began by assuming that children had to be *taught,* and that they would be taught *in groups.* It was no secret then that children differ, and learn at different rates and in different ways — though far less was understood about these matters in pre-psychology days. Relatively few persons were concerned with these differences: the popular view was that most children didn't want to learn, much as they didn't want to bring in wood for the fire or weed the garden, and that liberal use of the whip was the best way to change a "stupid" or "lazy" or recalcitrant child into one with a thirst for book learning. In schools of the day, a quarter to a third of the children might daily get whipped, birched, strapped, caned, or less formally clouted on the head or rapped on the knuckles to encourage mental processes. The procedure was accepted, just as the prison-school of today is accepted. We must remember that then, as now, only highly respectable persons applied the torture, for highly respectable reasons.

Teaching in groups had many advantages at that time. It

permitted the use of cheap help, and greatly lowered costs. It allowed some standards to be set (a welcome novelty), and some degree of order and plan to be introduced to replace the haphazard arrangements that had prevailed. These advances in turn won public willingness, if hardly eagerness, to pay taxes for educational purposes. We should remember that the public schools then, particularly in the East and more populous centers, were still to a great extent "poor schools"—more or less charitable enterprises supported by the wealthier (who did not send their children) for the benefit of the less fortunate and the poor. Only a few wild men dared suggest that the public schools had to be *good*—they needed only to be good enough for the classes of persons who filled them. The education intended was both minimal and terminal. Very few students carried their formal instruction further: the high school came into the picture several decades later.

So our present class-and-grade system took definite shape, without apology, as an expression of the fiction that children could be regarded and treated as alike, and so taught in fixed groups on a regimented, treadmill plan. It was the child's job to fit the school. If he didn't or couldn't, that was too bad. The child tried again or was simply sloughed off.

In part because the grade system was so new and attendance so ragged, these early schools were not as rigid as those "well run" institutions of the later part of the century. By this time population growth was exerting strong pressures and the tide of immigration was running strong. Classes of 60 and 70 were common. Schools prided themselves on "efficiency," which unfortunately applied to outward appearances and not to results. Teachers held their posts by sufferance and trembled at the merest hint of displeasure by their superiors. Little happened instructionally in the classroom that was not precisely ordered from on high.

But the counterforces became stronger. As the educational program grew larger in scope, the fiction of alikeness (which had broken down almost at once) became more and more difficult to act on. By about 1880 the "poor school" aspect had pretty much evaporated: the schools had become public in a wider sense. By the end of the century the roots of what was to be called the "Progressive" era were well planted, to bear assorted but potent fruit after World War I. Psychology and IQ testing came to public awareness; Thorndike set moving an avalanche of achievement testing; and the child development movement threw new light on individual differences. Despite the excesses, the schools were broadly humanized, modernized, and improved. The Progressive Education Association died in 1955 not because its basic tenets had been rejected, but because they had become accepted even by those who fought some of the extremes.

In the process the well-run school became the anarchistic school, in which the established teacher commonly "owned" her classroom and within wide limits did just what she pleased; and in which, as we have seen, a fifth-grade class might include some children working, in a particular subject area, at second grade level, while those around worked at all levels up to eighth or higher. "Grade" had become virtually meaningless; and "grade," of course, was the reason for "class."

Unfortunately, working educators are "brought up" in classes; often train in colleges that still make heavy use of classes (in contrast to the flexibility of the better universities, which use lectures, television, seminars, laboratory work, tutors, small conferences, and individual work); and then become teachers in classes. Some are unable to think in any other terms, or reluctant to consider working except in a class, however exacerbating its day-to-day demands. They seem unable to see the head-on collision between the class concept and individualized instruction.

"What do you *mean!*" a teacher almost wails. "I knock myself out trying to individualize instruction. Why, I have four reading groups now, and no one else teaching my grade has more than three." Blessing on the teacher for effort; but she misses the point that she is teaching four *groups.*

Another teacher, shocked by my suggestion that the school paid little heed to the individual, told me that that very day she and the principal had spent almost a half hour deciding what to do with one bright but "nervous" eighth-grade girl. The upshot was that they agreed to keep her in grade, rather than "special progress" her into ninth! This teacher could plainly see that the discussion had concerned an individual, and that both she and the principal cared about the individual; but she could not see, or refused to see, that in the end the choice boiled down to a crude grouping procedure. The child had to "fit" one class or the other—that was the limit of the school's resources.

As we noted in analyzing the classroom teacher's "job" in Part I, she is forced into a schizophrenic situation. On one hand she has been taught to recognize and honor individual differences, on the other she must move her class along as a unit, however much she may subdivide it. In the higher grades, even the pretense of teaching on more than one level is likely to vanish, though the differences in achievement become still more striking. There is also the "vexing dilemma" of *grade-expectation,* a factor that becomes particularly obnoxious and troublesome in ghetto schools. All the lip-service about individual variations fails to push aside the unrealistic, simple-minded, maddening assumption that because a child has been put into a group labelled "Grade X" he is to be evaluated on the basis of arbitrary or broadly averaged expectations of performance for that grade. He is viewed not as a student who is at a certain level, but as one who is at a level *relative* to an arbitrary standard. Few children are at the standard on any one factor—perhaps only one child in five. But the nonsensical standard still carries much administrative importance and constantly distorts and disguises the true situation. The yearbook *Elementary School Organization* notes:

> Grade-level expectations are built into curricular patterns and structural organization. They are built into the thought processes of children, parents and colleagues, and they are built into the materials and tests used each day. To ignore these expectations is to invite the misunderstanding and often the condemnation of everyone involved.

Outside her room the teacher can talk about the "child centered" school and the sacredness of individual differences. Let

her step inside her door, and she must grapple with grade expectations and group teaching.

It appears rather plain that young teachers typically come
to their work brimming with enthusiasm and good intentions,
highly aware of individual differences. Then they encounter
the weird realities of the classroom. As we have detailed (Chapter 8), a teacher soon discovers that the more diligent she is in
observing differences and individual needs, the more problems,
headaches, and frustrations she creates for herself. To maintain mental health (and an alarming percentage of teachers
don't—not to mention those who quickly withdraw because
"they can't take it"), the teacher must adopt an "I do what I
can" attitude. We can speculate that this may be a main factor
behind the fierce resistance of many teachers to having any adult
observe them or share their room, and the odd mistaking of
grouping for "individual" treatment we have just examined.
In the class-and-grade school, the teacher comes to *fear* any true,
vigorous recognition of individuals. The classroom may be
rough, but at least it is familiar, private, and *hers*—and in these
senses, protective.

We should consider at this point the "non-graded" form of
organization, long in use in some hundreds of more advanced
schools, especially in the elementary or lower elementary periods. The usual pattern is to set up classes that include a fairly
wide range of age, maturity, and academic achievement, on an
overlapping pattern:

MISS ABLE'S CLASS
MISS BAKER'S CLASS
MR. CHARLES' CLASS
MRS. DOGUE'S CLASS

If Miss Able has a child who seems to be pushing beyond the
upper limits of her class, the student can be transferred, at any
time of year, to Miss Baker's—where the median standards are
a bit higher. No grade designations are used. Ordinarily transfers are not made lightly or often; but since they can be accom-

plished anytime, and moves take place all year, there is far greater freedom to "adjust" children than in the rigid grade setup. If the non-grading is genuine (there are schools so called that use the term publicly but continue to operate in much the same way as before), the grade-expectation problem is reduced, although it slips back in through the materials used or the "subjects" taught, which have strong grade connotations. Non-grading is an advance — but a modification, not a quantum jump. The classroom and grouping and "teaching" remain.

The thought of the open school, with each student working and progressing as an individual rather than as a member of a fixed class, terrorizes many working educators. The first reaction usually is, "It would produce chaos!" This is nonsense, of course. Chaos is what we have *now,* in a system that is a mass of contradictions, dilemmas, and frustrations!

The open school, however it may be organized, does not simply modify grouping. It totally *discards* administrative grouping, which is what we have in the class-and-grade, or even nongraded, structure, and introduces purely *educationally*-dictated grouping. This *is* a quantum jump.

Another way to put it is to say we shift from "pre" to "post." We cease announcing, "These twenty-nine children are assigned to Mrs. K's class, where they will be taught in the ensuing nine months," and instead say, "Susie, having reached a certain point in her learning progress yesterday, will today go to Mrs. P's room to continue her progress." The class's assignment *preceded* any achievement; Susie's assignment *follows* achievement. It cannot be planned or predicted, because her individual rate of learning and maturing cannot be predicted.

The open school will have groupings, but they will be educationally-dictated, not administrative; "post" and not "pre"; and always fluid, not fixed in point of time or composition. An analogy may help us visualize. Imagine a large number of cross-country runners, who have begun the race at different times. They will be strung out along the route. If we watch from a helicopter we will see groups constantly forming and changing, as the runners progress at different speeds. Suppose there is a river, with boats to ferry the runners over. Each boat will "group" the runners who reached it about the same time; and each such group will dissolve on the other side as the runners resume different rates of advance. How much simpler it is to fill the boats this way, for the purposes of the moment, than to make up in advance lists of who shall be in each and sort them out clerically!

When a school is set up for this kind of "automatic" grouping, a great deal of administrative work becomes unnecessary.

Clearly this kind of grouping is like that used in the early one-room school — the strongest feature of that still admired system. It is simply employed on a much larger scale. The practical problems of organizing a school this way are by no means overwhelming. More serious are the human factors — not among the children, who react with appreciation reflected in greater effort and the evaporation of discipline problems, but among the staff. But as we have suggested in our fictional Isaac Newton school, once a teacher realizes what it means to be free of the maddening, crippling classroom, he or she is apt to rejoice mightily.

Once the "class" goes in the garbage can, a great new era in American education can begin.

3. FROM SEQUENTIAL TO RANDOM INSTRUCTION

This third quantum jump, I fear, may be the hardest to grasp and visualize, even after our visit to Isaac Newton. We have been brought up in a world in which "sequential" is good and "random" bad; it is not easy to reverse accustomed values. But if we would live in the world of today and tomorrow, we have to.

For long years, the function of the school was to provide almost all the academic inputs, to pump old skills and knowledge into new students. It sought to prepare them, to a very modest degree, for the *existing* world they would enter very shortly.

Life is not now so simple. *The mission of the school has changed.*

As we have seen, the school has become a minor factor in providing inputs.

Even in the basic skills, the demands have enormously increased (a thought the "basic education" partisans do not seem to have grasped). Once it was sufficient that the graduate could *compute* by arithmetic, reasonably accurately. No further ability in mathematics was required, no real understanding of mathematics or of its applications (especially those on the theoretical side). In reading, the barest facility was enough—ability to read a bill of sale or puzzle out a newspaper story would suffice for most. Today reading ability implies a capacity to know what reading materials are available, to find information, to select, check facts, evaluate, to survey, skim, summarize, to digest, relate new information to old, even foresee where still newer will come from. (The list suggests the true size of the problem of instructing disadvantaged children in "reading" if they are to be brought to a competitive level!) Even the college or technical student, not yet embarked on a career, had best be able to wolf down enormous amounts of reading. "Speed reading" corrective courses do a lively trade, with junior executives, technicians, scientists, and scholars the best customers.

Within the Establishment, many now publicly recognize that education covers so long a period and the world changes so fast, that the schools must prepare a child not for the present world but for conditions to come. The problem is far from abstract in effect. Even the Ph.D. who becomes obliged to seek a new job in his late thirties may find himself in trouble: the knowledge he acquired in great depth fifteen years before may be regarded as obsolete—and he with it. Old-style "vocational" courses in high schools flounder badly, because the methods and equipment used fall further and further behind those in commercial and industrial use. Yesterday's science has a quaint, museum quality.

We already have lip-service to the concept that the school can no longer "teach the past," but must equip children to learn on their own, to grapple with new problems, to adapt to and manage violently rapid change, to acquire and accept new facts and ideas in place of old ones, continuously. But lip-service will hardly suffice. The quality of education needed today must be enormously better. A major function of the school must be *integration:* the interweaving, evaluation, and correction of inputs, the structuring of skills and content on interconnected concepts. The mission has changed radically. It surely is futile to try to produce students with problem-solving and change-meeting abilities when we cling to the antique devices of "subject" and "course," and the *sequential* approach they demand.

Plainly enough, "subject" represents the exact opposite of integration: baloney-slicing of education into neat packages of convenient size for administrative purposes. "Course" means a portion of a subject—a fragment of a fragment—arranged in a certain "logical" sequence for teaching (not learning) purposes. Consider the whole process. Mathematics, for example, is broken down into subjects: arithmetic, algebra, geometry, trigonometry, and so on. Algebra in turn may be broken down into elementary, intermediate, or advanced. Each of these courses again is broken down into a syllabus, or outline of what is to be taught in sequence. Language arts similarly breaks down into reading, writing, spelling, composition, literature, and other subjects, which in turn fracture into courses. The higher one goes in grades, the more the courses proliferate.

"Teaching" is now supposed to reverse the process: the student is expected to synthesize an "education" by somehow melding these divergent "slices" of instruction into some kind of whole. It doesn't work. A vast part of the effort produces no effect whatever. Typically the student emerges with a diploma that certifies to the time he has served in his prison-school, but with only tatters of the education he needs.

The idea of teaching by sequence stems basically from the institution of the class. In the early class-and-grade school, the teacher taught the class as a whole—unlike the rural one-room school of fond affection. To direct the little-trained teachers, the administrators devised detailed sequences in each subject, planning out the year's instruction far in advance and far removed from the actual students. Even less was known then, of course, than now about how children actually learn, but the thought likely would not have bothered the administrator of the time. Had the sequence arrived at by "logical" considerations been challenged, the answer would have been, "In my school the pupils will learn in the order they are *told* to learn!"

Textbooks were few in these early class-and-grade schools,

but they soon appeared and their flood has still to abate. Hillel Black, the author of *The American Schoolbook,* a recent study of textbooks and their influence, estimates that a school child typically is supposed to absorb some 32,000 pages of text before he graduates high school! Naturally enough, textbooks picked up and "embalmed" the sequential approach—as McLuhan has stressed, books by their very format tend to be sequential. Over the years, the idea that *teaching had to follow a certain step-step-step order solidified, and along with it the notion that the same had to be true of courses and subjects.* Not until the Progressive movement had brought some sense of human realities into the school did the individual teacher acquire any liberty to vary the established sequence. But teachers, with rare exception, still think and teach in sequence terms. Usually they select from texts available to them (the choice may be narrow or wide, according to the State and the system) those with sequences they prefer—which they then follow with little deviation, especially in the higher grades. They may take brief excursions, and they backtrack frequently in "reviews," but overall they go by the text's sequence. Texts dominate instruction overwhelmingly. As a consequence, most instruction is by the traditional sequential approach.

The idea is first to teach fragment A; when A has been learned, the class can go to B; when B has been mastered, we can proceed to C, and so on. It sounds beautifully logical, but in use it breaks down immediately. To begin with, the students are not blank slates, ready to begin at A. They are at positions all through the sequence—in what they know, what they think they know, and what they know *wrong.* Re-teaching is surely a major source of the acute boredom referred to by Harold J. Noah, and by so many other observers today. In many subjects, perhaps most notably American history, rehashing is built into the curriculum. Daily practice, including plowing through a text, recitation, and reviewing, adds to mind-dulling repetition. But most of all, the school tends to ignore the huge amount of learning the child has acquired outside school.

Next comes the crushing fact that rarely if ever do *all* in a group master A before going on to B, or B before C. Each step involves failures; as the steps multiply the breaks in the sequential learning go up geometrically. Reviews, which usually consist of teaching the same way only faster, merely add to the boredom.

That this style of instruction is dreadfully ineffective has become all too apparent. Though the "creative" teacher tries to modify or depart from the textual sequence in response to class needs, she cannot really respond well to the differing needs of 30 very different individuals. "Class needs" is a myth. Always, in the conventional school, the teacher is locked within the limitations of the classroom situation. She can do only what is possible with 30 students at a time. However appealing "project" and "discovery" approaches may be, class and classroom tend to force the teaching into narrow channels, all highly sequential.

The ability to learn sequentially reflects a high order of sophistication. It is most possible for the broadly educated adult, least practical for the young student. As we have suggested at many points, this is *not* the way children learn—they are enormously more successful, and happy, with a *random* approach. This process is something like putting together a jigsaw puzzle. At first there are only many bits (raw input), largely meaningless; but as these are gradually fitted together to form clumps or blocks, a glimmer of meaning appears. Then comes the flash of insight or recognition, the exciting moment when one suddenly sees how two such blocks relate and rapidly builds links between them. Finally, when many such blocks have been organized into a structure, comes the filling in of voids. No two persons put together a jigsaw puzzle in the same order, no two children learn in the same order. Even with great effort and personal attention, a teacher cannot find out "the state of the child's puzzle"—what pieces he has, what clumps he has formed, some firmly, some tentatively, some incorrectly. John Holt makes the point in a March 1966 article in *Grade Teacher:*

> The reason why teaching in the conventional sense of the word—telling children things—is almost inherently impossible, is that we cannot know what the state of a young child's mind is. He hasn't got the words to tell us. . . . He has a great many more understandings that he cannot possibly verbalize—and a great many misunderstandings.

(Consider the child who learns the daily ceremony as "I will lead the pigeons to the flag," a version that makes more sense to him than the incomprehensible "I pledge allegiance . . . ." He is not aware of being in error. Given a free choice, he would prefer his version to the proper one. And only by lucky chance is his teacher likely to discover where this child "is" in this respect!)

Even as adults, we learn by this sort of jigsaw-puzzle assemblage, on the periphery of our knowledge, or by filling voids, or reorganizing. Our education can be only as good as the structure of *concepts* which supports and interrelates skills and information (content) and understanding. Most concepts transcend "subjects." Consider these, for example:

Reversibility	Equation
Model	Negative-positive
Checks and balances	Time development
System	Conservation
Inversion	Critical mass
Causal relationship	Feedback
Cycle	Democratic freedom

Negative-positive is a concept useful in mathematics, electricity and electronics, chemistry, photography, communications, and decision-making, to give a few instances; but how easily a subject-taught child may fail to realize, for a lifetime, that this is the *same* concept in many applications! The whole point of concepts is that once understood they become permanent tools of thought, keys to an infinite number of locks—including those to be encountered far in the future.

We have had the "subject-oriented school" and the "child-oriented school." Our need now appears to be the "concept-oriented school." To get it, we have to throw in the trash barrel not only the conventional *class,* but also *subject* and *course,* and all the ridiculous baloney-slicing apparatus dear to pedagogues.

The idea of organizing education around the three areas of skills, content, and concepts (whether these or other terms be used) is new, because it is only feasible in the open school. Team teaching has given it a great boost; but many who espouse team teaching have yet to take the full quantum jump and discard the "subject" and "sequential" approaches tied to the classroom. The random approach is still newer, but its day has come. We may note that it seems linked to allowing the students to *talk*. "Stop talking!" has long been the teacher's most frequent injunction. Today's advanced schools are at long last realizing that talking is *the* basic educational skill—far more so than reading. In teams of two or three, in seminar groups of up to ten, in "gaming," in one-to-one teacher conferences, and in free time, students are at last being allowed to talk—not in situations where one speaks and 29 listen, but in groups and places designed for talking. Such talk, of course, is characteristically *random*, not sequential.

As our look at Isaac Newton School suggested, the open school does not turn over control to the student, nor let him "run wild." Nor does it abandon rote and drill, or some sequential teaching (the alphabet and multiplication tables, for example!) where it still has point. But we face the plain fact that *students learn slowly and badly by sequential methods, and quickly and excellently when allowed, and assisted, to follow natural random methods.*

The mission of the school today is to assist the student, to facilitate his learning—not to teach or direct him except in certain limited areas. It is to help him develop concepts which will serve him whatever he does in later life. It is to help him integrate and organize his huge total input. Too, it must measure each student's progress—realistically and not by reference to any group.

We can get to this new kind of school only by a group of interconnected quantum jumps: from "teaching" to learning, from "class" to individual, from "sequential" to random instruction. The jumps call for boldness. The alternative is to "play it safe" by quietly watching the classroom disaster grow worse, day by day. Winston Churchill has been quoted as pointing out: "Things do not get better by being left alone. Unless they are adjusted, they explode with a shattering detonation."

We must step up the process of elimi-nating obsolete and outmoded teaching methods and curricula. This can only be done by educators, who need to cast off timidity, and, once and for all, inhale the ozone of courage and be willing to take the steps that are necessary.

Vice-president Hubert H. Humphrey at the White House Conference on Education, 1965

24

WHAT MUST BE DONE

The reader who has come this far without kindling a hot bonfire to burn this book as subversive, disaffecting, and threatening to established institutions may consider the author unsportsmanlike, if nothing worse, unless a suggestion is offered for action to help effect change.

Some shorter-winded radicals have proposed, "Burn down the schools!" The recipe is oversimple; and in any case disgruntled students are already giving it a try, to the extent of several hundred schools a year—a rate that could accelerate sharply as the present crisis worsens. In Part II, the problem of effecting change has been touched on. It may be worth analyzing a bit further at this point, although a thorough discussion would require a book in itself.

We can examine the question from two main points of view: that of those who labor within the schools, and that of the lay citizens outside who merely send their children and pay taxes. To be sure, one can count a third party—the students. A student revolt probably can produce action faster than almost anything else; but the mere thought calls to mind such late-show shockers as "Revenge of the Zombies" and is almost too horrible to contemplate. In any case, some students have already begun to experiment with the device, as with the torch; and small news stories of high schools that have had to suspend "to ease tensions" now appear fairly regularly in newspapers such as *The New York Times*. The crises usually have racial overtones. But can we suppose the college campus protests on other issues will not filter down? The banners of youthful protesters, as with adults, often state anything but the real cause of discontent. We can hardly expect to come on a forest of picket signs that read, "Bored!"

The odd notion that one might be able to learn something, or at least get some feedback, by listening to the students who are simultaneously the consumers, victims, and products of "education," is beginning to make some faint headway in the schools. Should it find nurture, if only as preferable to muddled, inchoate demonstrations, it could well begin to have some consistent effect in advancing change. Certainly the students overwhelmingly approve the newer instructional approaches. As we have seen, almost any move that gives the students more responsibility for their own education and that breaks away from classroom system rigidities usually produces a marked lessening of the "discipline problem."

But when we come to teachers, administrators, and others who are employed within the system, we run into massive and manifold resistance. So little effort has been made, relatively, for quantum-jump change rather than tinkering, that still less *thinking* has been done on this problem. Its bases seem poorly understood, and on the whole hardly identified.

There exists, to be sure, a considerable minority of school people who see the need for sweeping change, want to change, and will, if circumstances permit. But we must suspect that here again the curve is skewed towards the high-income community; in general the poorer in all senses a school system is, the less such push for radical change there will be, and the less chance of it bearing fruit. Vigorous individuals, wherever they turn up, can have remarkable effect, but commonly what they achieve is built on quicksand: let them move elsewhere, and it slowly sinks from sight as "the old way" fills in. Too many "experimental" schools owe too much of their results to the energy of one sponsor. *Enduring change has to be workable by ordinary mortals.*

Terms such as "retooling the teacher," bandied around today in the forward sectors, seem to evade the real issues. They skip lightly over the hard fact that we have no practical *means* to reshape people working in the schools. In-service efforts tend to be feeble and limited, and all too often window-dressed to hide their futility at least a little. What is announced as a seminar on "intrastaff cooperation-enhancement" may turn into a quarrelsome meeting on which groups should go first to the cafeteria. The administrator presiding is likely to be regarded by at least half those present as less qualified on any topic than they are. The "cooperative" approach, often a mass blind-lead-blind affair, has one frustrating weakness even when it works: it tends to be infinitely slow. And the whole notion that staff people can be trained in new ways while they put in exhausting days using old ways must be adjudged something short of realistic.

The trouble goes deeper, however. No aspect of teaching is better documented than that teachers interact with their pupils, emotionally. To some extent teachers do what they were taught or told to do, or what they have found "works"—but by and large teachers do what they *are*. In actuality the teacher talks and conveys attitudes on a subverbal level and makes hundreds of decisions a day mostly based on her personal values. Hundreds of thousands of teachers come from what roughly is called the "lower middle class," a stratum in which "proper" conformity is just about the highest of all behavioral virtues. To attempt to train such a teacher to respect and accept nonconformity by a few discussions must be considered an absurdity. Where the problem is a deep-seated conviction, dating from early childhood, that those who are "not like us" are inferior, retraining may at best lessen only the frequency of utterance of this idea. When we move into stickier areas the prospect becomes still dimmer. The teacher who hates anything male; the tyrant who lusts for assurances of power; the sadist; the disappointed who project lost dreams on their charges—these are among those only long psychiatric treatment would be likely to change. This is no special shortcoming of teachers except insofar as the occupation attracts certain types more than others. We would have the same difficulty retraining, say, a body of traveling salesmen.

To this we must add the problem of expertise. In any field, the person who has won some claim, however disputable, to being an expert can hardly be expected to cheerfully move into a new area as a beginner. A few brave souls, true, do love the challenge — the type who decide to take up the study of medicine at 40 or skiing at 60. For most, getting to where they are has been a hard struggle, and they will cling as to a life raft. Recently on a train I eavesdropped on two bright young teachers, animatedly discussing their work. To have suggested to them after half an hour that they were discussing not the education of their pupils but *classroom management* — the art of manipulating, controlling, and subduing their hordes — would I am sure have carried no meaning. They were obviously delighted with their skill, perhaps because only slightly earlier they had worried acutely, as beginning teachers do, over having their classes get out of hand. These were young teachers, presumably more flexible; but I for one would have hated being assigned to persuade them to abandon this newfound expertise, in an open school that didn't require it.

Teachers may *talk* willingness to change, until they find what it may cost them in loss of power and expertise. Then they may discover an amazing array of reasons why change should be postponed just a little while longer.

For administrators, rather different problems promise to arise. Their control over their schools or systems hardly approaches the dictatorship of the classroom teacher. Rather than being captains of their ships, they are usually nervous helmsmen often less concerned with where they are heading than with keeping the passengers from raising voices in anger. Nor is their expertise so closely linked to the classroom. Their duties are many, on many levels. However attenuated their authority, they are still managers; and the manager's expertise supposedly equips him to tackle situations and needs as they arise.

Probably, many school administrators find themselves rather intrigued by the prospect of introducing major change. Few may think the matter through consciously, but the sly thought may seep in that such a shift might *raise* their level of expertise relative to their nominal subordinates. On conventional affairs, the subordinates may scarcely conceal their feeling that *they* know best what to do, and need support rather than direction from above. If the administrator, however, is "up" on the new program and those under him are not, the tables must turn—the head man may be able to lead for once, rather than follow. The vision can be appealing.

But there are negatives. Offered the role of leader, the administrator may find his long-yearned-for power frightening as an imminent reality. "Cooperative" and "democratic" coaxing is one thing; giving orders and making large commitments quite another. In addition, the administrator's role is both public and political. He knows all too well that *any* change, however trivial or whatever its merits, will stir up a number of people and bring complaints, catcalls, and charges. He fears resistance from his staff, his faculty, his board or influential citizens that could halt or distort his plans and leave him far out on a limb. And since most administrators are past the period of fiery youth, he may decide that it is not up to *him* to rescue the children from the status quo—when by not rocking the boat he can take life easier as he gently glides to the charms of retirement. True, ambition pulls the other way: there is no faster way to attract national note and job offers from larger systems than to acquire a reputation as a forward-looking, successful innovator. The catch lies in "successful."

On balance, the administrator seems to present less of an obstacle than the typical teacher and, too, the administrator is more accessible.

The public, if we can trust large-scale polls taken for the Kettering Foundation, favors major change far more than those within the schools. Signs of disenchantment with the status quo appear in many forms, one of them being stiffening refusal to vote more money for schools, even while conditions are deplored and the need for better education is stressed. In April

1968, an Associated Press survey found this resistance "all across the land," confirming earlier conclusions of the Office of Education, and other studies.

The Educational Curtain and the traditional "everything is just perfect" attitude of school spokesmen have taken their toll. Evidence abounds that the public feels *something* must be awfully wrong—but nailing it down is another matter. Most parents understandably approach "education" in terms of their own children. Citizens with broader interests in the school system, save as taxpayers, are rare. Even fewer willingly undertake any study of local schools more penetrating than the bland reports of PTA or parent club committees. As has been pointed out, more meaningful information is not easy to come by; and reality is obscured by so many myths that the inexperienced investigator gets lost, often, at the first foggy turn. In my own experience, only sophisticated students of public education can begin to comprehend how bad things are—others keep assuming it must be *their* ignorance that makes their investigation so confusing! Honest, good-hearted citizens who have heard for years how horrible the slums are still react with utter shock when taken on a tour. Unfortunately, the corresponding tour of our educational disaster areas rarely can be arranged. The visitor sees at best the facades, not the crumbled interiors. Though occasionally "pure" citizens' committees have brought about major change, such instances are few.

Nevertheless, it seems to me that the indispensable element in a community is an *informed* body of citizens resolved to see change accomplished. By themselves they may not get far; but in combination with a genuine, motivated leader in the person of the superintendent, or a principal, or a member of the board of education, a program can get moving. Or the leader may be in some power position outside the school, as for example an influential business man, a Negro leader, an exceptional volunteer who has or builds a following, a militant clergyman with time, facts, and single-minded purpose. The citizen group need not be large, but it must be confident and vocal, ready to rush to the support of those developing new programs whenever necessary—as it often will be.

The task becomes easier when a crisis sets the stage: a money crisis, a scandal, a teachers' strike, minority issues, civil disturbances. These days, one need seldom wait long for a crisis — they come along like buses. The trick is to shift effort from "putting out the fire" to fundamentals.

The helpful effects of the Education Act of 1965 slowly become evident. Fresh blood is beginning to circulate. Title III and Title IV especially show results in making information and example more accessible — the Title III Regional Centers, now well established throughout the nation, provide a handy and useful starting place. So do the education schools or colleges of most universities, though the initial contact may be less easily made.

Perhaps the hardest aspect of the struggle (and struggle is the normal concomitant of change) centers on the need for *quantum-jump* change. To persons timid about change, a small shift seems safer, and even wiser, than a large one. The delusion can be devastating. Our need is to dump the classroom system, not to patch it up. But even on tactical, practical grounds, *large shifts are easier to effect than small ones.* If we put the people who staff our schools in a slightly modified situation, they will tend to slide back to where they were, to old accustomed ways. Far easier and more effective is to put them in new, very different situations, *where there is no way to regress.* As we take teachers out of the isolation of the classroom, put them under the observation of other adults and subject to feedback that cannot be ignored, we can achieve what "retraining" cannot. We can stop attempting to change *teachers* and instead change the *situation* that influences what they do. At present, to illustrate, we put a prejudiced teacher in charge of a class, whose members cannot escape. If instead we restructure the situation so the students can relate more to adults of their choice, they *can* escape, and do — forcing feedback upon the teacher that must be faced up to. The open school, we should remember, provides many *different* ways of using present teachers. We can expect that some teachers will be forced out, in one way or another — and high time they were. But most will adapt and once over the hurdle per-

areas—even if various projects headed in contrary directions. As we break out of the classroom-system rigidities and sterility, many paths beckon. We may find a lot of them lead to the same region, but it is too early to tell. And while we must "engineer," there is some need to avoid what Dean Theodore R. Sizer of the Harvard Graduate School of Education calls "a curious optimism." In his Dean's Report for 1966–67, issued early in 1968 he notes:

> An idea persists that we know what to do—that the research is in—and that the principal task is one of engineering and packaging the "proven" ideas for school use. There is a certain merit in this view as the task of "engineering" is a difficult and largely neglected one. But to assume that we have a clear grasp now of what to "engineer" is folly.

Dr. Sizer goes on to point out that the large corporations that rushed into the newly discovered "education business," such as IBM, Xerox, RCA, General Electric, and others as august, have stubbed their toes painfully on the realities. "The gadgetry of computers and teaching machines and the rest has yielded interesting, but financially intolerable, results," he observes.

While we can hardly doubt that the gadgetry will in due course, and probably quite soon, become useful technology, the organizational problems discussed in Chapter 21 strongly suggest that efforts in this area will *follow* structural reform rather than bring it about.

The key to implementation, in the final analysis, seems to rest on public comprehension of how bad our present schools are. Mere unhappiness for individual family reasons will not suffice. We must realize the full horror of the mess we are in: that our schools are prisons; that they systematically torture our children; that much of the money we give them is used to hold back and discourage children who would otherwise learn; that the schools' educational output is ridiculous in relation to the vast sums, time, and effort put in; that they widen the gap between have and have-not and foster racism and prejudice; that the whole vast operation is in a state of anarchy, unmeasured

haps rejoice in the advantages of a more rational, relevant and far less frustrating organization.

The "pilot" school is invaluable, especially if it is within the community or in one quite parallel. But we must clearly distinguish between *imitating* another school, which engenders many risks, and utilizing the same basic philosophy and structure to set up a new school, not a carbon copy. The pilot school, the "exemplary school" of Title III, ordinarily must be the first objective—not that all other change must wait on its success. Too, the pilot school should be projectable, not a special case by virtue of its student body, funds available, or special facilities. The criteria simplify to this: a pilot school aims to demonstrate superior results, at the same time that it refines techniques, materials, and equipment, and trains a cadre of staff. "School" may be an exaggeration at first, for a start can be made at the kindergarten end, or with the primary grades, thus beginning the conversion to open school with a modest number of children and converting further as they move ahead—a "bottom up" progression that allows an early, small-scale but quantum jump to new approaches and permits conversion to be spread over several years.

This is not intended to suggest that we can afford to wait 13 years to convert. Much can be done meanwhile to introduce new structuring in place of the higher grades, with emphasis on concept presentations, use of teams, skill labs, and much self-directed and free time for students. And I would make a strong plea that the pilot school should *not* be said to be "experimental." In a scientific sense it won't be; and in practical terms the problems fall more in the "engineering" area—the putting together, to compose a coordinated *system,* of parts that have been largely well tested in other uses. "Advanced" is a better term: it suggests successful use of newer resources, not the open-minded doubt of "experimental."

We cannot afford the strange double-think which holds that anything new must be proved out, preferably to perfection, while the old methods in use pile failure upon failure. Quite literally, almost any reasonably-conceived change promises to be for the better, if only because it stimulates the people involved, opens new doors, and provides Hawthorne effect benefits at least for awhile. The quick penalties of not changing are all too clear. They begin with bankruptcy and end with blood and ashes.

The technical problems of conversion demand respect. Even where there are approximate patterns and experience to follow, the details can prove overwhelming. The approach, I believe, must be "clean slate"—a total break with the past, a total systems approach to the future. There is no reason, of course, why the new school cannot use available materials, and even in some cases methods; but they must be used because they "fit," not because they are there. An architect friend assures me that it usually costs no more to build a new structure than to modify extensively an old one. The principle seems to apply to creating a new school.

The term "change agent" has come into use in education. Perhaps it should be given more specific meaning, and applied to a new kind of *executive* on the educational scene—one whose sole function is to effect the shift from classroom school to open school. Such a change agent would take complete charge, gathering the "parts" from all sources and forming them into a system with the active consultation of board, administration, staff, students, knowledgeable volunteers, and interested members of the community. The change agent, though not by that name, is familiar in management outside education: the role is well understood. The "pilot unit" approach is standard procedure, now supplemented often by use of computers to create models and simulation studies—a missile, say, can be "flown" on an analog or hybrid computer long before a single part exists. Within the schools we find little knowledge of the techniques of innovation for the good and simple reason that until very recently there has been slow drift, but seldom anything rapid enough to be called change.

Significantly, the Harvard Graduate School of Education now deliberately trains change agents, by that name, to work with school systems. Other leading training institutions are developing similar channels. Possibly a steady supply will soon

become available, and communities will hire a change agent a few years as a normal part of keeping their systems mo ahead. Likely, too, other change agents and stimulators come from outside education, bringing in needed new niques. But perhaps the greatest advantage of the change a is simply that his existence and use facilitates a "clean break with the past—something very hard to achieve pract except by creating a new power unit with uninvolved pe operating it. As the saying has it, "It's good to bring in a man because he doesn't know all the things that can't be d

Change, in and of itself, costs money. But in educ where plant costs relatively little of the whole, it is hard much fundamental reason why change need be very expe Unfortunately, the budget seldom includes an item to co so by the weird accounting of education it becomes "extr the school world, it is perfectly proper to argue that spend your money this year the way you did last year, y being wise, conservative, and frugal—no matter how w last year's method was, or how shocking the results. Truly ing is the proclivity of boards and superintendents to "We have no money for change!", even while most of their are being ceremoniously poured down the drain. "No m constitutes the first line of defense against change. The to be breached by demanding, "What are you doing w money you have?" and getting answers.

Menacing on the other hand are those, often of " persuasion, who have a naive faith in huge amounts of and who skip lightly over the awkward fact that funds substitute for program. Too many dollars tends to bureaucracy forthwith—the program gums up before gets going. The same ailment may also generate great tions that then painfully deflate, leaving proponents disc and intended recipients angry and frustrated.

We do not yet have the programs. We do not yet kn to do. Generations of puny research have left many a "ignorance gaps." The best we can do is push ahead istically, following the lead of the private foundations erally backed *any* innovation that held promise and ope

and out of control; that we can no longer staff it, pay for it, or suffer it to drag down our national strength and sunder our democracy.

We are in urgent need of new structures. The institution of the classroom blocks them: the classroom, an invention that served us well only briefly, must go.

Then, if we have not slipped too far over the brink, we can take a splendid leap forward. Public education can become as shining as it now is tawdry.

APPENDIX

A random sample of schools reporting significant departure from conventional classroom organization

This Appendix is presented by popular demand, as it were. In my experience, discussion of new techniques and ways of organizing provokes the insistent query, "Where are these ideas being used? Where can I see them in action?" Since I have said that this book is in large measure a synthesis of newer approaches put into practice by various schools, the request cannot be put aside. On the other hand I include this response with deep misgivings that reflect the kindly warnings of Professor Robert H. Anderson and others.

The reader must realize that to compile a reliable list of schools that have successfully innovated in these directions would require both visits to the schools and evaluation of the results — an inquiry far beyond the scope of this book, and one that would call for a team of investigators and many months of observation. A great many schools are innovating, and still more claim to. By the time such a study was completed, it would be no longer current. Nor is there any simple, quick way of evaluating results that would be widely accepted. This Appendix aims only to give a small, *unreliable* sample of the ferment of innovation that is clearly going on all over the country, revealed day by day in news sources that cover education.

I must also sound a loud, clamorous warning gong to alert those who, the instant a specific school is named, jump to the conclusion that it must be the shining embodiment of all that is perfect in team teaching, or individual progress, or flexible approaches, or whatever techniques it is utilizing. The critic then leaps upon the example, finds that problems exist, or that the school still uses some classroom approaches, or that some of the local people are disgruntled or less than content. "See?," he announces, "I *visited* the school. The idea doesn't work." One is reminded of the early days of our space effort, when skeptics seized happily on each rocket fizzle and destruct to ridicule the whole effort.

We can almost suspect that some who are impatient of theory and eager to inspect the example have more than a little hope that they will find some excuse for holding to comfortable ways and putting off the evil day of change. Curiously, they display a double standard, demanding that the new approach work flawlessly, even while the old system is wracked with problems to the point of imminent collapse.

Enthusiasts present even a worse hazard. They may exult over what they find. Visions of what can be becloud what is. Minor improvements, which actually lead nowhere, may be hailed with delight. And even when they find solid substance, they may advocate prompt imitation. Unfortunately, attempts to imitate or replicate without thorough grasp of the theoretical and operational bases of the new organization can lead to fiasco or gross distortions in the new locale. Genuine successes may reflect special circumstances, the impact of rare personalities, or expenditures too large to be projectable. Only theoretical analysis can disclose what advance has been made that can be generally utilized.

Visits to innovating schools, it seems sensible to suggest, should be made only after some discussion and clarification of what the purpose of the visit is. It can be useful to see with one's own eyes that there *are* other ways to organize a school than by class and grade, to inspect other than conventional plant and equipment, and to get the feel for a markedly different atmosphere. But a day in Rome does not make one an expert on the Italian people; nor does a visit to a school provide evaluation or understanding of its structure and functioning.

One further caution perhaps is needed: each situation can change rapidly. The school struggling today with new problems may be working smoothly a year or two from now; or temporary success, especially if over-publicized, may give way to difficulties as new factors play a role and Hawthorne effect lessens. Any specifics given in this Appendix must be considered valid only as of the date noted.

The main purpose, then, of the list that follows is merely to suggest the patterns of change, and to show that departures from the conventional class-and-grade system are being made, are in use, are successful, apparently, in many instances. The schools named are *not* offered as examples of the kind of school synthesized in Part II of the text, nor as instances to "prove" anything. The notes may, however, hint at the large body of experience that is being rapidly expanded. My list of schools could easily be enormously longer if any point were to be served. A survey in 1968 by the NEA's Department of Elementary School Principals gives some idea of numbers: more than a quarter of the sample of 2,300 principals reported use of non-graded primaries, team teaching, and television, with over half of these finding the innovations "very valuable" and only a small percentage reporting negatively. As a rule, secondary schools have tended to innovate more rapidly than elementary, and in more ways, so it seems safe to say that *thousands* of schools have some first-hand knowledge of newer approaches.

The notes that follow are based on a simple questionnaire, sent out to 100 schools in June 1968, and so reflect the status at the end of that school year. I wish to express my appreciation to the school executives who so kindly at that busy season took time to reply. Some also sent literature. For space reasons, I have not used all, but selected a modest sampling arbitrarily to suggest range, rather than pick the most successful. My interpretation of responses may involve some degree of error: again, the purpose of the listing should be borne in mind.

Some of the most noted innovative schools, even the Nova complex in Fort Lauderdale, Florida, have been omitted because so much material is available on them to provide more detail. The reader who would like to accumulate current information, obtain literature which some schools offer, or arrange visits, is urged to begin by contacting the nearest Regional Education Center (Title III, ESEA). If required, a query to state or federal Office of Education officials will help locate it. Or a local public or college librarian may be consulted. "Pacesetters in Innovation," an annual guide issued by ERIC (Educational Research Information Centers) obtains wider distribution each year as another valuable result of ESEA activity. Many libraries have or can obtain the latest issue.

A considerable number of schools or systems in all parts of the country are "demonstration" units, happy to assist, and usually staffed with a Dissemination Officer who can give time to those seeking information. Most of these demonstration schools are affiliated with a private foundation, university, or some other plan to facilitate new developments. The federal Title III center, however, should normally be the best channel to utilize first.

EXPLANATION OF NOTES

The questionnaire used began with these two multiple-choice entries:

1. We have departed from the conventional classroom structure and operation—
   ( ) In certain test areas
   ( ) In a number of ways
   ( ) To a large extent
   ( ) Almost entirely

2. We regard the results as in general—
   ( ) Highly successful
   ( ) Overall successful
   ( ) Successful in some areas
   ( ) Still to be judged
   ( ) Not successful

The answers checked are shown at the beginning of each note.

Checks and comments on 17 other points elicited an outline of approaches in use, or being tested.

Team teaching is clearly the most important general departure, since it permits breaking out of the one-teacher, fixed-group classroom. "Complete" team teaching denotes apparently vigorous use of organized teams as the prime means of carrying on instruction; "full" team teaching suggests a somewhat more restricted use. "Assistants" indicates all members of the team are not teachers on the same level. "Informal" conveys that teachers work jointly on a less organized team basis.

"Students work on their own" will usually mean that they are allowed to disperse and use unscheduled time (within the normally scheduled school day) to follow projects or interests of the moment, working alone or with one or two other students, or perhaps with a teacher. Unscheduled time usually is about one-quarter to one-third of the whole. Where this is permitted, students likely have free access, without requiring passes or special permission, to resource centers in the school. These include libraries, learning laboratories of various kinds, reading and discussion rooms (often with "soft" furniture), and audiovisual rooms where films, records, filmstrips, tapes, and the like may be used individually. "Carrels" are small booths at which a student may study or write. Some may be more elaborately equipped with audio-visual devices.

"Technology" refers to various types of electronic and visual equipment, often including television. "No four-wall classroom" means use is made of open space plans, pods, movable walls or dividers, or arrangement other than the old style room. Reference to plant is made in some cases where pertinent information is available.

"Flexible" refers to grouping plans of various kinds, all unlike the usual class in that groupings are changed readily and frequently as student needs dictate. "Nongraded" suggests freedom from the annual promotion, fixed-expectation pattern of the classroom school.

In many cases, newer innovations (for that school) may be in limited use and not necessarily applied throughout the school.

While this random small sample has no statistical value it may be worth noting that virtually all schools that reported "highly successful" or "overall successful" results also noted reduction, often to the vanishing point, of "discipline" problems within learning groups, although some arose elsewhere — probably as students reacted to unaccustomed freedom. (In some instances, existing individual problems became more visible.) In general, attendance remained or moved up very high, and the trend toward improved staff morale and enthusiasm was remarkable. In some cases comments have been quoted. (Where known, zip-codes for the schools or school districts are offered.)

FREMONT UNITED, CALIF. 94538
HS — John F. Kennedy

To a large extent; overall successful. Flexible, modular scheduling using various team teaching arrangements, including assistants. Individual progress with some choice of level and teachers. Students work on their own 20% of time. Free access to resource centers. Audio-visual and closed circuit television facilities; mass media used instructionally. Art studio, special activities program including guest speakers. "No classroom problems; staff morale very high."

GARDEN GROVE, CALIF.
Elem.

To a large extent; highly successful. Flexible grouping, team teaching using assistants and various size groupings for function, individual student conferences. Student progress evaluated by more than one teacher. Free student access to resource centers.

POWAY UNIFIED, CALIF. 92064
HS

Almost entirely; overall successful. Complete team teaching, using assistants, various sized grouping, much flexibility. Students work on their own, unscheduled time. Carrels, resource centers available. Students have some choice of level and teachers. Change reported to have brought "more visible problems," staff morale "outstanding."

SAN DIEGO CITY UNIFIED, CALIF. 92114
JHS

To a large extent; overall successful. 7th grade of 900 students using a flexible schedule changing each week. Full team teaching used, various sized groupings, individual conferences. Selected students have free access to resource centers. Carrels. Student progress evaluated by more than one teacher. "Great enthusiasm."

TIMBER, CALIF.
Elem. — Banyan School

Almost entirely; highly successful. School designed for flexibility, no four-wall classrooms, pods used. Complete team teaching approach. No conventional classes, no grades. Highly flexible, individualized, continuous progress. Students evaluated by teams. Parents assist.

JEFFERSON COUNTY SCHOOLS, COLO. 80014
Elem., JHS, HS

In a number of ways; overall successful. Complete team teaching approaches with emphasis on flexibility, using various size groupings for functions, assistants, individual conferences. Students work on their own in unscheduled time, have free access to resource centers, carrels. Other than four-wall classroom in use. Nongrading, further individualized progress being tested. Student progress evaluated by more than one teacher.

MEEKER SCHOOL DISTRICT, COLO. 81641
Elem., JHS, HS

In a number of ways; overall successful. Flexible grouping, full team teaching. Students work on their own in unscheduled time. Free access to resource centers, carrels. Working on K–12 individualized progress, in effect in some areas. Heavy use of technology. HS aides used in Elem. and JHS. Reports "drop-out rate much lower, much better morale and enthusiasm in teachers and students."

NORWALK, CONN. 06852

To a large extent; overall successful. Mixed effects in discipline, staff enthusiasm. Team teaching to limited degree, testing flexible grouping.

BARRINGTON DISTRICT #4, ILL. 60010
K–5 — Hough Street; Middle School

Almost entirely; highly successful. Complete team teaching approach with various sized groupings, unscheduled time for individual work. Carrels, resource centers available, four-wall classroom not used. Nongraded plan in use. Student has some choice of level and teachers. Progress evaluated by more than one teacher. Testing further individualized progress.

DECATUR, DISTRICT #61, ILL. 62521
HS — Lakeview

Almost entirely; highly successful. Full team teaching with assistants, various size groupings for function, individual student conferences. Students work on their own in unscheduled time. Free access to resource centers, carrels. Testing individualized progress.

EVANSTON, DISTRICT #65, ILLINOIS
Elem. — Laboratory School

To a large extent; successful in some areas. Various team approaches being used in an old classroom school, including full team teaching, various size groupings, individual conferences, some unscheduled time, some choice of level and teacher.

EVANSTON TOWNSHIP HIGH SCHOOL, ILL. 60204

In a number of ways; highly successful. Stanford Modular Schedule. Full team teaching in English department, using assistants, various size groupings. Study carrels, individual study.

MUNSTER SCHOOL TOWN, INDIANA 46321
HS, JHS

To a large extent; highly successful. Notable modern plant making heavy use of technology. Flexible grouping, considerable team teaching using various size groupings and assistants, individual student conferences. Free access to resource centers, carrels. Testing increased work by students on their own in unscheduled time.

FAYETTE COUNTY, KY. 40504
Elem.

To a large extent; overall successful. Team teaching combined with nongrading and individual student progress, evaluated by team. No fixed classes, flexible grouping. Students work on their own in unscheduled time. Carrels, free access to resource centers.

SILVER SPRING, MD. 20902
HS—John F. Kennedy

To a large extent; overall successful, some programs still to be judged. Fairly conventional plant providing many sizes and types of rooms, plus movable walls. Modular scheduling and complete team teaching. Much emphasis on student freedom and individual study. Some choice of level and teachers. Access to resource centers, carrels. Individual conferences, multiple evaluation, and counseling.

CAMBRIDGE, MASS. 02138 (Box 287)
Elem.—Fayerweather Street School (Independent)

Entirely; highly successful. Wholly individual progress, no fixed classes. Nongraded, unscheduled time permitting students to work on their own. Free individual access to resource centers.

LEXINGTON, MASS. 02173
Elem., JHS, HS

To a large extent; overall successful. System has worked with Harvard under SUPRAD organization for 10 years. Two completely team teaching elementary schools, one in classroom build-

ing, one in structure built for purpose. High school offers students
five-level plan, with unit arrangements to promote faculty contact.
New JHS will emphasize open space design. Cost studies of team
schools show them in middle range. Much individualization at all
levels. Carrels, resource centers available.

CARSON CITY, MICH. 48811
Elem.—Crystal School

To a large extent; overall successful. Organized team teaching,
various size groupings according to function. Four-wall classroom
not used. More than one teacher evaluates student progress.

HOLLAND, MICH. 49423
HS

In a number of ways; highly successful. Limited use of team teaching. Students work on their own in unscheduled time, have some
choice of level and teachers, free access to resource centers,
carrels.

LIVONIA PUBLIC SCHOOLS, MICH. 48150
HS—Franklin

To a large extent; successful in some areas, others still to be judged.
Recently introduced 15-minute modular plan. Voluntary teams,
no leaders, various size groupings including small "inquiry"
groups. Individual use of resource centers being developed, carrels. Student has some choice of level. Other innovative programs
at Bentley and Stevenson schools, and more planned.

MINNEAPOLIS, MINN. 55404
HS—South

Almost entirely; highly successful. Complete team teaching, with
assistants, various size groupings, individual conferences. Flexible
groupings, students work on their own in unscheduled time. Some
choice of teachers. Carrels, free access to resource centers.

LADUE PUBLIC SCHOOL DISTRICT, MO. 63124
Elem., JHS, HS

In a number of ways; still to be judged. Full team teaching using assistants and various size groupings in use at secondary level, and less complete team teaching. Nongraded plan in elementary. Under Title III experimental plan, some student choice of level and teachers, and unscheduled individual study. Horton Watkins HS has addition built for various size groupings, including audiovisual and closed-circuit television facilities. Innovative program will be expanded in 1968–69. Staff enthusiasm reported "extremely high."

CLARK COUNTY, NEVADA
Elem.—Ruby Thomas School

Almost entirely; overall successful. Team teaching, various size groups according to function, individual student conferences. Four-wall classroom not used. Carrels, resource centers available. Student progress evaluated by more than one teacher. Testing individual progress, unscheduled time, some choice of teachers.

GLEN RIDGE, NEW JERSEY 07028
Elem., Middle, HS

To a large extent; overall successful with newer programs still to be judged. Flexible grouping, team teaching approaches, some use of assistants. Various size groupings for function, individual conferences. K–4 and 5–8 nongrading, testing progress evaluation by more than one teacher. Expanding carrels and unscheduled time independent study. Student has some choice of level, testing choice of teachers.

LOS ALAMOS, NEW MEXICO 87544
Elem.

In a number of ways; overall successful. Chamisa School built for complete team-flexible approach. No four-wall classrooms; pod clusters, no fixed interior walls. Grade labels, but children move freely, are grouped by achievement as needed. Groups vary from small to large, by function. Developing independent work. Some study carrels and complete audio-visual carrels. Student and staff enthusiasm reported high.

AMHERST CENTRAL #1, NEW YORK 14226
HS

In a number of ways; overall successful. Moving towards full team teaching by gradual stages. Two and three teacher teams, using large group and seminars in certain areas. Some carrels, planning more.

FLUSHING, N.Y. (NEW YORK CITY) 11542
Elem.—P.S. 219

Almost entirely; highly successful. Radically new design, "satellite" plant, domed with no interior walls. Complete team teaching approach, with various size groupings, assistants, individual conferences. Free access to resource centers, carrels. Student progress evaluated by more than one teacher. Modified nongrading.

GREECE CENTRAL #1, NEW YORK 14612
Elem., JHS, HS

Almost entirely; overall successful. Full team teaching, assistants, various size groupings, individual student conferences. Students do work on their own, have free access to resource centers, carrels, four-wall classroom not used.

PLAINEDGE, N.Y. 11714
Elem.

Almost entirely; highly successful. 25 classes in three elementary schools. Nongraded, inter-age classes, no annual promotion, no fixed groupings, free access to resource centers. Informal student and teaching teams. Highly individualized progress. Disciplinary problems reported "practically non-existent."

WILLIAMSVILLE-MAPLE, N.Y. 14051
Elem. — Maple

Almost entirely; highly successful. Complete team teaching approach in a conventional building. (Cafeteria converted to carrels and independent study area.) Nongraded. Moving towards increased individualization. Staff morale reported "extremely positive."

PORTLAND, OREGON 97266
HS — John Marshall

Almost entirely; highly successful. Complete modular scheduling and team teaching approach in a conventional structure. Teams use assistants, use various size grouping for function, full provision for individual conferences. Students work on their own during unscheduled time, have free access to resources centers and also Student Union. Some choice of level. Carrels. Heavy use of technology.

LOWER MERION, PENNA. 19003
Elem., JHS

In a number of ways; overall successful. Ungraded primary. Team teaching in JHS, various size groupings for function. Emphasis on flexibility. Student progress evaluated by more than one teacher. Morale reported "greatly improved."

MEMPHIS, TENNESSEE 38127
HS

Almost entirely; highly successful. No fixed classes, flexible grouping, team teaching approaches. Students work on their own in unscheduled time. Free access to resource centers, carrels. "Attendance up to 98%."

OAK RIDGE, TENN. 37830
Elem., JHS, HS

To a large extent; overall successful. Team teaching approaches, flexible groupings of various sizes. Carrels. Departing from four-wall classroom. Access to resource centers, student evaluation by more than one teacher.

IRON COUNTY SCHOOL DISTRICT, UTAH 84720
HS — Cedar City

To a large extent; overall successful. Three-level plan, with student option. Full team teaching in several departments, with flexible, various size groupings. Some continuous progress, using seminar groups. Nongraded programs to extend student choice of interests. Modular scheduling from 20 to 180 minutes; over 15% of time unscheduled. Carrels, resources centers. School designed for flexible programs. Attendance reported 96%; staff morale "much higher."

WEBER COUNTY SCHOOL DISTRICT, UTAH 84067
HS — Roy

Almost entirely; overall successful. Complete team teaching, assistants, various size groupings for function, individual conferences, flexibility. Students work on their own in unscheduled time. Individualized progress, some choice of level and teachers. Nongraded. Free access to resource centers. (JHS on similar, less completely flexible plan, reported "highly successful.")

CHAMPLAIN VALLEY UNION, VERMONT 05482
HS

To a large extent; highly successful. Flexible grouping, considerable team teaching with various size groupings by function. Students have some choice of level, access to resource centers, carrels. Testing more unscheduled time, individual conferences.

SEATTLE, WASH. 98109
Elem., JHS, HS

In a number of ways; overall successful. Secondary students have some choice of teachers and level, unscheduled time, access to resource centers, carrels. Elementary testing team teaching, flexible groupings; aiming at non-graded, individual progress.

SPOKANE DISTRICT #81, WASH. 99203
HS

Almost entirely; highly successful. Flexible grouping, complete team teaching using assistants, various size groups for function, individual conferences. Some student choice of level. Students work on their own in unscheduled time. Free access to resource centers, carrels. Testing some nongrading. Other than four-wall classroom arrangements used. Permissive attendance. "High morale, eager and anxious to innovate."

DELAVAN-DARIEN HIGH SCHOOL DISTRICT, WIS. 53115

In a number of ways; overall successful. Full team teaching using assistants, various size groupings, individual student conferences. Students have some choice of level of work, unscheduled time, carrels.

SELECTED BIBLIOGRAPHY
AND QUOTATION REFERENCES

In the course of planning and writing this book, hundreds of books, articles, papers, speeches, reports, and press stories were consulted. A good part of this exploration served only to document the existence of acute educational problems and shortcomings and the lack of critical, analytical, or speculative thinking about our schools' classroom organization and its effects. Also painfully evident was the dull, insipid, and repetitious character of most of the conventional educational literature.

The listing that follows has therefore been limited to sources directly quoted, plus some other material that seemed to me of more than usual interest or importance. This is not to suggest that much more of value could not be named. The more recent literature, I have happily observed, seems to attain a much higher level of quality. Here as elsewhere there has been great progress in the last ten years.

An asterisk indicates that the work is quoted from; page reference in the source is given in parentheses followed by the page number for the appearance in my text. I wish to thank the many publishers and authors who kindly granted specific permission to quote.

*Abraham, Willard, *Common Sense About Gifted Children*. New York, Harper & Row, Inc., 1958. (75) 118

*Ayers, Albert L., *Administering the People's Schools*. New York, McGraw-Hill Book Co., 1957. (107) 69

*Bany, Mary A., and Johnson, Lois V., *Classroom Group Behavior*. New York, The Macmillan Co., 1964. (195) 115

*Baron, Denis, and Bernard, Harold W., *Evaluation Techniques for Classroom Teachers*. New York, McGraw-Hill Book Co., 1958. (14) 119; (253) 120

*Beggs, David W., and Buffie, Edward G., eds., *Nongraded Schools in Action: Bold New Venture.* Bloomington, Ind., Indiana University Press, 1967. Roy A. Larmee quoted. (77) 185

*Briggs, Thomas H., and Justman, Joseph, *Improving Instruction through Supervision.* New York, The Macmillan Co., 1952. (321) 75

*Bruner, Jerome S., *Toward a Theory of Instruction.* Cambridge, Mass., Harvard University Press, 1966. (157) 12; (158) 295; (113) 297

*Carnegie Foundation for the Advancement of Teaching, Annual Report, 1958–59. (3) 108

*Caswell, Hollis L., and Foshay, Arthur W., *Education in the Elementary School.* Third Edition. New York, American Book Co., 1957. (297) 202

*Chamberlain, Leo, and Kindred, Leslie, *The Teacher and School Organization.* Third Edition. Englewood Cliffs, N.J., Prentice-Hall, Inc., 1958. (259) 72

*Conant, James B., *The American High School Today.* New York, McGraw-Hill Book Co., 1958. (51) 178

*DeHaan, Robert F., and Havighurst, Robert J., *Educating Gifted Children.* Revised Edition. Chicago, University of Chicago Press, 1961. Reprinted by permission of University of Chicago Press. (23) 135; (79) 135

*Downie, N. M., *Fundamentals of Measurement.* New York, Oxford University Press, 1967. (264) 130; (10) 137

*Edman, Irwin, *John Dewey.* New York, The Bobbs-Merrill Company, Inc., 1955. Reprinted by permission of Mrs. Meta Markel, executrix of the estate of Irwin Edman. (31) 186

Elementary School Organization. Washington, D.C., Department of Elementary School Principals, National Education Association, 1961. All rights reserved. (16) 10; (17) 10; (69) 143; (89) 303

Flanagan, John C., ed., *The American High School Student.* (Project Talent.) Pittsburgh, University of Pittsburgh Press, 1964. Referred to, 29 and 291.

*Friedenberg, Edgar Z., *The Dignity of Youth and Other Atavisms.* Boston, Beacon Press, 1965. (185) 7

*Fuller, Louis, ed., *Horace Mann on the Crisis in Education.* Yellow Springs, Ohio, The Antioch Press, 1965. (149) 118

*Gans, Dr. Roma, *Common Sense in Teaching Reading.* New York, The

Bobbs-Merrill Company, Inc., 1963. Reprinted by permission of the publishers. (115) 201

*Gardner, John W., *Self-Renewal: The Individual and the Innovative Society.* New York, Harper & Row, Inc., 1963. (20) 251

*Getzels, Jacob W., and Thelan, Herbert A., *The Dynamics of Instructional Groups.* 59th Yearbook of the National Society for the Study of Education. Chicago, University of Chicago Press, 1960. (56) 9

*Glogau, Lillian, and Fessel, Murray, *The Non-Graded Primary School.* West Nyack, N.Y., The Parker Publishing Co., 1967. (62) 290

*Goodlad, John I., *School, Curriculum, and the Individual.* Waltham, Mass., Blaisdell Publishing Co., 1966. (115) 53; (17) 107

*Goodlad, John I., and Anderson, Robert H., *The Nongraded Elementary School.* New York, Harcourt, Brace and World, Inc., 1959. (3) 142

*Goslin, David A., *Teachers and Testing.* New York, Russell Sage Foundation, 1967. (19) 127; referred to, 134

*Haan, Aubrey, *Elementary School Curriculum.* Boston, Allyn and Bacon, Inc., 1961. (293) 115

*Hagman, Harlan L., *Administration of Elementary Schools.* New York, McGraw-Hill Book Co., 1956. Used by permission of McGraw-Hill Book Co. (186) 168; (195) 170

*Hansen, Carl F., *The Amidon Elementary School.* Englewood Cliffs, N.J., Prentice-Hall Inc., 1962. (xi) 26

*Holt, John, *How Children Fail.* New York, Pitman Publishing Co., 1964. (39) 13; (24) 295

*Holt, John, *How Children Learn.* New York, Pitman Publishing Co., 1967. (vi) 3; (148) 95

Innovation in Education: New Directions for the American School. New York, Committee for Economic Development, 1968. (17) 261

*Johnston, Edgar G., Peters, Mildred, and Evraiff, William, *The Role of the Teacher in Guidance.* Englewood Cliffs, N.J., Prentice-Hall, Inc., 1959, (5) 145

*Jones, Arthur J., *Principles of Guidance.* New York, McGraw-Hill Book Co., 1963. (17) 12

*Keppel, Francis, *The Necessary Revolution in American Education.* New York, Harper & Row, Inc., 1966. (99) 72

*Knight, Edgar W., *Education in the United States.* Third Edition. Boston, Ginn & Company, 1951. (331) 47

*Kowitz, Gerald T., and Kowitz, Norma G., *Guidance in the Elementary Classroom.* New York, McGraw-Hill Book Co., 1959. (27) 120; (108) 175

*Landreth, Catherine, *The Psychology of Early Childhood.* New York, Alfred A. Knopf, Inc., 1960. (353) 139

*Lindgren, Henry Clay, *Educational Psychology in the Classroom.* New York, John Wiley & Sons, Inc., 1967. (295) 116

Lynd, Robert S., and Lynd, Helen M., *Middletown in Transition.* New York, Harcourt, Brace & World, Inc., 1937. (Table 37, Appendix III) Chart on 46

*McLuhan, Marshall, *Understanding Media.* New York, McGraw-Hill Book Co., 1964. Copyright © by Marshall McLuhan, 1964. Used with permission of McGraw-Hill Book Co. (vii) 281

*Martinson, Ruth A., and Smallenburg, Harry, *Guidance in Elementary Schools.* Englewood Cliffs, N.J., Prentice-Hall, Inc., 1958. (132) 137

*Miles, Matthew B., *Innovation in Education.* New York, Teachers College Press, 1964. (661) 193; Paul R. Mort quoted. (318) 31

*Miller, Richard L., ed., *The Non-Graded School.* New York, Harper & Row, Inc., 1967. Maurie Hillson quoted. (88) 223

*Mills, Herbert H., and Douglass, Harl R., *Teaching in High School.* Second Edition. New York, The Ronald Press Co., 1967. (66) 211; (66) 118; (211) 88

*Otto, Henry J., and Sanders, David G., *Elementary School Organization and Administration.* New York, Appleton-Century-Crofts, 1964. (64) 10; (98) 11; (101) 31

*Prescott, Daniel A., *The Child in the Educative Process.* New York, McGraw-Hill Book Co., 1957. (x) 148; (23) 149

Professional Administrators for America's Schools. American Association of School Administrators 1960 Yearbook. Washington, D.C., National Education Association, 1960. (101) 30

Report of the National Advisory Commission on Civil Disorders. ("Riot Report.") New York, Bantam Books and The New York Times Co., 1968. (425) 21

Schools for the Sixties: A Report of the Project on Instruction of the National Education Association. New York, McGraw-Hill Book Co., 1963. (75) 141

*Sexton, Patricia J., *Education and Income.* New York, The Viking Press, Inc., 1961. (viii) 36

*Sizer, Theodore R., *Dean's Report, 1966–67.* Cambridge, Mass., Harvard University Graduate School of Education. (4) 324

*Spain, Charles R., Drummond, Harold D., and Goodlad, John I., *Educational Leadership and the Elementary School Principal.* New York, Holt, Rinehart & Co., 1956, (258) 69; (261) 73

Staff Relations in School Administration. American Association of School Administrators 1955 Yearbook, Washington, D.C., National Education Association, 1955. (135) 174

*Stoddard, Alexander J., *Schools for Tomorrow.* (pamphlet) New York, Fund for the Advancement of Education, 1957. (17) 40

*Stoops, Emery, ed., *Guidance Services: Organization and Administration.* New York, McGraw-Hill Book Co., 1959. (191) 157

*Thomas, R. Murray, *Judging Student Progress.* New York, David McKay Co., 1954. (90) 163

*Trump, Lloyd, *Images of the Future.* (pamphlet) Washington, D.C., National Association of Secondary School Principals, 1959. (15) 92; referred to, 259

*Wheatley, George M., and Hallock, Grace T., *Health Observation of School Children.* New York, McGraw-Hill Book Co., 1965. (192) 121

*Wiles, Kimball, *Supervision for Better Schools.* Third Edition, Englewood Cliffs, N.J., Prentice-Hall, Inc., 1967. (210) 70

*Woodring, Paul, *New Directions in Teacher Education.* New York, Fund for the Advancement of Education, 1957. Reprinted by permission of the Fund and the author. (14) 41; (20) 49; (71–72) 65

*Woodring, Paul, and Scanlon, John, eds., *American Education Today.* New York, McGraw-Hill Book Co., 1963. Alvin C. Eurich quoted. (vii) 273

Periodicals and articles quoted from:

*Holt, John, *Grade Teacher,* March 1966. (70) 310

*Hopper, Robert L., *American Education,* June 1966. (21) 28

*Ianni, Francis A. J., *Perspectives in Education,* Winter 1968. (21) 19

*Koerner, James D., "Teachers Get the Worst Education," *The Saturday Evening Post,* June 1, 1963. (8) 51

*Morgan, H. Gerthon, *National Education Association Journal,* November 1959. (16) 237

*Noah, Harold J., *Teachers College Record,* May 1967. Reprinted in *The Education Digest,* September 1967. 85

*Sarason, Seymour B., *National Education Association Journal,* November 1959. (261) 131

*Skinner, B. F., "Why Teachers Fail," *Saturday Review,* October 16, 1965. Copyright 1965, Saturday Review, Inc. (81) 292

*Torrance, Paul E., *Theory Into Practice,* December 1966. (218) 209

*Traxler, Arthur E., *National Education Association Journal,* November 1959. (19) 129

*Tumin, Melvin, "Teaching in America," *Saturday Review,* October 21, 1967. Copyright 1967, Saturday Review, Inc. (77) 23

The following have not been quoted from directly:

Beggs, David W., ed., *Team Teaching.* Indianapolis, Ind., Unified College Press, 1964.

Bellack, Arno A., ed., *Theory and Research in Teaching.* New York, Teachers College Press, 1963.

Black, Hillel, *The American Schoolbook.* New York, William Morrow, 1967.

Brown, B. Frank, *The Nongraded High School.* Englewood Cliffs, N.J., Prentice-Hall, Inc., 1963.

Bruner, Jerome S., *The Process of Education.* New York, Random House, 1960

Chall, Jeanne, *Learning to Read.* New York, McGraw-Hill Book Co., 1967.

Changes in Teacher Education. Report of the National Committee on Teacher Education and Professional Standards. Washington, D.C., National Education Association, 1963.

Conant, James B., *The Education of American Teachers.* New York, McGraw-Hill Book Co., 1963.

Cremin, Lawrence A., *The Transformation of the School.* New York, Alfred A. Knopf, Inc., 1961.

Dufay, Frank R., *Ungrading the Elementary School.* West Nyack, N.Y. The Parker Publishing Co., 1966.

Elam, Stanley, and McLure, William P., eds., *Educational Requirements for the 1970's.* New York, Frederick A. Praeger, 1967.

Full, Harold, ed., *Controversy in American Education.* New York, The Macmillan Co., 1967.

Greene, Maxine, *The Public School and the Private Vision*. New York, Random House, 1965.

Gross, Ronald, and Murphy, Judith, eds., *The Revolution in the Schools*. New York, Harcourt, Brace and World, Inc., 1964.

Hawes, Gene R., *Educational Testing for the Millions*. New York, McGraw-Hill Book Co., 1964.

Heald, James E., and Moore, Samuel A., II, *The Teacher and Administrative Relationships in School Systems*. New York, The Macmillan Co., 1968.

Henry, Nelson B., ed., *The Dynamics of Instructional Groups*. 59th Yearbook of the National Society for the Study of Education (Part II). Chicago, University of Chicago Press, 1960.

Herndon, James, *The Way It Spozed To Be*. New York, Simon and Schuster, 1965.

Hillson, Maurie, ed., *Change and Innovation in Elementary School Organization*. Holt, Rinehart, and Winston, 1965.

Hillson, Maurie, *Elementary Education: Current Issues and Research*. New York, The Free Press, 1967.

Jackson, Philip W., *Life in Classrooms*. New York, Holt, Rinehart, and Winston, 1968.

Jenson, Theodore J., and Clark, David L., *Educational Administration*. New York, Center for Applied Research in Education, 1964.

Jersild, Arthur T., *When Teachers Face Themselves*. New York, Teachers College Press, 1955.

Kagan, Jerome, ed., *Creativity and Learning*. Boston, Houghton Mifflin Co., 1967.

Kephart, Newell C., *The Slow Learner in the Classroom*. Columbus, Ohio, Charles E. Merrill Books, Inc., 1960.

Kozol, Jonathan, *Death at an Early Age*. Boston, Houghton Mifflin Co., 1967.

Krumboltz, J. D., *Learning and the Educative Process*. Chicago, Rand McNally and Co., 1965.

Mayer, Martin, *The Schools*. New York, Harper & Brothers, 1962.

Miller, Richard I., ed., *The Nongraded School*. New York, Harper & Row, Inc., 1967.

Pines, Maya, *Revolution in Learning*. New York, Harper & Row, Inc., 1966.

Rosenthal, Robert, and Jacobsen, Lenore, *Pygmalion in the Classroom.* New York, Holt, Rinehart, and Winston, 1961.

Stoops, Emery, and Johnson, Russell E., *Elementary School Administration.* New York, McGraw-Hill Book Co., 1967.

Tanner, Daniel, *Schools for Youth: Change and Challenge in Secondary Education.* New York, The Macmillan Co., 1965.

Thomas, R. Murray, and Thomas, Shirley, *Individual Differences in the Classroom.* New York, David McKay Co., 1965.

Trow, William Clark, *Teacher and Technology.* New York, Appleton-Century-Crofts, 1963.

INDEX

Boldface numerals indicate the pages on which major discussions begin.

haps rejoice in the advantages of a more rational, relevant and far less frustrating organization.

The "pilot" school is invaluable, especially if it is within the community or in one quite parallel. But we must clearly distinguish between *imitating* another school, which engenders many risks, and utilizing the same basic philosophy and structure to set up a new school, not a carbon copy. The pilot school, the "exemplary school" of Title III, ordinarily must be the first objective — not that all other change must wait on its success. Too, the pilot school should be projectable, not a special case by virtue of its student body, funds available, or special facilities. The criteria simplify to this: a pilot school aims to demonstrate superior results, at the same time that it refines techniques, materials, and equipment, and trains a cadre of staff. "School" may be an exaggeration at first, for a start can be made at the kindergarten end, or with the primary grades, thus beginning the conversion to open school with a modest number of children and converting further as they move ahead — a "bottom up" progression that allows an early, small-scale but quantum jump to new approaches and permits conversion to be spread over several years.

This is not intended to suggest that we can afford to wait 13 years to convert. Much can be done meanwhile to introduce new structuring in place of the higher grades, with emphasis on concept presentations, use of teams, skill labs, and much self-directed and free time for students. And I would make a strong plea that the pilot school should *not* be said to be "experimental." In a scientific sense it won't be; and in practical terms the problems fall more in the "engineering" area — the putting together, to compose a coordinated *system*, of parts that have been largely well tested in other uses. "Advanced" is a better term: it suggests successful use of newer resources, not the open-minded doubt of "experimental."

We cannot afford the strange double-think which holds that anything new must be proved out, preferably to perfection, while the old methods in use pile failure upon failure. Quite literally, almost any reasonably-conceived change promises to be for the better, if only because it stimulates the people involved, opens new doors, and provides Hawthorne effect benefits at least for awhile. The quick penalties of not changing are all too clear. They begin with bankruptcy and end with blood and ashes.

The technical problems of conversion demand respect. Even where there are approximate patterns and experience to follow, the details can prove overwhelming. The approach, I believe, must be "clean slate" — a total break with the past, a total systems approach to the future. There is no reason, of course, why the new school cannot use available materials, and even in some cases methods; but they must be used because they "fit," not because they are there. An architect friend assures me that it usually costs no more to build a new structure than to modify extensively an old one. The principle seems to apply to creating a new school.

The term "change agent" has come into use in education. Perhaps it should be given more specific meaning, and applied to a new kind of *executive* on the educational scene — one whose sole function is to effect the shift from classroom school to open school. Such a change agent would take complete charge, gathering the "parts" from all sources and forming them into a system with the active consultation of board, administration, staff, students, knowledgeable volunteers, and interested members of the community. The change agent, though not by that name, is familiar in management outside education: the role is well understood. The "pilot unit" approach is standard procedure, now supplemented often by use of computers to create models and simulation studies — a missile, say, can be "flown" on an analog or hybrid computer long before a single part exists. Within the schools we find little knowledge of the techniques of innovation for the good and simple reason that until very recently there has been slow drift, but seldom anything rapid enough to be called change.

Significantly, the Harvard Graduate School of Education now deliberately trains change agents, by that name, to work with school systems. Other leading training institutions are developing similar channels. Possibly a steady supply will soon become available, and communities will hire a change agent for a few years as a normal part of keeping their systems moving ahead. Likely, too, other change agents and stimulators will come from outside education, bringing in needed new techniques. But perhaps the greatest advantage of the change agent is simply that his existence and use facilitates a "clean slate" break with the past—something very hard to achieve practically except by creating a new power unit with uninvolved persons operating it. As the saying has it, "It's good to bring in a fresh man because he doesn't know all the things that can't be done."

Change, in and of itself, costs money. But in education, where plant costs relatively little of the whole, it is hard to see much fundamental reason why change need be very expensive. Unfortunately, the budget seldom includes an item to cover it, so by the weird accounting of education it becomes "extra." In the school world, it is perfectly proper to argue that if you spend your money this year the way you did last year, you are being wise, conservative, and frugal—no matter how wasteful last year's method was, or how shocking the results. Truly amazing is the proclivity of boards and superintendents to holler, "We have no money for change!", even while most of their funds are being ceremoniously poured down the drain. "No money!" constitutes the first line of defense against change. The wall has to be breached by demanding, "What are you doing with the money you have?" and getting answers.

Menacing on the other hand are those, often of "liberal" persuasion, who have a naive faith in huge amounts of money, and who skip lightly over the awkward fact that funds are no substitute for program. Too many dollars tends to create a bureaucracy forthwith—the program gums up before it even gets going. The same ailment may also generate great expectations that then painfully deflate, leaving proponents discouraged and intended recipients angry and frustrated.

We do not yet have the programs. We do not yet know what to do. Generations of puny research have left many and large "ignorance gaps." The best we can do is push ahead pluralistically, following the lead of the private foundations who generally backed *any* innovation that held promise and opened new areas—even if various projects headed in contrary directions. As we break out of the classroom-system rigidities and sterility, many paths beckon. We may find a lot of them lead to the same region, but it is too early to tell. And while we must "engineer," there is some need to avoid what Dean Theodore R. Sizer of the Harvard Graduate School of Education calls "a curious optimism." In his Dean's Report for 1966–67, issued early in 1968 he notes:

> An idea persists that we know what to do—that the research is in—and that the principal task is one of engineering and packaging the "proven" ideas for school use. There is a certain merit in this view as the task of "engineering" is a difficult and largely neglected one. But to assume that we have a clear grasp now of what to "engineer" is folly.

Dr. Sizer goes on to point out that the large corporations that rushed into the newly discovered "education business," such as IBM, Xerox, RCA, General Electric, and others as august, have stubbed their toes painfully on the realities. "The gadgetry of computers and teaching machines and the rest has yielded interesting, but financially intolerable, results," he observes.

While we can hardly doubt that the gadgetry will in due course, and probably quite soon, become useful technology, the organizational problems discussed in Chapter 21 strongly suggest that efforts in this area will *follow* structural reform rather than bring it about.

The key to implementation, in the final analysis, seems to rest on public comprehension of how bad our present schools are. Mere unhappiness for individual family reasons will not suffice. We must realize the full horror of the mess we are in: that our schools are prisons; that they systematically torture our children; that much of the money we give them is used to hold back and discourage children who would otherwise learn; that the schools' educational output is ridiculous in relation to the vast sums, time, and effort put in; that they widen the gap between have and have-not and foster racism and prejudice; that the whole vast operation is in a state of anarchy, unmeasured